Chartist drama

Manchester University Press

Chartist drama

EDITED BY GREGORY VARGO

Manchester University Press

Copyright © Gregory Vargo 2020

The right of Gregory Vargo to be identified as the author of this work has been asserted by him in accordance with the Copyright, Designs and Patents Act 1988.

Published by Manchester University Press
Oxford Road, Manchester M13 9PL
www.manchesteruniversitypress.co.uk

British Library Cataloguing-in-Publication Data
A catalogue record for this book is available from the British Library

ISBN 978 1 5261 4206 1 hardback
ISBN 978 1 5261 6410 0 paperback

First published 2020
Paperback published 2022

The publisher has no responsibility for the persistence or accuracy of URLs for any external or third-party internet websites referred to in this book, and does not guarantee that any content on such websites is, or will remain, accurate or appropriate.

Typeset by
Servis Filmsetting Ltd, Stockport, Cheshire

In memory of my father, Albert Vargo

Contents

List of figures	*page* viii
List of tables	ix
Acknowledgements	x
A note on the texts	xiii
Introduction	1
1 *Wat Tyler* (1794/1817) – Robert Southey	50
2 *John Frost* (1841) – John Watkins	87
3 *The Trial of Robert Emmet* (1841)	159
4 *St John's Eve* (1848) – Ernest Jones	181
Appendix 1: Chartist dramatic performances	227
Appendix 2: Newport sonnets	236
Appendix 3: Passages omitted in Cleave's trial version as they appear in Cleave's source, *The Life, Trial and Conversations of Robert Emmet, Esq., Leader of the Irish Insurrection of 1803*	241
Appendix 4: Advertising placard for a performance of *The Trial of Robert Emmett, Esq.*	248

Figures

1.1 'Scenes from Southey's "Wat Tyler"', *Cleave's Penny Gazette of Variety and Amusement*, 10 March 1838, p. 1, British Library *page* 55
2.1 Title page of John Watkins's *John Frost: A Chartist Play in Five Acts* (London: n.p., 1841), Columbia University Rare Book and Manuscript Library, Seligman Collection 94
3.1 Frontispiece and title page of *Memoir of Robert Emmett and the Irish Insurrection of 1803; with the Trial of Emmett for High Treason, his Memorable Speech, &c.* (London: Cleave, n.d.), Columbia University Rare Book and Manuscript Library, Seligman Collection 164
4.1 First page of Ernest Jones's *St John's Eve* in the *Labourer* (1848), Columbia University Rare Book and Manuscript Library, Seligman Collection 187

Tables

0.1	Plays known to be performed multiple times	*page* 11
0.2	Chartist performances' fundraising beneficiaries (when indicated)	13
0.3	London and Manchester theatres with Chartist benefit performances	15
0.4	Chartist performances identified by year	22
0.5	Chartist dramatic performances by locality (in localities with two or more performances)	32
5.1	Chartist dramatic performances	228

Acknowledgements

The work of many people has brought this book into being. I would like first to thank my research assistants, who have each made substantial contributions to the project at different times over the last four years. Emma Dollery prepared the typescript of *St John's Eve* and assisted in notetaking. Gabriela James Noguera conducted research at libraries in London and her native Manchester and helped copyedit the introductions and footnotes for British usage. Charline Jao contributed invaluable research from the project's earliest stages, working especially on material on female Chartist associations. She also prepared the typescript for three plays and helped resolve formatting questions that arose in anthologising four texts with idiosyncratic styles. Finally, Athena Pierquet has been involved with the volume for the last two years, and her thoughtful and insightful work has made a real difference to me. She researched and wrote many of the footnotes, checked the anthologised works against the original texts, and photographed three of the images. I am also grateful for assistance from librarians, archivists, and staff at the British Library, the Working Class Movement Library in Salford, the Manchester County Record Office, the Rare Book & Manuscript Library at Columbia University, and New York University's Fales Library and Special Collections. Charlotte Priddle at Fales and NYU's English subject librarian Amanda Watson are trusted and valuable colleagues. Thanks also to the staff in NYU's English Department and Gallatin School of Individualized Study for much support and guidance, especially Alyssa Leál, Lissette Florez, Patricia Okoh-Esene, Mary Mezzano, Jaysen Henderson-Greenbey, and Will Huntington.

Conversations with many supportive and generous colleagues at NYU have enriched my thinking about Chartist drama. In particular, John Waters helped orient me in the world of nineteenth-century Irish radicalism and greatly assisted my research on re-enactments of Robert Emmet's trial. Julia Jarcho offered a chance for me to teach one of the anthologised plays in her theatre history class, and I profited from discussions with her about theatre and performance. I am also thankful to Elaine Freedgood, Lenora Hanson, David Hobbs, and Dara Regaignon for engaging with this material at the CUNY Victorian seminar.

Thanks also to Anne Humpherys for her invitation to speak at that seminar as well as her support for the project over a period of years. I would also like to thank Joseph Alban, Peder Anker, Gianpaolo Baiocchi, Nick Boggs, Pat Crain, Patrick Deer, Anne DeWitt, Lisa Gitelman, Hannah Gurman, Wendy Lee, John Maynard, Maureen McLane, Crystal Parikh, Sonya Posmentier, Dara Regaignon, Bryce de Reynier, Catherine Robson, Pacharee Sudhinaraset, Simón Trujillo, Eugene Vydrin, and Jini Kim Watson for their friendship and engagement.

My research has profited from the opportunity to discuss it in a variety of contexts, especially at conferences hosted by the Northeast Victorian Studies Association and the North American Victorian Studies Association (NAVSA). I am especially grateful for the work of Sharon Weltman and other members of the NAVSA theatre caucus and to my fellow scholars of radicalism, Mark Allison, Rob Breton, Ian Haywood, and Mike Sanders. William St Clair and Matthew Roberts generously answered queries concerning sources. Thanks also to Mary McAvoy for sharing her pre-publication proofs of her excellent *Rehearsing Revolutions: the Labor Drama Experiment and Radical Activism in the Early Twentieth Century*.

Institutional support was critical for the completion of the volume. An NYU Center for the Humanities Faculty Fellowship helped launch the project. I would like especially to thank Uli Baer, Gabriela Basterra, Cécile Bishop, MC Hyland, Joan Flores, Ayasha Guerin, Mikiya Koyagi, Heather Lee, Gwynneth Malin, Christine Mladic, Wendy Muñiz, Wendi Muse, Kaitlin Noss, Simón Trujillo, and Hannah Zeavin for their engagement with the project. The Gallatin Research Scholars program and the Gallatin Faculty Enrichment Fund, along with the English department, provided crucial monies for hiring research assistants. I am grateful, moreover, to Susanne Wofford, Dean of the Gallatin School, and to Millery Polyné, Dean of Faculty at Gallatin, and to John Archer and Tom Augst, successive chairs of the English department, for their encouragement and support.

The tables in the volume's introduction first appeared in an article about Chartist drama in *Victorian Studies*, from which I have also drawn an occasional sentence and one or two paragraphs. My thanks to the journal's editor Rae Greiner as well as the article's anonymous readers, for their helpful suggestions, and also to Indiana University Press for permission to republish. I gratefully acknowledge permission from the British Library Board to reproduce Figure 1; and from the Rare Book & Manuscript Library, Columbia University in the City of New York, to reproduce Figures 2, 3, and 4 (all from the Seligman collection).

I feel fortunate that this book has found a home at Manchester University Press. Thanks to my editors Matthew Frost and Paul Clarke for their commitment to the project; to the anonymous readers of my proposal and manuscript for their suggestions; to Humairaa Dudhwala for her efforts overseeing production; to the art department for their work on the cover, which reproduces an image from Kenneth Budd's 1978 *Chartist Mural*; and to Doreen Kruger for her insightful and meticulous copyediting.

Last, I would like to thank my family for their love and support, especially Susan and Bill Howe, Mark and Barbara Vargo, Benin Ford and Jesse Phillips-Fein, Charlotte Phillips and Oliver Fein, and my mother Geraldine Vargo. My children Clara and Jonah are inspirations. Kim Phillips-Fein has accompanied me through every stage of this project, and her insights about theatre and politics have helped make the plays and their world come alive.

Finally, my efforts on the volume are dedicated to the memory of my father Albert Vargo, who shared with me his love of learning and his kindness and gentleness. Born an ocean away from the coal fields of Wales and a century after the Newport rising, my father grew up in the mining town of IdaMay, West Virginia. The son of a coal miner, he was a lifelong educator and lover of theatre. Among the dozens of playbills he collected from London playhouses are four from the Victoria, the site, 160 years ago, of several benefit productions organised to raise funds for the Chartists.

A note on the texts

The texts in this anthology are all taken from editions produced by Chartist publishers, advertised in movement newspapers, and sold in radical bookstores. John Cleave's 2d. edition of Robert Southey's *Wat Tyler* (from the mid- to late 1830s) stood in a long line of pirated versions of Southey's notorious play. Cleave, however, largely followed the text as it appears in Southey's *Collected Works* of 1837 instead of utilising, except in a few instances, the many previous radical versions. In any case, only slight differences separate the unauthorised editions and Southey's *Collected Works*. Although a manuscript version exists for the *Collected Works* edition of *Wat Tyler*, it has not been consulted; this volume is not concerned with Southey's intentions but how the play circulated and was performed in the context of 1830s and 1840s working-class radicalism.

No manuscript papers survive relating to the other texts in the collection. John Watkins himself published a 6d. edition of his drama *John Frost* due to circumstances described in the work's introduction. He first advertised the play in the *Northern Star* in March 1841. *The Trial of Robert Emmet* derives from two chapters of John Cleave's *Memoir of Robert Emmett and the Irish Insurrection of 1803*. This text was almost certainly published in 1841 (when advertisements for it first appear in the *Star*). As is explained in more detail in the work's introduction, Cleave largely plagiarised a popular chapbook (that was also sold by Cleave and more widely in Chartist circles) to produce his version. Because the chapbook was likely used in its own right for Chartist performances, portions of it that Cleave omits are included in Appendix 3. Never published as a single volume, Ernest Jones's *St John's Eve* appeared serially in the 6d. Chartist monthly the *Labourer*, which Jones co-edited.

Obvious and minor errors are silently corrected in all texts. The only significant emendations concern *The Trial of Robert Emmet* and *Wat Tyler*. In *The Trial of Robert Emmet*, Emmet's name is spelled with one 't' rather than two as it appears (incorrectly) in Cleave's text. For *Wat Tyler*, this edition regularises the treatment of lines when two characters share a single unit of iambic pentameter. Cleave's version treats these lines haphazardly; instead of beginning the second character's speech directly below where the first character's speech ends (as is customary), he places the second character's speech essentially at random, sometimes directly below and sometimes indented various amounts. *Wat Tyler* and *John Frost* both contain inconsistencies in terms of capitalisation, for respectively, such phrases as 'king' and 'Christian', and 'Whig' and 'Tory'. As both texts seem to capitalise or omit capitalising these words based on which character uses them or the ideological stance of the author or publisher, the irregularities are generally maintained.

Introduction

Shakespearean Chartists

In the autumn and winter of 1842–43, the poet and activist Thomas Cooper faced legal prosecution on three separate occasions for matters related to his activities in the Chartist movement. First, in October, Cooper was tried unsuccessfully for committing arson in Hanley, Staffordshire during the massive strike wave of August 1842.[1] The following March, in a trial that 'commenced on [his] birthday', Cooper was convicted of seditious conspiracy for speeches made during that same summer and sentenced to two years' imprisonment in Staffordshire Gaol.[2] But even as he awaited his second trial, the activist was summoned to Leicester's town hall to answer a seemingly unrelated accusation: on 30 January 1843, Cooper was charged with performing Shakespeare's *Hamlet* 'on the 9th and 16th inst., for profit and gain, contrary to the statute' that restricted the staging of tragedy and comedy to theatres with a royal patent.[3] These performances grew out of the cultural world of Leicester Chartism. Under Cooper's leadership, the local movement combined advocacy for the Charter, which sought a set of political reforms to establish democratic rule, with a vibrant counter-culture that included a school, frequent lectures, and 'sections ... for the cultivation of singing, study of the drama, &c.'.[4] Members of the latter group performed a series of plays in December and January, culminating with the controversial production of *Hamlet*.

Although the stakes of Cooper's court appearance on 30 January were undeniably lower than the other prosecutions, in which if convicted Cooper faced penal transportation or imprisonment, the idea of the impoverished stockingers who made up Leicester Chartism's rank-and-file staging serious drama provoked scandal in the town.[5] Such was the cultural trespass that on the day of the trial, the 'Town-hall ... was crowded with persons anxious to hear the information against Mr. Cooper for unlicensed theatrical performances!'[6] Although the prosecutor asserted that Cooper not only 'caused plays to be acted' but took 'the part of "Hamlet"' himself, the proceedings ended anti-climatically when charges were withdrawn in exchange for Cooper's 'public pledge' that all dramatic performances 'should cease from that time forth'.[7]

Cooper's appropriation of Shakespeare was hardly unique. Chartist writers celebrated the bard as an artisan poet and republican genius, conscripting him into the service of democratic reform.[8] Nor was Leicester alone among Chartist localities in performing Shakespeare. Groups in Failsworth, Lancashire and Kilbarchan, Scotland staged *Othello* at least one time each.[9] While Leicester's branch styled itself the 'Shaksperean Brigade' after the name of their (idiosyncratically spelled) meeting room, a troupe of 'Shaksperean ... amatures' in Nottingham raised nearly two pounds for the 'local Defence Fund' by performing an unnamed play.[10] In London, a Chartist benefit at the Strand Theatre paired *Henry IV* with *Damon and Pythias* to raise money for the 'National Victim and Defence Committee'.[11] Beyond actual performances, Cooper himself frequently lectured on Shakespeare, once reciting 'the entire first act' of *Hamlet* to a London audience, which required that he 'personate the whole of the characters who figure in the first act – the *Ghost* included', a task made especially arduous 'considering the total absence of those essential helps, dress, scenery, stage, and the other aids, real and illusive, which are to be found only in the theatre'.[12] Finally, in spring 1840 the Chartist newspaper the *Northern Star* ran a column that culled egalitarian sentiments from *Henry IV*, *Coriolanus*, *Julius Caesar*, and other plays, thus purporting to deduce 'Chartism from Shakespeare'.[13]

Nevertheless, the Shaksperean Brigade's production of *Hamlet* in the massive Leicester Amphitheatre carried a particular charge. Termed 'the most spacious building in a theatrical form out of London', the Amphitheatre was 'crowded to excess each night'.[14] Hamlet's fated destruction must have resonated with the coming trial and anticipated imprisonment of the Shaksperean Brigade's 'General' for the 3000 people who nightly witnessed Cooper in the title role, a part he took, as he later recalled, because he 'knew the whole play by heart'.[15] The Chartist context would have called to the fore the insurrectionary import of a play about a contemplated regicide, and Rosencrantz and Guildenstern's surveillance of the hero would have taken on special significance in the midst of the wave of trials of Chartist activists following the 1842 strikes, many of which relied on testimony by informants and police spies. The fundraising purpose of the production – which sought 'to raise money for [Cooper's] law expenses' – would only have strengthened these associations.[16]

More speculatively, one might consider the play's 'Mousetrap' sequence an apt metaphor for Chartist literary and dramatic culture, which adapted a wide array of texts and genres for new purposes. Hamlet, in order to test Claudius's conscience about the death of his father, commissions a group of travelling actors to perform the 'The Murder of Gonzago' and has them learn 'a speech of some dozen or sixteen lines, which [he] would set down and insert in't'.[17] This introduction argues that just as Hamlet turns to theatre to articulate truths that cannot be voiced in other contexts, Chartist performance of both received and original texts offered a way of considering ideas, especially about political violence, that were subject to prosecution when expressed openly in oratory or journalism. Drama served the Chartists in many fashions: as a means of political education, a way to raise money, and a method of bringing their democratic message to the broader public. But perhaps most importantly, it granted opportunities for creativity and self-expression, encouraging both participants and audience members to engage in acts of imagination akin to the movement's efforts to transform society.

The texts collected in this volume were each written or performed by members of the largest working-class protest campaign in nineteenth-century Britain. At its most basic, Chartism sought the adoption of the six points of the Charter: universal male suffrage; secret ballots; no property qualification for Members of Parliament; payment to Members; equal electoral districts; and annual elections. These measures promised to reshape British political life at a time when a small fraction of the population had the right to vote. The Chartists further believed that by establishing democracy they would initiate a host of social and economic reforms and protect the interests of 'the people' against the privileged orders.[18] In particular, they hoped to end the social austerity of the New Poor Law, secure the right to participate in unions, raise wages, and reform working conditions in factories. Beyond a political and economic programme, however, Chartism represented a cultural mobilisation. The flowering of educational and literary activity in Leicester's 'Shaksperean Brigade' was matched in localities throughout Britain. Chartist associations founded 'Democratic chapels', organised alternative schools, formed musical groups, participated in theatrical clubs, and hosted innumerable tea parties, dances, and literary soirees.[19]

Growing out of this extraordinary milieu, each of the plays in this collection represents an important work in Chartist dramatic culture. Stagings of Robert Southey's *Wat Tyler* (1794/1817), which concerns the Great Rising of 1381, were part of a broad array of Chartist efforts to re-imagine the past from the perspective of ordinary people. Performances of the play connected the Chartists to earlier generations of British radicals: the Jacobins of the French revolutionary era – Southey's contemporaries when *Wat Tyler* was written – and the reformers of the post-war period, who first published the text in pirated editions. Chartist stagings are also the only documented productions of Southey's important Romantic text. John Watkins's *John Frost* (1841) treats a crossroads in the history of Chartism, the Newport rising of 1839, which resulted in the last mass treason trial in British history. Written by a Chartist poet, the play illustrates the intense debates within the movement about the implications of Newport for the future of Chartism. *The Trial of Robert Emmet*, which was the most frequently staged Chartist production, also deals with questions of political violence and state repression. Even though the Chartists never published a text for this work, this volume reprints their source material, popular and inexpensive editions of memoirs of the Irish revolutionary's life and trial. Those works offer a good sense of what performances might have looked like. Finally, *St John's Eve* (1848) by Ernest Jones is notable as the only extant drama of this influential Chartist writer, journalist, and politician. It also represents the sole play published in its entirety in a Chartist journal and speaks to the way the Chartists sometimes staged less explicitly political drama.

The range of genres represented in the volume – the texts include a history play, a tragedy, a gothic melodrama, and a trial re-enactment – testifies both to the eclecticism of Chartist literary culture and the dynamism of early Victorian theatre. As Jane Moody has shown, the 'illegitimate' theatres of London fostered an array of experimental genres as ways of circumventing the patent monopoly.[20] Conflicts over legal restrictions of theatrical performance came to a head in the early 1840s. In 1843, the Theatres Regulation Act overturned the century-old Theatre Licensing Act, which had restricted the performance of tragedy and comedy to theatres possessing a royal patent. Just as in the 1830s, a forceful campaign against the patent monopoly played out against the crisis around the Reform Bill of 1832, efforts at theatrical reform in the 1840s found echoes in the decade's broader upheaval.[21] Appreciating Chartism's links with London theatrical culture sheds light on the politics of commercial theatres during this critical period.

The remaining sections of this introduction take up a number of questions. In the next part, I situate the volume's texts in the wider context of Chartist culture and drama, exploring the relationship between print and performance in Chartist life and describing what can be gleaned about the social setting and dramatic practices of Chartist theatre. In the third section, I assess the connections between Chartist and commercial drama. While most Chartist performances were amateur, activist groups in London hosted two dozen benefits at many of the city's most important working-class theatres, including the Standard, the Pavilion, and the Victoria. A smaller number of professional benefits took place in Manchester while the Glasgow Chartists commissioned an acting troupe to stage re-enactments of the *Trial of Robert Emmet* in several Scottish towns and cities. Beyond these collaborations, professional theatre inevitably influenced Chartist amateur performance in terms of the kinds of plays performed and the styles utilised.

The concluding sections of the introduction turn to thematic subjects from the plays. The fourth part looks in depth at the question of 'physical force' in Chartist drama. Texts in the collection centre on the Great Rising of 1381 (*Wat Tyler*), the failed Dublin rising of 1803 (*The Trial of Robert Emmet*), and the Newport rising of 1839 (*John Frost*). The spectre of the latter sits over all Chartist theatre, which obsessively explores issues of state violence and repression while repeatedly embodying revolutionary crowds on stage. Approximately 80 per cent of Chartist performances (where titles of pieces are available) included at least one play that explicitly depicts revolution, insurrection, or conspiratorial plotting. Finally, I explore women's participation in Chartist theatre. Although no text in this collection was written by a woman and several articulate a masculinist perspective that situates political agency with martial men, women played important roles in bringing Chartist drama to the stage. Beyond organising theatrical benefits, women performed a wide range of parts, several of which complicate Chartist discourse that figures the radical movement as the protector of distressed femininity and the patriarchal family, thus countering Chartist celebrations of heroic masculinity.

Chartist dramatic culture

Chartism had a paradoxical relationship with the world of writing. On the one hand, the campaign fostered a massive print culture that comprised over one hundred journals and newspapers, including some of the most widely read in Britain in the late 1830s and early 1840s. Beyond editorialising about contemporary politics and recording Chartist rallies and other events, these papers provided a forum for writers to publish a huge array of poetry and fiction. On the local level, Chartist classes and schools promoted literacy as a tool in the struggle for democracy. In Leicester, for example, nearly three hundred people attended an adult school that Cooper superintended, at which class sections were named for poets and radical heroes.[22] Finally, the national petitions of 1839, 1842, and 1848 staked a claim to political legitimacy partly on the ability to write.[23] Patrick Brantlinger evocatively describes the national petitions as 'acts of symbolic literacy' for a democratic mass.[24] While all this highlights the importance of reading and writing within Chartism, a substantial portion of the movement's ranks were nevertheless unlettered. James Vernon estimates that 'in 1840 something like 50 per cent of women and 33 per cent of men were still illiterate'; among the coal miners, factory proletariat, and distressed textile outworkers who formed important constituencies within Chartism, the proportion was likely higher.[25]

So if Chartism promised members the possibility of educational uplift and cultural citizenship, it simultaneously attempted to mobilise people who could not read or write. Chartist groups did so by fostering an oral culture that included such participatory spectacles as protest marches, ceremonial dinners, and mass rallies.[26] Robert Lowery's description of a giant meeting in late September 1838 on Kersal Moor outside Manchester captures the theatrical nature of such occasions: 'When we got out of the streets it was an exciting sight to see the processions arriving on the Moor from different places, with their flags flying and the music of the bands swelling in the air, ever and anon over-topped by a loud cheer which ran along the different lines.'[27] Speaking from a raised platform, Lowery looked out on the crowd (estimated at 300,000 by *The Times*) while other speakers mounted some 'half-a-dozen' wagons distributed throughout the multitude. From these improvised stages, orators combined ostentatious gesture with passionate speech in ways that provoked, in Lowery's words, a 'response … swelling up from [the spectators'] very hearts depths'.[28]

While in recent years historians have come to appreciate the ways the Chartists sutured divisions between the movement's literate and illiterate members, literary scholars of radicalism have had less to say about the interplay between orality, performance, and print.[29] As a literary art uniquely accessible to those who cannot read, drama demands such a reckoning. John Watkins's *John Frost*, takes up potential divisions within the movement around the question of literacy. Notably, the play begins with Frost, a Chartist leader, '*solus*' in 'a library room' but moves in Act 2 to the public space of an outdoor meeting.[30] When at the meeting the discussion turns to the national petition, a working-man declares 'I can neither read nor write; but I can work, / and, maybe, fight' while another admits he 'cannot write' though he 'can read'.[31] In this way, Watkins draws attention to the exclusions petitioning entails. The soon-to-be martyred Shell – a character based on a Chartist aged 19, killed at Newport – advances a separate critique that echoes throughout the play.[32] Suggesting petitions are a paltry alternative to physical force, Shell promises: 'Next time I write, I'll dip my pen in blood— / The blood of tyrants, and a pike my pen.'[33]

Chartist drama emerged out of and remained connected to the movement's broader performance culture. In October 1842, the *Star* declared that 'concerts, Balls, Raffles, &c. are constantly taking place in all quarters of the metropolis, for the benefit of the victims … and London is fast redeeming her character'.[34] Such events, along with ubiquitous Chartist tea parties and soirees, included many different kinds of cultural expression. Typical was an 1845 ball in Burnley where 'the gay lads and bonny lasses enjoyed themselves with singing, reciting, &c., until one o'clock, when they reluctantly separated to hold themselves in readiness for the tinkling of the factory bells at five o'clock'.[35] Similarly, political dinners involved ceremonial toasting, oratory, recitation, and song.[36] Although drama sometimes occurred as a stand-alone event, it frequently formed part of larger festivity.[37] After the performance of *The Trial of Robert Emmet* at an 1841 Christmas Day gathering 'in the Working Man's Hall' in Keighley, Lancashire, 'the Hall was thrown open for general entertainment, and songs, recitations, and dancing were continued during the remainder of the evening, the whole enlivened and assisted by an excellent quadrille band'.[38] On Easter Tuesday, 1842, 'several pieces were performed … from Wat Tyler, William Tell &c.' at 'a tea and dancing party' in Coventry.[39] And as part of a concert in the London Chartists' 'City Rooms, Old Bailey', a 'Mrs. and Miss Ford, with Mr. Ford' performed a scene from *John Frost* during an evening that featured a recitation of Byron's 'The Gladiator' (from *Childe Harold's Pilgrimage*), a second scene from

Watkins's play, and the performance of 'a number of patriotic songs', including 'the Marseilles Hymn'.[40]

Even as Chartist drama was grounded in a culture of conviviality and political spectacle, it also depended on writing. Two texts in this collection, Robert Southey's *Wat Tyler* and the anonymous *The Trial of Robert Emmet* (or rather the *Memoir of Robert Emmett* from which the latter is drawn) were some of the most widely read literary works in Chartist circles.[41] Southey's text had been a staple of the radical press since its publication in a pirated edition in 1817, the circumstances of which is discussed in more depth in the play's introduction. In the 1840s, ads for 2d. editions featured regularly in several Chartist periodicals, including the *Star*, the *Charter*, *Cleave's Gazette of Variety*, the *Northern Liberator*, and the *Odd Fellow*. In 1851, the Manchester publisher, bookseller, and Chartist Abel Heywood testified to a parliamentary committee that he sold 450 copies of the play each week (three times the sales of Shakespeare in penny numbers).[42]

Memoirs of the Irish revolutionary Robert Emmet were also very popular. Emmet owed his celebrity to the failed Dublin rising of 1803 and the treason trial that followed, at which, following the verdict, he made what would become one of the most famous speeches in Irish history. Bronterre O'Brien recalled 'the sensation which the publication of that speech excited in England – the avidity with which every copy of the [*Poor Man's*] *Guardian* ... was bought up'. 'Since then,' O'Brien claimed with little exaggeration, 'the speech itself has been reprinted over and over again – each edition circulating in the tens of thousands.'[43] Based on the anonymous *The Life, Trial and Conversations of Robert Emmet* (1836), John Cleave's *Memoir of Robert Emmett* appeared in a variety of formats. Cleave sold the memoir as a 1s. chapbook alongside a 1d. edition of Emmet's courtroom speech, both of which he advertised extensively in the *Star* and the *Northern Liberator*. The *Memoir* also ran serially in Cleave's own *English Chartist Circular* as well as the Glasgow *Chartist Circular*, the latter paper selling 20,000 copies per issue.[44] Notably, Chartist groups from Glasgow and Greenock toured Scottish towns with competing productions of Emmet's trial within a year of the *Chartist Circular*'s series.[45] Such was the perceived propaganda value of Emmet's life that activists also distributed the texts for free. In Gateshead, the local branch of the National Charter Association provided 'weekly missionaries' with a dozen copies of 'Emmett's Speech after his sentence' to loan to interested readers, and when William Beesley was arrested for seditious libel in Burnley in early September 1842 'two or three dozen of Emmet's life and trial' were discovered on his person.[46]

Chartist drama was thus able to reach audiences who never attended a performance. The movement's print culture interacted with drama in other ways as well. Tickets for productions were available at radical bookstores, including at Heywood's in Manchester and Cleave's in London.[47] Additionally, movement papers advertised benefit performances, reviewed the commercial stage and weighed in on such issues as the patent monopoly and the question of copyright for dramatic adaptation. The London-based *Charter* sided with the playwright W. T. Moncrieff in a controversy over his use of Charles Dickens's *Nicholas Nickleby* as the basis of a script. 'It is somewhat illiberal and ungrateful', Moncrieff reasoned in a letter the *Charter* published, 'that being indebted to the stage for so many of his best characters … [Dickens] should deny it a few in return.'[48]

Feargus O'Connor and Ernest Jones's literary journal the *Labourer* gave more space to drama than any other Chartist paper. Besides serialising Jones's own *St John's Eve*, the magazine displayed a literary internationalism by introducing readers to Friedrich Schiller's *Fiesco* and *The Robbers* and publishing a scene from Count Sigismund Krasinski's *Infernal Comedy* translated from Polish.[49] An essay by Jones called for the democratic renovation of the 'expiring drama – expiring, because it has been dedicated to an expiring cause'. Urging Chartist writers to go beyond 'combating the fallacies of opponents', he exhorted them 'to do *something more*, – more in the matter they treat of – more in the moral they deduce. We have had the misfortunes of younger sons, the mishaps of injured daughters of noble houses, but when has the Bastile victim, when has the lost child of labour, when has the hapless operative (the martyrs of the nineteenth century,) when have these been brought before the public eye in the drama, or when will they?'[50]

The significance of drama for Chartism lay partly in the form's capacity for exploring social relationships and imagining ways these might change. In this regard, drama was allied with poetry, which occupied a central place in Chartist culture. Mike Sanders has theorised the importance of poetry in Chartism in terms of the aesthetic experience it offered, the way it functioned as 'an incarnation of the process of becoming'. In other words, the catharsis involved in reading verse helped reveal 'the creative potentialities and possibilities inherent in social-historical being, namely that life can be different'.[51] Drama too served as an attempt to improvise alternative worlds. The former Chartist Ben Brierley's memoir describes theatre's transformative potential for audience members and performers alike. His account of the 'wonders that were held out to us as if by the hand of some mighty magician' during his first visit to the Theatre Royal in Manchester evokes the way drama transported many nineteenth-century theatregoers beyond the realm of the ordinary.[52] And his description of performing *William Tell* and Southey's *Wat Tyler* with a Chartist group suggests theatre's capacity to reframe the given: 'only fancy two armies meeting, fighting, and subverting a government, on three or four planks; and you will think less of the glories of the battlefield, and the dignities of rulers'.[53]

The spaces in which Chartist drama occurred heightened this sense of possible transformation. Chartist association rooms, working men's halls, Democratic chapels, and similar locales offered opportunities for conviviality, creativity, and self-expression often lacking in other arenas of working-class life, especially the workshops and 'cotton bastiles' which dominated daily experience.[54] Chartist meeting rooms were elaborately decorated for special occasions in ways that would have heightened the contrast between the makeshift theatre and outside neighbourhood, potentially replicating the experience of awe commercial venues inspired in playgoers such as Brierley. For a tea party in Sheffield, a Chartist meeting room 'was beautifully ornamented … small arches of evergreens being formed on the walls, in the centre of which arches, were placed garlands of white muslin decorated with flowers. … From the centre of the ceiling was suspended a large and beautiful garland of evergreen flowers, fruit and ribbons.'[55] At the same time, the avowedly political context of Chartist drama underlined its ambition to reconfigure the present state of things. 'EVERY CHARTIST IN LONDON TO HIS POST' and 'IT IS THE CAUSE! IT IS THE CAUSE!!' blared advertisements in the *Star* for benefits held at the Victoria and Standard Theatres.[56] By overlaying spectatorship with political action, the *Star* rejected the idea of art as apolitical, a posture that explicitly countered the aims of theatrical censorship, which sought to ban controversial subjects from the stage. Occurring in spaces of holiday celebration (and often on holidays themselves), Chartist drama simultaneously set itself apart from, criticised, and attempted to transform the outside world.[57]

Just as poetry within Chartism helped make the movement 'culturally intelligible to its constituencies', drama provided a shared experience that could powerfully interpret past and present life.[58] Key differences, however, separated the genres. Anne Janowitz observes that as Chartism matured 'a process of poetic stratification set in', so that a small number of 'laureates of labour' received more and more attention in the movement press.[59] Theatre, on the other hand, necessitated the participation of large numbers of people who remained largely unheralded. To bring drama to life required the labour not only of actors and directors, but of musicians; ticket-sellers; and committee members, who arranged practical details, decorated the performance space, and prepared and served refreshments. We have already encountered the 'dramatic section' of the Shaksperean Chartists in Leicester and the 'Shaksperean amatures' in Nottingham. Other Chartist theatre troupes formed in the neighbouring Lancashire mill towns of Failsworth and Hollinwood, which performed *The Trial of Robert Emmet*, *Wat Tyler*, and several other plays; in London, where the Amateur Dramatic Society made its debut performance at the Standard Theatre; and in Ashton, where the Juvenile Chartist Association staged *The Trial of Robert Emmet* over a dozen times.[60]

Shannon Jackson's work on contemporary performance provides a helpful framework for considering the situated labour of these Chartist thespians. Jackson emphasises the way performance requires participants to 'think deliberately but also speculatively about what it means to sustain human collaboration spatially and temporally'.[61] Her focus on art that foregrounds its institutional and organisational support is suggestive for Chartist theatre because movement papers gave as much attention to work preparing for dramatic benefits as to performances themselves. Readers of the *Star*, for example, learned scant details about the performance of *Othello* by the Chartists of Kilbarchan. Instead, the paper focused on a meeting following the event when a committee gathered in the 'Chartist vestry' to pay expenses, disperse profits to various causes, and '[return] their best thanks to ... members of the Historonic [sic] club of Paisley, for ... the loan of their scenery'.[62]

While the Chartist press stressed the preparatory work that made theatre possible, Chartist plays depicted collaboration as a constitutive element of democratic politics. On stage, the Chartists instantiated meetings, depicted conspiratorial plots, and personified revolutionary crowds, thus using theatre to explore the limits and possibilities of various kinds of mass action. Indeed, the capacity or inability of people to sustain mutual efforts in the face of economic hardship and political persecution form a central problematic of *Wat Tyler*, *John Frost*, and *The Trial of Robert Emmet*. Other plays the Chartists staged, including *William Tell*, *Henry IV*, and *Venice Preserved*, take up similar questions.

As much as any work in the Chartist repertoire, *John Frost* explores the process through which political groups come into being. The play is framed with opening and closing scenes that foreground the protagonist's isolation. The action begins with Frost at home, alienated from his wife and disconnected from 'the people' he would aid. By the end, the radicalised hero is again cut off from the outside world, now awaiting exile in a prison cell. In contrast, the middle portion of the play shows a collective force arising that promises not only to dissolve the protagonist's estrangement but to redress the antagonisms that define society. Act 2 shifts from the private space of Frost's home to a Chartist meeting 'in the open air'. 'Here only we can meet', declares Shell, 'but meet we will, / In spite of wind and weather, or the whigs'.[63] The Chartists resort to the outdoor location, because the 'gagging whigs won't let us have a room, / A place to meet in to discuss our griefs'.[64] By calling attention to the restrictions on the right to assemble Chartist groups faced, Watkins delineates how barriers to working-class organisation are both material and political. Act 4 extends this theme by highlighting how ruling-class efforts to restrict access to politics are underwritten by violence. The police, armed with 'orders from the magistrates / Not to allow assemblages like these', disrupt a second meeting and arrest the leader Albion in the middle of his speech.[65]

In these and other instances, Watkins emphasises the fraught and contingent nature of efforts at radical change. Beyond external pressures, ethnic and ideological differences within the movement pose a threat to unity, albeit ones that are, at least temporarily, superseded.[66] In these ways, *John Frost* confronts

Table 0.1 Plays known to be performed multiple times

Play and author (when stated or otherwise unambiguously known)	Number of performances
The Trial of Robert Emmet. Anonymous	36 (possibly an additional 21 or more)
William Tell. James Sheridan Knowles (×1)	8
Wat Tyler. Robert Southey (×1); John Watkins (×1); others presumably Southey	7
Hofer, the Tell of the Tyrol. Edward Fitzball?	3
Wallace, the Hero of Scotland. William Barrymore	2
Douglas. John Home	2 (likely 3)
Black-Eyed Susan. Douglas Jerrold	2
Venice Preserved. Thomas Otway	2
Hamlet. Shakespeare	2
Othello. Shakespeare	2

issues of social agency that Chartist verse frequently elides, a problem taken up in more detail in the introduction's penultimate section.[67] Crucially, however, Watkins suggests that the obstacles that confront democratic politics cannot be addressed theoretically (as in Frost's solitary reflections in Act 1). They must rather be surmounted through collective action, which the collaborative space of the meeting (and the stage) typifies.

The ambition of Chartist theatre to imagine social transformation was reflected in its subject matter. While Chartist performance spanned the range of Victorian genres – including melodrama, pantomime, burletta, farce, comedy, tragedy, and opera – history plays occupied the pride of place (see Table 0.1).[68] *The Trial of Robert Emmet*, *Wat Tyler*, *William Tell*, *Wallace*, and *Hofer, the Tell of the Tyrol* were each performed multiple times while *Henry IV* and two French revolutionary dramas (*Robert le Grange* and *The Black Doctor, or the Siege of the Bastile, and Revolution of 1793*) were staged at least once. Notably, these plays each concern a revolt thirty or more years in the past in Britain, Ireland, or elsewhere in Europe. Even *John Frost* might be deemed a kind of history play, especially considering its prologue, which situates the Newport rising in a *longue durée* of oppression and resistance.[69]

Wat Tyler and *The Trial of Robert Emmet* best illustrate the dynamic relationship the Chartists imagined between past, present, and future. Both conclude by suggesting the history they have recounted remains open-ended even in the face of the revolt's defeat. The close of Emmet's speech from the dock turns to the future as the arena in which the rising's failure will be made comprehensible:

> Let no man write my epitaph; for as no man who knows my motives dare now vindicate them, let not prejudice or ignorance asperse them. Let them and me

repose in obscurity and peace, and my tomb remain uninscribed, until other times, and other men, can do justice to my character. When my country takes her place among the nations of the earth – then, and not till then – let my epitaph be written.[70]

The complex temporality in play here animates much Chartist drama. A voice from the past looks forward to a time (potentially the moment of performance) that will prove capable of redeeming history's wreckage. *Wat Tyler* ends with a parallel gesture when the condemned priest John Ball bequeaths to an unknown generation the work of liberation: 'the destined hour must come, / When [the truth] shall blaze with sun-surpassing splendour, / And the dark mists of prejudice and falsehood / Fade in its strong effulgence.'[71]

So far I have focused on the cultural and ideological significance of drama within Chartism, but it also possessed practical importance. As theatre was a popular form of working-class entertainment, staging plays offered a way to raise funds and, potentially, to broaden the base of the movement. The venues the Chartists chose for benefits testified to this popularity; in many instances activists selected the largest space available. Beyond the Leicester Amphitheatre, which held 3000 and was the site for at least four performances, Chartist groups staged productions at the Owenite Hall of Science in Manchester, which also sat 3000; in the Ashton Chartists' Charlestown meeting room, which accommodated 1600; at the Dundee Democratic School where 'from 1,000 to 1,200 attended' a 'soiree' featuring the school's 'scholars' performing *The Trial of Robert Emmet*; in the 'Democratic Chapel' in Nottingham, which seated between 650 and 800 and witnessed one or more performances of *John Frost*; and at Cook's Circus in Glasgow, which was 'capable of holding 2000 [and] was crowded to suffocation' for an 1843 performance.[72] In London, benefits performances occurred at several prominent working-class theatres, including a minimum of six at the Standard, said by the *Star* to be the East End's 'most commodious House', four at the Victoria, and two each at the City and the Pavilion, all venues with capacities around 2000.[73] Although performances also took place at many smaller locations, it is safe to assume that tens of thousands of people at one time or another attended a dramatic performance associated with Chartism.

In certain cases, drama took on a more important role than even these numbers suggest. A remarkable experiment in amateur performance helped revitalise the movement in Lancashire following the devastating setbacks of 1839, which saw the defeat of the national petition, the failure of the Newport rising, and the arrest of hundreds of activists. Between 1840 and 1842, Ashton's Juvenile Chartist Association toured factory towns around Manchester, staging *The Trial of Robert Emmet* over a dozen times in a production with a cast of twenty-seven (on one occasion at least).[74] Composed of mostly young adult men and women, the Juvenile Association combined militant politics with a cultural programme that included a night school, frequent lectures, and drama.[75] As the group prepared to launch its theatrical venture, an Ashton representative reported to the South Lancashire delegate meeting that 'they were going on a great deal better now than they had for a long time. They were getting up a trial of Robert Emmet ... and he had no doubt but in a short time there would be a most numerous society again at Ashton.'[76]

The Trial proved a success, attracting enthusiastic audiences in Ashton, Manchester, Stockport, Oldham, Middleton, and Hyde. The Ashton troupe also inspired imitators in four nearby localities (Keighley, Failsworth, Hollinwood, and the slightly further Bierley), where groups staged their own productions (performances in Preston may or may not have been by the Ashton group). In sum, the tour raised funds, improved morale, and forged deeper connections between associations in the region. Advertising placards invited 'friends' and the 'public in general', making explicit the Chartists' effort to appeal to people outside the movement's core.[77] Performances succeeded in this regard too. In Middleton, between '150 to 200 men, women and children' attended the re-enactment, a figure representing, according to the *Manchester Courier*, 'by far a greater number than have attended any Chartist meeting in that town for some time past'.[78]

Like most aspects of Chartist drama, fundraising was tied to local circumstance and therefore idiosyncratic. At the same time, nearly half of all benefits went to defray legal expenses or support prisoners and their families (see Table 0.2). Such was the case for the performance of scenes from *John Frost* as part of a concert on 'behalf of Bronterre O'Brien' upon the publisher's release from prison in 1841 and of a performance in Nottingham of Watkins's play held to alleviate debts 'contracted in defending the Mapperly [sic] Hill Victims'.[79] Two performances of *Wat Tyler* at the Darlington Theatre raised money for 'Durham political prisoners', and a production of *Robert Emmet* in Bierley supported a similar cause.[80] Notably, these three plays feature show trials and state prisoners

Table 0.2 Chartist performances' fundraising beneficiaries (when indicated)

Beneficiary	Number of performances
'Victims' (Prisoners, ex-prisoners, and their families)/ defence funds	30
Organisational expenses/debts (non-building related)	20
Charity (including orphans and refugees)	7
Expenses related to buildings	6
Individual activists	3
Schools	2
Costumes for future performances	2

(though the trial occurs offstage in *John Frost*). The second most common object for theatrical benefits was meeting organisational debts, especially associated with the cost of securing meeting places.[81] Finally, drama supported a variety of charitable causes. Funds raised by *The Trial Robert Emmet* contributed to the 'Oldham Relieving Society', the Keighley Chartist Sunday school, 'Hungarian and Polish refugees', and three orphans whose 'last parent was killed a short time since in Ashton'.[82]

The amount of money raised also varied. Some productions were highly lucrative. In Glasgow, two performances of *The Trial of Robert Emmet* before 'crowded houses' at Cooke's Circus cleared a tidy £70, a figure roughly equalled by the sole event at a professional theatre in London for which a detailed breakdown of ticket sales, receipts, and expenses is available.[83] While other performances at professional venues likely earned significant amounts, amateur productions netted far less, often between 10s. and £5. These modest totals reflected low ticket prices (usually threepence and sometimes less) and relatively high outlays for costumes and other expenses. Performances of *The Trial of Robert Emmet* at the Greenock 'Mechanic's Institution', for example, incurred 'considerable debt ... for dresses and room, and the proceeds barely covered them'.[84] Similarly, because actors in Thomas Cooper's *Hamlet* 'demanded payment, both for the cost of their dresses and their time ... the income hardly covered expenses'.[85] In fact, Cooper had already abandoned the idea of future theatrical exploits when he appeared at Leicester's town hall and foreswore additional performances. Money, not the law, proved decisive. By contrast, three lectures Cooper delivered at the Amphitheatre charging only 'one half-penny' for admission paid the expense of the hall while leaving £10 for the 'suffering wife of the exiled William Ellis'.[86]

With these factors in mind, Thomas Martin Wheeler had the narrator of his Chartist novel *Sunshine and Shadow* voice frustration at the 'expensive and ill-judged' nature of 'benefits at theatres, balls, concerts, tea parties, lotteries, raffles, &c' as a means of raising money.[87] One might, however, see the slender takings of theatrical benefits in a different light: they suggest the Chartists turned to drama as much for its own sake as to alleviate the movement's chronic financial needs.

Chartist drama and early Victorian theatre

Unlike Chartist drama outside London, which was overwhelmingly amateur, 80 per cent of benefits in the capital occurred at professional establishments. Those amateur performances that did take place, moreover, consisted largely of 'dramatic recitations' or the staging of individual scenes rather than full-length plays. The availability of relatively high quality theatre with sophisticated production values seems to have discouraged the more ambitious amateur efforts

Table 0.3 London and Manchester theatres with Chartist benefit performances

Theatre	Number of performances
Standard	6
Victoria	4
City	3
Astley's	2
Marylebone	2
Milton Street	2
Pavilion	2
Queen's (Manchester)	2
Strand	2
Thespian (Manchester)	2
Albert	1
Grecian Saloon	1
Pantheon	1

characteristic of Chartist drama elsewhere. The theatres too proved willing accomplices. Save the important exceptions of the Surrey and the Britannia, almost all major houses catering to working-class audiences hosted one or more Chartist benefits between 1842 and 1851, which stands as a remarkable measure of mainstream establishments' openness to radical politics, though a fact previously absent from both general histories of London theatre and accounts of particular houses (See Table 0.3).[88]

While professional venues hosted all manner of benefits to boost sales and strengthen ties to the local community, implicitly endorsing Chartism presented a more charged decision than aiding such charitable organisations as the Lambeth Philanthropic Institution, a group that held a benefit at the Victoria the same 1845–46 season as a Chartist event there.[89] Unlike evenings supporting humanitarian causes, Chartist benefits risked attracting attention from the licensing authorities or the police.[90] Such was the case for the Milton Street Theatre, which was approached by 'detectives who did their best to prevent the manager from letting the theatre' to the Chartists for a 'grand concert and entertainment' for the wife and family of the prisoner John Bezer in 1848.[91] 'Surely the liberal Whigs', the *Star* opined, 'ought to be satisfied with the incarceration of their victims without satiating their vengeance by the starvation of their wives and families'.[92]

No matter the risk, Chartist events offered a good business opportunity, given the movement's popularity among working-class playgoers, which, thanks to falling ticket prices, represented an ever larger portion of the audience in the 1840s.[93] Following an account of the Victoria's crowd, Henry Mayhew records a conversation with a costermonger about the politics of his fellows: 'you might say, sir … that they *all* were Chartists, but as its [*sic*] better you should rather be under than over the mark, say *nearly* all'.[94] For his part, the Milton Theatre's proprietor, who frequently rented the space for political lectures and meetings, not only refused to comply with the police's request but 'offered the theatre to the committee at a lower rate than usual' for a benefit the following week.[95]

As might be expected, Chartist benefits concentrated in the working-class East End: the Grecian, the Pavilion, the Standard, and the City of London all saw performances. Benefits also took place on the southern side of the Thames at the Victoria and Astley's. Each of these establishments were neighbourhood institutions, drawing their audiences in part from local residents. As Jim Davis and Victor Emeljanow document, police reports conducted during the lead-up to the passage of the Theatre Regulations Act of 1843 describe how 'weavers' and others from Whitechapel frequented the City of London Theatre while the 'Standard drew tradesmen, mechanics, their children, and silk weavers from Spitalfields'.[96] The fare companies offered often dealt with subjects that would have appealed to local residents or neighbourhood workers. The Pavilion, which catered to sailors and labourers from the nearby docks, staged frequent nautical melodramas (as well as regular doses of Shakespeare).[97] The Victoria, which drew mechanics from its Lambeth neighbourhood, featured many melodramas exploring social issues such as poverty and alcoholism. Charles James Mathews called the theatre 'the incarnation of the English "domestic drama", or rather of the drama of English domestics. There you will always find the truest pictures of virtue in rags, and vice in fine linen.'[98] In 1842, the Vic literally advertised to 'female domestics', promising that a performance of *Susan Hopley*, whose heroine was a maid, would end by 8 30, allowing servants to return in time to satisfy punctilious mistresses.[99] Chartist benefits thus grew out of the working-class milieux in which theatres operated.

The extent and nature of collaboration between professional houses and the Chartists varied.[100] At a minimum, Chartists groups publicised events and sold tickets 'at most Chartist-halls and other places of meeting'.[101] But evidence also points to activists occasionally taking a more active role in the evening's entertainment. 'Aided by several members of the "Standard Company"', a troupe of Chartist amateurs performed the melodrama *Ella Rosenberg* and the fourth act of *Venice Preserved* at a benefit for the 'National Victim Fund' at the Standard in 1843.[102] In other cases, activists might deliver 'an appropriate prologue' before the beginning of a play.[103] At a union benefit at the Victoria Theatre, a mason read a poem provided by the Chartist writer John Watkins, which linked a recent strike with the coming performance of *William Tell*: 'Tyrants no warning take, – / Their hardened hearts no judgments can awake, – / Save when wronged labour rises in its might, / And hurls oppression from its harmful height. / Thus did bold Tell!'[104] Finally, it seems plausible that Chartist groups sometimes weighed in on their preferred programme. Although chosen pieces were usually part of the house's repertoire, they seem often to have been selected as appropriate for Chartist audiences. Benefit performances at the Victoria featured such topical plays as John Walker's *The Factory Lads*, which dramatised, in the words of a contemporary review, 'the misery of the working classes, arising from reduced wages and frequent discharges'.[105] Plays about revolution were also common, and indeed many titles overlapped between professional venues and Chartist amateur theatre. Performances included *William Tell*; *Hofer, the Tell of the Tyrol*; *Venice Preserved*; and *The Black Doctor or the Siege of the Bastile*, in which a scene featuring the Bastille's destruction 'elicited the loudest applause'.[106]

Only in rare instances did Chartist benefits feature no overtly political works. Such was the case for a fundraiser for 'assembly and reading rooms' at the Marylebone Theatre in December 1846 'under the patronage of T. S. Duncombe, MP', a frequent ally of the Chartists.[107] More typical were evenings that paired lighter fare with one or more plays concerning political or industrial strife.[108] Like other early Victorian theatre, Chartist benefits also included 'singing, dancing, and other entertainments' between plays.[109] A Chartist event at the Victoria, for instance, incorporated a '"Highland Fling" in national costume' and an amateur performance of 'several admired airs on the accordion' alongside two revolutionary dramas.[110] Such interludes could be less innocuous. At a Chartist benefit at the Pavilion, 'the Ethiopian Serenaders' performed the crude racial caricatures of blackface minstrelsy.[111] That the *Star* singled out these performers for 'special praise' while noting that the audience was 'evidently delighted with the entertainments of the evening' underlines how racist elements in popular culture could enter the Chartist milieu as well.[112] Yet the paper's coverage of theatre makes clear that ideas about race within the movement were far from monolithic. The *Star* lauded the 'highly-creditable' performance of John Home's tragedy *Douglas* by an all-black amateur company at the Theatre Royal in Jamaica and noted that the singing of the important London activist William Cuffay – a black man whose father had been enslaved in St Kitts – 'was warmly encored' at the 1843 benefit at the Standard mentioned in the preceding paragraph.[113]

Beyond the business potential of Chartist events, the politicised nature of London theatre encouraged collaborations with the Chartists. Ironically, contests over the state's efforts to regulate and censor the stage had contributed to this politicisation. The Stage Licensing Act of 1737, which stayed in place until 1843, restricted the performance of comedy and tragedy to theatres possessing a royal patent. Lacking patents, so-called illegitimate theatres could only legally perform such genres as farce or melodrama. These establishments had long associations with democratic politics. In the 1790s, the theatrical monopoly became sharply contested as the right to stage drama increasingly resonated with questions of political representation, a set of associations forcefully renewed in the early 1830s when efforts to abolish the patent monopoly ran in harness with the campaign for political reform.[114] During the period between the Jacobin and Chartist decades, non-licensed theatres transgressed many aesthetic, generic, and political boundaries.[115] Unlike the Theatres Royal, the minor houses did not have to submit scripts to the Lord Chamberlain's office, a freedom that permitted them to stage plays about industrial strife, rebellion, and mutiny, subjects likely to be censored if ventured at patent houses.[116]

At the same time, unlicensed theatres defied the patent monopoly in a number of ways, including by performing Shakespeare under such thinly disguised titles as *The Moor of Venice* and *The Three Caskets; or the Jew of Venice*, both offered by the Coburg (later renamed the Victoria) in 1827.[117] Finally, unlicensed theatres developed an array of new genres in response to the monopoly's strictures. Melodrama, pantomime, burletta, musical comedy, extravaganza, hippodrome, and other hybrid forms made illegitimate theatres a site of dynamic innovation. Ironically, the patent houses of Drury Lane, Covent Garden, and the Haymarket found that in order to compete financially with the minor theatres they had to abandon their pretensions to being home to the nation's dramatic heritage and mount the same kind of spectacles that captivated large audience at unlicensed venues.[118] So in some sense the 1843 abolition of the patent monopoly merely recognised a de facto reality: the minor houses routinely staged legitimate plays, and the patent theatres shamelessly borrowed from their more successful competitors.[119] At the same time, the Theatres Regulation Act of 1843, passed partly in the hopes of reigning in the anarchic culture of the illegitimate stage, greatly expanded censorship by requiring that all new plays be submitted to the Lord Chamberlain; although theatres were no longer required to have a patent to perform comedy and tragedy, all theatres became subject to greater control.

Venues hosting Chartist benefits often had specific traditions affiliating them with radical politics. The Victoria had waged a campaign against the patent monopoly in the late 1820s, establishing a 'fighting fund' to deter prosecutions, and occasionally weighed in on issues in the wider political realm.[120] Six months after the 'Tolpuddle martyrs' suffered penal transportation for swearing a secret oath to an agricultural labourers' union in Dorset, the Victoria placarded its walls 'with a very large bill' announcing that 'Unionists' had recently made a set of 'extensive alterations' to the theatre, demonstrating 'their skill, industry, and sobriety'.[121] In 1839, the theatre more explicitly supported victims of the repression of unions by hosting a performance for five Glasgow cotton spinners transported the previous year for assaulting strike breakers and another for the Dorchester labourers after their return from penal transportation.[122] Nine years later, the theatre responded to the 1848 revolution in France by rapidly mounting *Vive la Liberté*, a play that promised to bring to stage 'two glorious days of the French Revolution! And the wonderful and rapid results of the Grand Struggle of the People in the cause of liberty.'[123] The Queen's Theatre in Manchester, the site of at least two Chartist benefits, also held fundraisers for trade unions as well as for the 'relief of the distress in Ireland' during the famine years. The theatre, moreover, allied itself with far-left unionism by selling tickets at the office of the *Voice of the People*, the organ of the Owenite National Association for the Protection of Labour.[124] As these examples make clear, the Chartists inherited a rich set of connections linking radical groups to the world of popular theatre, connections they exploited and deepened with their frequent benefits.

What might amateur Chartist performance have drawn from professional productions? The remainder of this section explores Chartist drama in relationship to the professional stage, considering in particular the spectacular nature of Victorian theatre, the behaviour of audiences, and the question of censorship. Given the popularity of theatre with working-class people, commercial plays assuredly served as models to which amateurs aspired. Recollecting a visit to the Theatre Royal in Manchester with fellow members of a Chartist 'mutual improvement society', Ben Brierley rhapsodised: 'our first acquaintance with the legitimate stage led us to aspire to be specks of light in the milkyway about which the constellations revolved'.[125] At the same time, amateurs could not straightforwardly emulate some aspects of professional theatre and Chartist groups surely rejected others due to political or aesthetic concerns.

In the 1830s and 1840s, ever larger auditoriums encouraged a grandiose acting style in the tradition of the famous tragedian Edmund Kean while increasingly sophisticated stage technology enabled spectacles on a massive scale. Staged fires, explosions, avalanches, naval battles, pursuits on horseback, and the appearance of ghosts using 'lantern-slide projections, mirrors … and traps' were all common.[126] Needless to say, amateur productions could attempt few of these feats, although Chartists in Longton bravely staged Matthew Lewis's 1797 *Castle Spectre*, which owed its continued popularity to an apparition sequence.[127] Instead of the technically ambitious spectacles of established houses, Chartist stagecraft likely resembled the humble penny gaffs, which in Henry Mayhew's estimation had 'no very great scenic embellishment' on their tiny stages.[128] An account by the Nottingham artisan and radical Christopher Thomson of the first production of his amateur troupe gives a sense of the challenges that would have confronted aspiring Chartist actors. Thomson, who went on to work as a scene painter and 'strolling player', recounts how the troupe's stage manager was able to befriend and borrow costumes from 'the wardrobe-keeper of the Theatre Royal'.[129] Scenery presented more formidable difficulties. Though a cast member was 'by profession a coach herald painter', the group could only afford one scene, requiring the 'painter … to show his skill in design, by contriving a picture, "Which served us for parlour, and kitchen, and all"'.[130]

Aspects of the two most frequently staged Chartist plays, *John Frost* and *Robert Emmet*, seem well suited to amateur performance in that they obviate the need for large-scale spectacle. Instead of staging the Newport rising's climactic confrontation, in which soldiers exchanged fire with a Chartist crowd, Watkins's play retrospectively narrates the attack through the hero's confused perspective. Similarly, *The Trial of Robert Emmet* does not represent the 1803 Dublin rising on stage but instead reconstructs events via eyewitnesses' fragmentary accounts, the prosecutor's opening address, and Emmet's final speech. If these plays permitted minimalist staging, however, Chartist drama sometimes embraced an aesthetics of spectacle, a style to which Chartist crowds (whose members would themselves have participated in protest marches and other political displays) were not strangers. The considerable expense some groups dedicated for costumes and the massive settings of certain performances (including the Leicester Amphitheatre and the Glasgow Circus) suggest something more than threadbare productions. Newspaper accounts of the Ashton *Trial of Robert Emmet* stress the way the performance recreated the elaborate rituals of a treason trial. The large cast included jury members, 'six soldiers', judges, and attorneys, all of whom exercised 'the greatest decorum' and adhered to the 'regular court' forms.[131] One Irish paper remarked that 'the appearance of the court, with the necessary number of witnesses, counsel for the crown, judges and their attendants arranged in gowns, wigs, &c. was very well got up'.[132]

Furthering a sense of spectacle, Chartist performances sometimes included music. An orchestra performed for a Leicester production of John Home's tragedy *Douglas*, and 'the patriotic Winlaton band ... played several appropriate airs during [a] performance' of *John Frost*.[133] As Michael Pisani describes, such extra-diegetic music was ubiquitous in Victorian theatre and assisted 'the actors in establishing and sustaining the [play's] emotional pitch'.[134] Music accompanied characters' entries and exits, helped define the heroine, the villain, and other parts, and punctuated climaxes. For *John Frost*, music would have called to the surface the play's melodramatic elements. Doleful melodies might have accented scenes representing suffering or dissonant chords signalled highly wrought emotion. Either strategy would suit a worker's speech at a public meeting in Act 2, which describes his penal transportation for swearing a union oath, his return to England, and his wife's descent into madness, which culminates with the murder of their starving children. Similarly extraordinary situations can be found in each text in this collection and such events would have encouraged a melodramatic acting style defined by broad gestures and extreme emotion, a style common in professional theatre.

Early Victorian theatre audiences shared an affinity with political crowds. Accounts of popular theatre by both working- and middle-class observers describe boisterous playgoers interacting with the performance in numerous ways, thus helping to shape its meaning and significance.[135] The gallery would call for tunes from the orchestra, stamp in time during dances, and join in the choruses until 'the ears positively ache[d] with the din'.[136] 'Showers of applause' greeted characters' 'worthy' sentiments while 'cowardice and falsehood' met hissing.[137] Other interventions might break drama's 'fourth wall'; Mayhew describes how at one show at the Victoria a 'lady begging for her father's life was told to "speak up old gal"'.[138] A working-class memoir similarly records how someone at a melodrama called out following a death scene: "'Die again, my bold Bricks! die again!" and the cry being taken up by the other gods, was repeated with a frequency and strength of lungs, that proved sufficient to wake the (stage) dead. For, in obedience to the call, Bricks got up and *did* "die again".'[139]

Interruptions could also have political import. The gallery might demand the *Marseillaise*, and applause or expressions of displeasure could transform the meaning of particular lines. The most notorious example of this practice occurred in 1794–95 when Jacobins succeeded in inverting the significance of Thomas Otway's *Venice Preserved* by cheering the sentiments of characters conspiring to overthrow Venice's senate. The radicals' efforts were so successful that they forced the cancellation of successive runs at Covent Garden and Drury Lane. After the incident became part of the prosecution's case in the treason trial of John Thelwall, the play remained controversial for decades.[140] By performing *Venice Preserved* twice in the autumn of 1843, once in an amateur production that cast the novelist and activist Thomas Martin Wheeler as the lead conspirator, the Chartists affiliated their dramatic culture with a tradition of radical theatre arising with the audience. The re-appropriation had become so complete that the crowd's cheers were no longer against the grain.

The controversy around *Venice Preserved* brings up a crucial difference between Chartist amateur drama and the professional stage. Although illegitimate theatres tested the bounds of the patent monopoly and theatrical censorship, they nevertheless had to contend with the Lord Chamberlain and local magistrates, who could impose fines, jail actors, or revoke an establishment's licence. Censorship became especially acute in times of political upheaval. Jenna Gibbs describes how 'in the face of Chartist agitation' the Lord Chamberlain vigilantly policed East End theatres and 'became intolerant of licensing violations'.[141] From the early 1840s, the police repeatedly raided the Britannia; later in the decade, the Lord Chamberlain cancelled performances of George Dibdin Pitt's *Revolution in Paris* (1848); Pitt's *Terry Tyrone* (1845), which concerns an Irish rebellion; and *The Chartist; or, a Dream of Every-day Life* (1848), although the latter shows the ruinous consequences of an artisan's embrace of radicalism.[142]

The Chartists, on the other hand, routinely staged plays that celebrated a revolutionary tradition linking Britain, Ireland, and Europe. Yet the overwhelming majority of amateur Chartist productions met no interference from theatrical authorities or the police. Indeed, the Chartists staged plays on subjects that were suppressed in commercial venues for decades to come. In 1881, the Lord Chamberlain refused the Lyceum permission to perform Frank Marshall's *Robert Emmet*, and films about the Dublin rising encountered censorship through the 1910s.[143] Several factors contributed to the Chartists' relative freedom. First, censorship was less easily enforced outside London, though local elites could exercise a kind of soft censorship by denying space to planned productions, a circumstance which frustrated efforts to stage William Cobbett's *Surplus Population* in Tonbridge, Kent a few years before the rise of Chartism.[144] Second, the informal spaces and irregular schedules of Chartist performances likely shielded them from unwanted attention. Third, after 1843 the Chartists could simply refuse to submit scripts to the Lord Chamberlain, a stratagem established theatres sometimes used to circumvent the law.[145] Finally, prosecuting the Chartists under the Theatre Licensing Act must have struck authorities as wasted resources, given how members of the movement routinely faced far more serious charges. Together, these factors created a rich irony: while other kinds of Chartist speech and writing were heavily surveilled and served as the basis of hundreds for prosecutions, the movement turned to theatre – the only art form in Britain subject to statutory censorship – as a way for members to express themselves freely.

Political violence and state repression in Chartist drama

Chartist drama began in the shadow of the Newport rising of November 1839 and served as one of the ways the campaign took stock of itself in the aftermath of the rising's failure. As Table 0.4 indicates, the first burst of Chartist performance occurred in 1840, a year of crisis for the movement.

While Watkins's *John Frost* made Newport its explicit subject, the Chartists staged numerous plays that reflected on violence as a political strategy as well as

Table 0.4 Chartist performances identified by year*

Year	Number of performances
1839	3
1840	11
1841	14
1842	17
1843	17 (possibly an additional 21 or more)
1844	3
1845	1
1846	5
1847	4
1848	6
1849	4
1850	6
1851	6
Unknown year	8

* *Note:* The ambiguity surrounding 1843 concerns a tour of *The Trial of Robert Emmet* the *Star* ceased covering. See Footnote 68.

on governmental repression, which many believed had set the rising in motion and which only intensified following the outbreak's defeat. Reckoning with Newport involved first understanding what had actually occurred on the night of 3 November and the morning of 4 November when some nine thousand armed miners and iron workers marched on the economically critical Welsh port, which connected the Monmouthshire coal and iron fields to Britain and the wider world. In Newport, the Chartists attacked the Westgate Hotel (in the hope of liberating a group of Chartist activists who had been detained by police forces). They were repelled by soldiers who killed at least twenty-two and wounded approximately fifty, leading to the rising's collapse. Did these events, as many contemporaries believed and historians deem probable, represent a misfired 'signal' for other parts of the nation 'to rise in insurrection also'?[146] Or were they, as the defence claimed at trial, a protest or riot that led unintentionally to tragic consequences? Whatever the case, Newport sent shockwaves through the nation. Over the following months, what proved to be the last mass treason trials in British history transfixed the public. Before a Special Commission in Monmouth that included the Lord Chief Justice Nicholas Tindal, sixteen Chartists stood accused of capital crimes. Three leaders, Zephaniah Williams, William Jones, and John Frost were sentenced to death. Although a petition campaign (or the government's calculation that a degree of conciliation might purchase peace) saved the men's lives, they were transported to Van Diemen's Land under life sentence.

Newport marked a strategic and ideological turning point in Chartism's history. As several scholars note, the disastrous consequences of the rising and juxtaposed success of the petition campaign that rescued Frost, Williams, and Jones bolstered the movement's moderate wing while prompting figures identified with physical force to temper their opinions.[147] At the same time, Chartist positions on violence represented a continuum rather than a set of simple oppositions. Anticipating a modern scholarly consensus, the *Charter* wrote in the wake of the rising: 'the difference between moral and physical force is not so *wide* as writers seem to think'.[148] Moral force strategies could include confrontational tactics or contain the threat of escalation, and physical force language might signal militancy without prompting concrete steps towards armed rebellion. Nevertheless, at a point when insurrectionary politics appeared discredited, it is striking that Chartist performers in several localities staged plays that lauded a revolutionary tradition.

Among the plays the Chartists performed, John Watkins's *John Frost* was extraordinary in a number of ways. Not only was Watkins himself a Chartist activist, the temporal and geographic proximity of the play's subject matter separated it from works set in different times and places. Where *Wat Tyler* concerned the Great Rising of 1381, *Wallace, the Hero of Scotland* recounted the war for Scottish independence at the end of the thirteenth century, and

William Tell depicted legendary events that supposedly brought Switzerland independence, *John Frost* treated episodes barely one year old and still very present in Chartist consciousness when the play appeared in spring 1841. Watkins's text, furthermore, staked out extreme positions even within Chartist discourse. Watkins himself believed the play's politics led 'the chief Chartist publisher in London [to shrink] from the responsibility of publishing it', a circumstance that forced the author to self-publish.[149] At issue was political violence. In Malcolm Chase's account, 'Watkins articulated sentiments as close to open advocacy of revolution in print as any Chartist at this time'.[150] Although the play registers ambivalence about physical force (primarily in the voice of John Frost following the rising's defeat), it ultimately justifies insurrection, a stance the prologue unambiguously endorses.[151] Reconstructing a history of British resistance to oppression by the Romans, Normans, and others, the prologue projects this history into the future, declaring: 'Silurian Frosts again shall lead us on, / And Freedom's baffled battle yet be won!'[152]

Yet the calamitous course of the rising made it a challenging subject with which to advocate revolt. How democratic rule might be achieved forms a central problem of Watkins's play, which scrutinises and complicates notions of agency prevalent in Chartist verse. As Mike Sanders argues, Chartist poetry typically elides the question of what 'social force' would be 'capable of securing the Charter'.[153] Naturalistic metaphors of apocalyptic change, for example, suggest the inevitability of revolution while '[mystifying] the actual political obstacles which Chartism has already encountered'.[154] Other poems skirt the question of agency with recourse to a 'voluntarist paradigm', which attributes social power to an abstracted will of 'the people'.[155] Such language appears in Watkins's essay, *The Five Cardinal Points of the Charter*, which declares: 'When they [common people] all unite as one man, moved by one will, to obtain one object – nothing can drive them back, nothing can stand before them.'[156]

John Frost, on the other hand, grapples more seriously with the obstacles blocking change, even if it fails to satisfactorily resolve the issues raised.[157] In the play's opening scene, the protagonist himself ascribes to voluntarism, musing that 'Combined for freedom, we at once were free', but the action that follows presents combination as a difficult process threatened both by internal divisions and outside forces.[158] Tellingly, Watkins recasts naturalistic metaphors, literalising a figure for divine justice as a form of human action. When the Chartist leader Albion asks: 'Just Heaven, where was thy thunder? Sleeps it, God? / Oh, at our cries awake it, let it fall!' the worker-activist Shell responds: 'We'll launch it forth – our hands shall deal the bolt! / We are not passive, non-resisting slaves.'[159] Yet if the 'people' cannot simply will its own liberation nor await divine power to overthrow tyranny, the question remains what exactly might be capable of bringing about democracy. In Act 2, the eponymous hero encounters a series of allegorical figures, who articulate alternative models of change. Frost finds common cause with Aquarius, who recommends abstinence from alcohol, and Utopian, who propounds Owenite socialism, but Middleman's advocacy of political gradualism – 'the course of rational reform' – is shown merely to cover a commitment to class rule.[160]

In satirising Middleman – a figure for Whig politicians who had allied with working-class radicals to win the franchise for a segment of the middle classes only to abandon the cause of further reform – Watkins stands on safe ground with the Chartist public. His text becomes controversial, however, in its attacks on petitioning as a political strategy, a set of critiques that position Watkins outside a constitutionalist tradition by declaring the impossibility of change within the present system. If in Act 2 the Chartists place their hopes in 'our National Petition, / Wherein [our] wants, [our] woes, [our] wrongs are writ, / The cause set forth, and quick redress implor'd', by the next act the Privy Council dashes those hopes when it treats the document as an object of ridicule, notable only for its 'ludicrous size'.[161] Lord Littlejohn (a figure for John Russell) describes to his fellows the presentation of the petition in Parliament: 'The members stared aghast awhile, and then, / Burst into laughter fit to shake the house.'[162] More damning still, Shell articulates the self-defeating nature of seeking redress from an anti-democratic body: 'Petitions do no good, but harm; as this – / They are acknowledgments of unjust power, / As if usurp'd and fraudful force were legal.'[163] This critique echoes the preface, in which Watkins declares the 'uselessness as well as mean-spiritedness of petitioning those who had banished' Frost for his return.[164] To advance this case, the play elides the seeming efficacy of the petition for Frost's pardon, making the commutation of the death sentence a cynical calculation by the Privy Council, rather than a concession to the popular will. With other modes of redress foreclosed, only revolt remains. On the eve of Shell's death, the young man resolves to

> Send no more papers begging of my own,
> To get no answer but a curse or scoff –
> Spurn'd from the door of our own House by Thieves,
> Who revel on the booty that's within!
> I'll take a pike, next time, for my petition;
> And knock so loud with it, the door shall fly.[165]

At Frost's treason trial, the defence claimed that the march on Newport was intended as a demonstration seeking the release of Henry Vincent and other political prisoners, an idea the Chartist press promulgated widely.[166] Watkins's treatment of this theme is revelatory; the play accepts the premise that Vincent's rescue (in the figure of Albion) is the Chartists' immediate goal but unpacks the revolutionary logic behind this demand, which defines the state's monopoly of violence as illegitimate. 'Because we were defenceless', Shell declares, 'they have dragg'd / Our friend to gaol for advocating us. / … Now we are arm'd to meet them on their terms. / If we can't rescue Albion let us die.'¹⁶⁷ When Frost warns the crowd to 'Obey the law, or you arm tyrants with't', Shell replies, 'We'll break the law and make a better one'.¹⁶⁸ Watkins thus places the Chartist debate about force in the context of violence upholding the present system. At Albion's arrest for breaking 'the Queen's good peace', the Chartist leader retorts, ''Tis you have broke the peace and people's heads, / Ye peace preservers!'¹⁶⁹

Beyond the coercion upon which the state depends, *John Frost* articulates a vision of violence permeating the economic sphere. In Frost's opening monologue and the conversation with his wife that follows, the hero describes inequality as founded on property relations akin to theft: '[Workers] must die off, or quit their native land, / That drones may revel on their labour's produce. / And shall the idler feast upon their store, / And spurn away the plundered working men?'¹⁷⁰ Though Frost initially holds such beliefs abstractly, labourers at the Chartist meeting make clear how violence pervades their everyday lives. One speaker describes his respiratory illness arising from work processing coal; another recounts how his wife wastes away due to starvation wages; a third bemoans his homeless children; another recalls his transportation for joining a union; and a last laments his degradation as a street sweep, though he lost a leg 'in the glorious' wars.¹⁷¹ Taken together, the testimony lays bare the violence intrinsic to the present order. When Frost's daughter asks her father to consider the 'peace' of their family before taking the fatal step of joining the Chartists, Frost responds that 'peace' can only be illusory in society as constituted: 'Peace? War! peace is not, cannot, shall not be / Until Britannia's slaves have food and freedom.'¹⁷²

Other Chartist drama broadened Watkins's critique of the violent nature of British society to include the state's militarism and commitment to empire. In *The Trial of Robert Emmet*, Emmet speaks from the dock about his effort 'to extricate [his] countrymen from [the] doubly-rivetted despotism' of foreign rule and 'a domestic faction, which is its joint partner'.¹⁷³ The Ashton Chartists emphasised this aspect of the trial, advertising performances in Manchester with placards headlined 'Arise! Ye sons of Erin! Your brave patriots are gone.'¹⁷⁴ Southey's *Wat Tyler* also associates anti-democratic rule with violence on the world stage. The play repeatedly stresses that the poll tax which sets the revolt in motion is implemented to raise funds for war with France. Tyler points out the class politics of the conflict by asking: 'What matters me who wears the crown of France? / Whether a Richard or a Charles possess it? / They reap the glory – they enjoy the spoil – / We pay – we bleed!'¹⁷⁵

If *The Trial of Robert Emmet*, *Wat Tyler*, and *John Frost* all contextualise revolutionary violence in terms of the brutal systems their protagonists seek to overthrow, the works reach different conclusions about the possible consequences of force. In particular, *Wat Tyler* presents a more multivalent view of violence than *John Frost*, offering, in Ian Haywood's account, 'various political fantasies

... of violence ranging from regicide to patriarchal self-defence'.[176] In Southey's narrative, the revolt of 1381 originates in Tyler killing a tax-collector who has sexually assaulted his daughter, an account that casts the outbreak as fundamentally defensive. This posture resonates with Chartist discourse that characterised the movement's recourse to violence as a last stand against aggression, sometimes even justifying insurrection as a means of restoring usurped rights.[177] The Manifesto of the Chartist Convention of 1839, for example, walks a rhetorical tightrope: 'We have resolved to obtain our rights, *"peaceably, if we may – forcibly, if we must"*: but woe to those who begin the warfare with the millions, or who forcibly restrain their peaceful agitation for justice – ... in one brief contest their power will be destroyed.'[178] In a similar key, Southey's John Ball inverts who is rebel, who sovereign, declaring that 'The nobles lose their pretext, nor will dare / Rebel against the people's majesty.'[179]

Wat Tyler repeatedly asks the audience to consider the role of violence, exploring at different points in the rebellion's progress whether force appears warranted or efficacious. At the height of the rebels' success, Ball attempts to restrain the crowd, urging them to execute no prisoners and forswear 'the calm deliberate murder of Revenge'.[180] When Piers reasons that the nobles 'would not argue thus humanely on us, / Were we within their power', Ball replies, 'we must pity them that they are vicious, / Nor imitate their vice'.[181] At the same time, the text poses Ball's moderation as potentially misguided. The priest himself expresses doubt three times (echoing Peter's three denials of Christ): 'my frail and fallible judgment / Knows hardly to decide if it be right, / Peaceably to return, content with little, / With this half restitution of our rights, / Or boldly to proceed, through blood and slaughter, / Till we should all be equal and all happy. / I chose the milder way: – perhaps I erred!'[182]

Ball's very next speech is interrupted by 'Great tumult', as the king, who had promised amnesty, breaks 'his plighted vow' and moves to crush the rebellion.[183] The rising's defeat thus encourages a reconsideration of the rebel's restraint. The play asks, along with Ball, whether the insurgents' moderation has 'been like the weak leech, / Who, sparing to cut deep, with cruel mercy / Mangles his patient without curing him'.[184] *John Frost* is notably less self-reflective than *Wat Tyler*. Even as the play dramatises the tragic outcome of the rising, key characters express their continued faith in an insurrectionary strategy without articulating how it might succeed in the future. Shell's own 'last death-utter'd words' affirm his commitment to physical force, demanding his death be revenged.[185] And Frost's wife Mary, previously hostile to Chartism, converts to physical-force doctrines; on the eve of her husband's exile, she tells him she will not 'petition Majesty' for his return but would 'sooner take a sword and lead [the people] on'.[186]

If drama intervened in Chartist debates about force, a question arises as to the ways performance affected the kinds of political acts the movement was able or willing to take. Brian Maidment and Mike Sanders have speculated that rather than encouraging confrontational acts, poetry when recited might have served a 'cathartic role' through which 'social aggression in the poem was sublimated or acted out rather than developed into action'.[187] Drama too might have '[discharged] anger which [could not] be vented in any other form', but intriguing evidence suggests that in certain cases Chartists groups turned to drama in the hope of revitalising the movement's most militant traditions.[188] In particular, the popularity of *The Trial of Robert Emmet* in the Lancashire cotton district situates performances at associations that saw significant arming and drilling in 1839 and that played central roles in the general strike of 1842.[189] In fact, the Ashton Juvenile Association, which toured area mill towns with a production of the trial in 1841–42, formed following a split in the local movement when older Chartists, objecting to drilling by younger members 'expelled the individuals so offending'.[190]

In this light, *The Trial of Robert Emmet* appears as the extension of Jacobin politics to the cultural sphere. No less formidable an opponent of Chartism than the Irish politician Daniel O'Connell understood productions in these terms. At a Manchester meeting, he condemned performances as offering 'the principles of the torch and the dagger'.[191] The local O'Connellite Association passed a resolution urging 'all Irishmen to refrain from attending'.[192] When Chartist orators invoked Emmet's memory, the authorities understood the revolutionary implications equally clearly. Allusions to the Irish martyr became part of the prosecution's case against Francis Looney, who advised his audience to acquire pikes and pistols in 1848, and Alexander Challenger, who claimed that 'less than these turnouts [i.e. the 1842 strikes] had brought on revolutions … The time was very near when a Cromwell, an Emmett, or a Fairfax would be found amongst the people'.[193] Similarly, Chartist orators invoked Wat Tyler as an insurrectionary example, and such invocations were used against them at sedition trials.[194] Chartist ultra-radicals too became associated with the historical Wat Tyler. A Chartist branch in Sheffield honoured their deceased leader Samuel Holberry, who led an abortive rising in the town, by constructing a 'shrine' that featured a bust of the fourteenth-century hero.[195] In Bradford in 1848, a major riot ensued when the police attempted to arrest the activist Isaac Jefferson, who went by 'Wat Tyler' and was 'the reputed principal Chartist pike-maker of the district'.[196]

What to make of the fact that so many Chartist plays featured unsuccessful revolts? Does this suggest the plays might have served as both inspiration and warning?[197] John Cleave's *The Memoir of Robert Emmett* (from which the trial in this volume is drawn) speaks of 'the danger as well as the necessity of resistance'.[198] In a review of Cleave's memoir, Bronterre O'Brien cautions that 'the failure of the scheme of the United Irishmen ought to be a warning to the reformers of all times and countries. It ought to teach them never to attempt to revolutionize a country by means of secret organisation, or otherwise than by fair and open appeals to the reason and natural feelings of the people themselves'.[199] Yet caution hardly seems the lesson learned from Emmet's story. In Cleave's *Memoir*, Emmet himself speaks proleptically, warning his comrades that 'should I fall on the scaffold, let not the coward or the knave intimidate you from again and again appealing to Heaven in behalf of your rights and liberties by appealing to my recent failure'.[200] If the *Chartist Circular* regretted Emmet's 'reckless ... enterprise', it imagined that had he acted at a more propitious moment he might have become 'an Atlas ... [capable of lifting] this world of tyrants ... into the cycle of freedom's undying sun'.[201] More broadly, Chartist culture celebrated martyrs and viewed their sacrifices as redemptive.[202]. An address by the Nottingham Female Association was characteristic: 'The martyrs of liberty never die ... The murdered Emmett and Fitzgerald still live, and are communed with on every mountain, and in every dell.'[203] For the *Circular*, fallen rebels performed a tangible service: 'Wretchedly enslaved as the world is, it would now have been in a more deplorable condition had there never been resistance to the aggressions of tyrants. ... The salutary influence of Wat Tyler, rude as he was, was felt in England for hundreds of years after he was dead: it is even felt to this day.'[204]

A further element linking *Wat Tyler*, *The Trial of Robert Emmet*, and *John Frost* is that each includes a treason trial. As many Chartist performances raised funds for prisoners or their families, this emphasis overlaid the plight of the plays' protagonists with that of the evening's beneficiaries. Notably, all three works turn away from a popular tradition of trial parodies, which included books such as William Hone's *Non Mi Ricordo! Or, Cross-Examination Extraordinary* and mock trials performed in taverns by judge and jury clubs.[205] Instead of parody, Chartist dramas utilise a variety of strategies to undermine the legitimacy of the proceedings they represent. In *Wat Tyler*, verbal irony satirises Ball's 'fair, free, open trial, where the King / Can choose his jury and appoint his judges'.[206] Ball, like many radicals of Southey's time and later, turns 'the vain and empty insult of a trial' into a platform from which to condemn his persecutors and propound 'the electric truth' he possesses.[207] *John Frost*, on the other hand, simply refuses to stage the protagonist's appearance in court, an ironic deflation of the most important political trial in a generation. Watkins's omission makes clear that the verdict has been decided elsewhere – the privy councillors inform the audience of Frost's conviction and death sentence.

Finally, *The Trial of Robert Emmet* turns sharply from parody. Newspaper accounts emphasise how performances attempted to recreate the ceremonies of justice and power that constitute a treason trial. Ashton productions, for example, began with the 'judges' entering the court, the grand jury being 'sworn', the 'Attorney-General [opening] the proceedings in the regular court style', and the prisoner being 'brought forward in chains, attended by an officer, and six soldiers'. All actors appeared 'in full uniform'. According to the *Star*, the audience 'could not but be struck with the reflections of reality'.[208] Yet despite this verisimilitude, *Robert Emmet* offers a devastating critique of the judicial apparatus. As a courtroom drama, the trial is haunted by Emmet's refusal to mount a defence. At Emmet's instruction, his counsel declines to call witnesses, offer a closing statement, or cross-examine most witnesses for the prosecution. This silence begs several questions. Does it signal Emmet's despair and recognition of his guilt? Should the audience accept the prosecution's narrative in which the conspirators appear alternately sinister and naive, murderous and quixotic? Or is the silence disruptive – an act of non-participation that highlights the emptiness of the ritual of due process the trial enacts? Emmet's closing speech makes explicit his refusal to take part in the proceeding on the state's terms. Offered the opportunity to plead to mitigate the sentence, Emmet replies that he has 'nothing to say that can alter [the judges'] predetermination'.[209] Indeed, instead of speaking simply to the court, he repeatedly addresses posterity, a temporal leap that paradoxically situates the re-enactment's audience in Emmet's courtroom in so far as the spectators embody the future to which Emmet appeals, the 'other times and other men' of the speech's close.[210] As Emmet denounces British rule in Ireland and the right of the court to judge him, the Lord Justice attempts to cut short his speech, which in turn becomes evidence of the trial's illegitimacy:

> Why did your Lordships insult me – or rather, why insult justice, in demanding of me why sentence of death should not be pronounced? I know, my Lord, that form prescribes that you should ask the question; the form also prescribes the right of answering. This, no doubt, may be dispensed with, and so might the whole ceremony of the trial, since sentence was already pronounced at the Castle before your jury was empanelled. Your Lordships are but the priests of the oracle, and I submit: but I insist on the whole of the forms.[211]

Emmet's awareness of a trial's inherent theatricality, his ability to manipulate its rules, and his recognition of the historical contingency upon which those conventions depend in the first place, allow him to transform the courtroom into a site of counter-spectacle, in which he invites the audience to imagine an alternative future – when Ireland 'takes her place among the nations of the earth' – springing from his sacrifice.[212]

'Not wisely but too well': Women and Chartist drama

Chartist drama, like Chartist discourse more broadly, often defined politics as a male domain. In Edward Fitzball's *Hofer, The Tell of the Tyrol* (1832), a play the Chartists performed at least three times, the hero reprimands his wife Marie for pleading with him to make peace with occupying French and Bavarian forces. Although Marie earlier set fire to the family home rather than let it fall into the hands of foreign soldiers, Hofer dismisses her perspective: 'no woman's voice should ever turn a patriot from his duty. Go, ply thy distaff! love, and be beloved; all that is beautiful and fond, I grant ye; but never meddle with affairs of state – thy hand is all too feeble for the helm.'[213] The protagonist of James Sheridan Knowles's *William Tell* speaks in similarly masculinist language when he refuses to bow to the tyrant Gesler's cap, hectoring the frightened crowd: 'Why gaze you still with blanched cheeks upon me? / Lack you the manhood even to look on'?[214]

Although these plays originally appeared in contexts distant from working-class radicalism, they nevertheless make explicit a set of suppositions that structured Chartist ideas about politics. In debates within Chartism, proponents of confrontational tactics celebrated militancy and courage as masculine virtues while deriding opponents as womanish.[215] At the height of the 1842 strike wave, for example, an address by the National Chartist Association exhorted: 'Brethren, we rely upon your firmness; cowardice, treachery, or womanly fear would cast our cause back for half a century', language wilfully ignorant of the thousands of women on strike throughout the cotton district (where a large majority of operatives were female).[216] Such rhetoric resonated with broader narratives that fashioned Chartism as the protector of working-class families under siege from the factory system and the austerity of the New Poor Law.[217] Benefits held to raise money for Chartist 'widows' and 'orphans' accorded well with this self-image.[218]

Dramatic productions, however, complicated narratives of female distress and male rescue in several ways. First, radical groups staged a number of plays which feature male protagonists who represent threats to women and their families. Such works as *Othello*, *William Tell*, and *John Frost* suggest the potential costs of celebrating heroic masculinity. Drama's dialogism, moreover, would have opened a forum for audiences to reflect on tensions and contradictions within Chartist attitudes towards gender. While Chartist life granted women few opportunities to speak publicly to mixed-sex groups, theatre allowed them to voice passionate emotions and articulate perspectives different from their male counterparts.[219] Furthermore, female actors sometimes inhabited roles of rebellious wives and daughters (alongside more conventional parts of domestic angels or passive victims). Finally, women helped shape Chartist dramatic culture through their work preparing for and hosting benefits. Although such labour represented something akin to 'separate spheres' within activist politics, it nevertheless afforded women the opportunity to organise on behalf of fellow women and leave a mark on Chartist life.[220]

For many middle-class observers, the prominent place women occupied within Chartism was a distinctive feature of the campaign.[221] Female Chartists attended meetings (both mixed-sex and otherwise), marched in processions, joined strikes, and formed their own organisations. Notably, several Chartist locales with theatrical traditions, including Ashton, Leicester, Greenock,

Table 0.5 Chartist dramatic performances by locality (in localities with two or more performances)

Locality	Number of performances
London	32
Ashton	13–16 (4 in Ashton and 9–12 in surrounding localities by Ashton troupe)
Failsworth	9
Manchester	7
Glasgow	6
Leicester	4
Nottingham	4
Oldham	3
Clitheroe	2
Hamilton (Scotland)	2
Hyde	2
Kilbarchan (Scotland)	2
Keighley	2
Vale of Leven (Scotland)	2
Preston	2

Manchester, and Nottingham, had active female associations or otherwise robust participation by women (see Table 0.5).[222] In Nottingham, the site of two stagings of *John Frost*, the Nottingham Female Political Union (NFPU) drew on local traditions of female activism that went back to at least 1820.[223] At NFPU meetings, women chaired the proceedings, proposed and debated resolutions, and delivered lectures and speeches. At its first gathering on 23 October 1838 the room 'was electrified by the able and energetic address of Mrs Oakland', who moved a resolution that all taxpayers (a category implicitly including women) should have the right to vote.[224]

Female associations were particularly active in the cultural life of Chartist localities. The *Star* frequently reported that 'the fair sex [was] strongly predominant' at festivals and tea parties.[225] Although the press sometimes employed condescending language to describe female participation on such occasions – 'the house was crowded in every part with female beauty' – women did more than grace meetings with their presence.[226] Rather, female associations organised all manner of events, making fundraising for prisoners' families a special mission. In the weeks following the Newport rising, the Nottingham Female Association – the descendant of the NPFU – published an address 'to the men and women of Nottinghamshire' calling attention 'to the condition of the wives and families of our incarcerated brethren ... Let us show our enemies that every act of coercion, only binds the advocates of justice more firmly together'.[227]

Benefits depended on much behind-the-scenes work by women, who frequently decorated meeting rooms and sometimes sold tickets. Although the former activity signalled Chartists' willingness to exploit traditional divisions of labour, women's efforts meant that female activists greatly influenced the movement's visual culture. At a holiday party in Manchester, 'The Female Chartists of Brown-Street' trimmed their room 'with evergreens, paintings of various descriptions, portraits, flags, and banners'.[228] Selling tickets too involved more than simple bookkeeping. It constituted a kind of political organising in which women activated their social networks, inviting friends and neighbours to share in conviviality and a project of mutual support. For a benefit at the Standard Theatre, the *Star* expressed its 'trust' that 'our female friends, who invariably are diligent in the great cause of humanity and philanthropy, will take care that all their acquaintances are supplied with box or pit tickets, on the occasion'.[229]

Beyond preparatory work, women also contributed to events as performers. Historians rightly emphasise that female Chartists were excluded from making toasts or speeches at ceremonial dinners.[230] They did, however, participate in a variety of other ways at dinners and similar events. Women played instruments, recited poetry, sang songs (including original compositions), and acted on stage.[231] At the same time, much female labour received little or no attention in the movement press, a mark of the sexual inequality that assigned women to less public roles in the first place. The reader, for example, only learns that it was women who organised a benefit for Polish and Hungarian refugees at Astley's Theatre in London, because the refugee committee invited Feargus O'Connor 'to attend and occupy the Queen's box on that occasion, in company with the wives of the Committee, who had got up the benefit'.[232]

Though many plays the Chartists performed contain few female parts, they also feature such significant characters as Desdemona in *Othello* and Lady Randolph in John Home's *Douglas*. These tragedies and several other works in the radical repertoire reveal conflicts frequently papered over in Chartist discourse. Isolated in worlds of politics and warfare, Home's and Shakespeare's heroines navigate their environments with constricted forms of agency; their fates highlight the dangers represented by male milieux where violence is celebrated and women barred from positions of authority. One might see the plays, then, as reflecting on exclusions women confronted within activist culture and Victorian society more broadly. Home's Lady Randolph expresses anger over the constraints that govern her existence. After the death of her first husband Douglas, she is denied her 'strong desire / To lead a single, solitary life' when she relents to Lord Randolph's suit and her dying father's pleas.[233] Nevertheless, she asserts autonomy in her second marriage, wearing widow's dress for seven years and maintaining a haughty independence by forswearing 'admiration, dear to womankind'.[234] Dominating many scenes, she stands at the center of a plot to restore her foundling son to his rightful title, thus stripping her second husband of estates acquired in marriage. After her son's death, the play concludes when 'fearless as the eagle' she climbs a precipice, and casts herself 'headlong down', her suicide simultaneously an act of protest and negation.[235] One can only speculate how Chartist audiences in Leicester and Failsworth might have responded to this heroine, but the reception of the song 'I'll be no Submissive Wife' at a benefit at the City of London Theatre provides some clue. '[Eliciting] an unanimous encore', the song concludes: 'Should a humdrum husband say / That at home I ought to stay / Do you think that I'll obey / No no no no no no no no no no not I'.[236]

Stories about men rescuing women in distress recurred on the early Victorian stage, but such plots are surprisingly rare in the Chartist dramatic repertoire. Beyond *Wat Tyler*, which (as already described) situates the origin of the Great Rising in a father protecting his daughter, only James Kenney's *Ella Rosenberg* and Jerrold's *Black Ey'd Susan* (both performed at benefits in London) conform to this narrative pattern. In Matthew Lewis's gothic melodrama *The Castle Spectre* (staged by Chartist amateurs in Longton), the hero attempts to rescue his beloved Angela, who is confined by her murderous uncle, but the intervention of the girl's (ghostly) mother proves decisive and Angela herself strikes the blow that kills the villain.

Rather than rescuing helpless women, the heroes of the Chartist stage act with a recklessness that itself poses a threat. Indeed, it is frequently the hero's patriotism or political activism that endangers his family. *Hofer, the Tell of the Tyrol* begins with Hofer's marriage, but by Act 2 his wife and child are captured by the French, who promise their execution unless Hofer surrenders. The climax of *William Tell* has the hero shoot an apple from his son Albert's head, which raises the possibility that he will 'Murder his child with his own hand! – This hand! / The hand I've led him when an infant by!'[237] When Tell later learns that Albert is held hostage against a Swiss attack, the patriot declares, 'I see him not! – / I see my country ... not my son! / She holds her arms to me – with piteous cries', the last image recuperating the language of melodramatic rescue in order to disregard claims of kinship.[238] Watkins's protagonist exposes his family to less severe consequences than Hofer or Tell, but Mary Frost repeatedly complains that her husband's actions will 'bring disgrace and ruin on his house'.[239] For his part, the Chartist leader relishes the prospect of sharing martyrdom with his family, whether or not they are so inclined. Eager for a tragic role, he imagines himself an Agamemnon, telling his daughter – the possible Iphigenia: 'By Heaven, I'd put away the wife that thwarts me, / Doom my own son to death, nay thee, my daughter, / And sacrifice myself, for my poor country.'[240]

Frost, Hofer, and Tell represent indirect threats to their families in that their actions inspire public censure or provoke collective punishment. A number of protagonists of plays produced by Chartists, however, pose more immediate danger to women's lives. With unremarked irony, the Chartists of Kilbarchan, Scotland staged *Othello* 'for the benefit of the wives and families of the victims'.²⁴¹ The tragedy might have appealed to the Chartists for the way Iago resembles an agent provocateur, scripting violent plots into which he seduces Roderigo and Othello. The play's racial politics also would have resonated with the identity of the important black leader William Cuffay, who participated in the Orange Tree conspiracy, for which he was transported in 1849. At the same time, *Othello* problematises a number of Chartist assumptions about male agency and female virtue. In a sense, Desdemona falls victim to the martial attributes she admires in Othello. Iago's method of only half-articulating his suspicions highlights how the villain's ideas exist as troubling possibilities within the hero himself. Meanwhile Desdemona, surrounded by men and increasingly estranged from her husband, transforms from a confident young woman, able to challenge her father and demand of the Duke's Council the right to accompany the Venetian expedition, into a self-abnegating heroine who asks in dying only to be 'commend[ed] ... to [her] kind lord'.²⁴² To a Chartist audience, Desdemona's servant Emilia might have provided an alternative vision of femininity, both for her defiance towards Iago (and Othello) and her delight in puncturing her mistress's sanctimonious regard for sexual virtue: 'Let husbands know / Their wives have sense like them. They see, and smell, / And have their palates both for sweet and sour.'²⁴³

Desdemona was not alone among Chartist heroines victimised by male figures whose public life appears heroic. Belvidera of Thomas Otway's restoration tragedy *Venice Preserved* dies of madness after one of a group of conspirators seeking to overthrow Venice's senate attempts to rape her, and her lover Jaffier threatens her life. Shakespeare's Ophelia (whose performer would have played opposite Thomas Cooper in Leicester) suffers a similar fate when Hamlet's machinations, seduction, and abandonment leave her 'divided from herself and her fair judgment'.²⁴⁴ In both these cases, the relationship between domestic and political life is distant from rhetoric that casts radicalism as the champion of distressed femininity. At best, women appear as collateral damage, easily cast aside by men seeking to remedy public wrongs. At worst, virile masculinity becomes actively threatening. In *Venice Preserved*, Jaffier agrees to his fellow plotters' demand that they hold Belvidera hostage to insure his loyalty, even offering his dagger so that 'whene'er [he] prove unworthy – / You know the rest – Then strike it to her heart.'²⁴⁵

Ernest Jones's *St John's Eve*, the only original play published in a Chartist journal, provokes many of the same questions concerning female agency and victimhood explored on the Chartist stage. Jones's gothic melodrama comments ironically on plots of male rescue by revealing threatening undercurrents in the hero's efforts on the heroine's behalf. The first scene adumbrates a melodramatic scenario: Gemma suffers the rule of her tyrannical father Rupert and awaits an arranged marriage to 'the cavalier', despite her love for the penniless Rudolf. Gemma's faith, passivity, and fidelity to her oppressive parent indicate her virtue while underlining her need for outside aid. At the same time, Jones dramatises the problematic nature of these qualities. Rudolf remarks that Gemma is 'Too good, too pure, too beautiful for earth', a pronouncement nearly literalised in a sickness the hero helps precipitate.[246] When Rudolf muses that the death of Gemma's father would make the lovers happy, a Mephistophelean stranger (who is, in fact, the cavalier), appears; together, they perform a graveyard ritual which summons apparitions of those who supposedly will die within a year. Though undertaken on Gemma's behalf, Rudolf's actions doubly threaten her. First, during the rite he spies Gemma's ghostly image; inadvertently revealed to Gemma, this knowledge functions as a self-fulfilling prophecy, precipitating her decline. Worse yet, Rudolf's traffic with sorcery exposes the lovers to blackmail. When Rupert discovers Rudolf's actions, he forces Gemma to renounce him and agree to marry the cavalier. Although the play ends formulaically with Gemma's faith saving the lovers, their projected union is haunted by the way the protagonist and his rival double one another and by the striking 'bridal train' of the final scene, which forms a visual parallel to the procession of ghosts Rudolf summons in Act 1.[247] In many ways distant from the explicitly political theatre the Chartists staged, *St John's Eve* nevertheless interrogates the ability of men to act as women's protectors, a question Chartist performance frequently raised.

Even while criticising plots of male rescue, *St John's Eve* relies on a stereotypically helpless heroine, who is ultimately saved by the conclusion's *deus ex machina*. Watkin's *John Frost* imagines a more combative mode of female subjectivity in the figure of Mary Frost. Although Mary initially embodies a set of misogynistic clichés, playing the part of 'brimstone virago' found in other drama by Watkins, she ultimately models a version of militant female agency lacking in most Chartist drama.[248] The audience first encounters Mary when she tries to turn away the 'ragged wretches' who visit the house to recruit John to the movement, provoking her husband's rebuke that she is 'Unfemininely chilling, callous, cruel'.[249] These negative attributes, moreover, implicitly define an ideal wife as a generous caregiver set apart from the world: 'She, who should heal with balmy sympathy / The wounds my spirit must sustain abroad ... / rankles them with venom of her own.'[250] While Mary's depiction seems to reinscribe the opposition between family life and political commitment we saw in Knowles's *William Tell* and Fitzball's *Hofer*, Watkins complicates the dichotomy. For one thing, unlike the women in Knowles's and Fitzball's works Mary is as assertive and opinionated as her husband. Where exchanges between the Chartist leader and various ideological opponents resemble the sentential dialogues of didactic fiction, the spouses argue passionately with both advancing political and personal claims. Mary's repeated warnings about the dangers of the rising, moreover, prove correct. She predicts the protesters will suffer casualties; her husband, incarceration; the family, disgrace; and the movement, failure, warnings that forecast the action of the play.

Mary's willingness to express dissent makes sense of an incongruous element at the play's close, in which following John's incarceration she changes to become the idealised wife absent in Act 1. Offering to accompany her husband into exile, Mary promises she will 'minister [his] wants ... / listen to [his] feeble plaints / ... [and] soothe [him] with heart-sympathy'.[251] At the same time, Watkins complicates any simple opposition between Mary in Acts 1 and 5 by making clear she remains strong-minded and confrontational. She challenges the jailer's authority to part her from her spouse and complains to John that the people 'wish me to petition Majesty! / I'd sooner take a sword and lead them on.'[252] Given this finale, one might understand Watkins's earlier portrait of Mary, for all its sexism, as expressing an intimation that a mass movement requires passionate, combative women rather than 'angels in the house'. Similar tensions animate Watkins's popular 1841 essay 'Address to the Women of England', which circulated widely as a tract and in movement periodicals. Although the essay begins by declaring 'the proper sphere of woman is home', it quickly justifies female participation in politics: 'when home is affected by any of the causes before mentioned – when it is no longer a home – when it is changed into a hell, shall not women come forth and enquire the causes of this'.[253] Using the language of 'militant domesticity', the address ultimately inverts masculinist rhetoric by celebrating female warriors, including Deborah, Queen Philippa, and Joan of Arc, who 'saved [her] country, when given up for lost by men'.[254]

The female Chartists of Nottingham – who helped bring Watkins's play to the stage – themselves pushed the movement in confrontational directions. They participated in local protests that turned riotous and appropriated the language of force, in a posture that exacerbated fractures in the local campaign.[255] An early address by the NFPU 'to the Patriotic Women of England' predicts that 'the time must and will arrive when your aid and sympathies may be required in the field to fight, for be assured a great and deadly struggle must take place ere our tyrant oppressors yield to reason and justice ... We shall glory in seeing every working-man of England selling his coat to buy a sword or a rifle to be prepared for the event.'[256] These women, then, might have heard their own language echoed in *John Frost* when a worker describes how 'my wife herself gave me this pike and said, / Kill the police if we all die for it.'[257] Yet even this fleeting evocation of an anonymous woman's embrace of physical force troubles ideas of heroic masculinity protecting working-class families. The worker recounts how his children looking on 'stopp'd their cry [for food] in fear for me'.[258] In a similar spirit, a woman responded to Watkins's 'beautiful Address to the Women of England' by pointing out the way physical conflict inflicts continued suffering on the survivors it leaves behind: 'The courage which takes a man to the field of battle ... is of a coarse character when compared to ... that self-same quality, which enables the war-made widow calmly to settle herself to support, it may be, her three or four fatherless-ones, well knowing that her persevering struggling with poverty and wretchedness must endure – not for a day, but for years.'[259]

The plays that follow open a window on to an extraordinary theatrical subculture, one of the first examples of a protest campaign turning to theatre as part of its mobilisation. Drama served the Chartists as a practical way to raise money while extending the democratic agitation into a domain of popular culture that touched the lives of tens of thousands of working-class people in London and elsewhere. It offered the chance to bring new participants into the movement, including those whose lack of reading made them hard to reach through the printed word. And it provided a space where some of the campaign's most challenging ideas could be aired and debated – where the politics of violence could be considered and questions about women and their political role brought forward. Chartism, a movement that took pride in its literate culture, thus looks different in light of its drama, a collaborative art through which activist groups reimagined British history and advanced their own interpretations of society.

Notes

1. Thomas Cooper, *The Life of Thomas Cooper* (New York: Humanities Press, 1971), pp. 213–18.
2. Ibid., p. 229.
3. 'Cooper, the Leicester Chartist', *Stamford Mercury* (3 February 1843), p. 2.
4. Cooper, *Life*, p. 169; 'Leicester', *Northern Star* (3 December 1842), p. 1; Stephen Roberts, *The Chartist Prisoners: The Radical Lives of Thomas Cooper (1805–1892) and Arthur O'Neill (1819–1896)* (New York: Peter Lang, 2008), pp. 69–80.
5. See, for instance, reviews of the Chartists' performance of John Home's tragedy, *Douglas*: 'Cooperian Theatricals', *Leicestershire Mercury* (17 December 1842), p. 3; 'Shaksperean Theatricals', *Leicestershire Mercury* (24 December 1842), p. 3.
6. 'Cooper, the Leicester Chartist', *Stamford Mercury* (3 February 1843), p. 2.
7. 'The Unlicensed Drama', *Leicester Chronicle* (4 February 1843), p. 1.
8. Anthony Pennino, 'The Reconstructed Bard: Chartism and Shakespeare', *Monograf*, 1 (2014), 12–38; Andrew Murphy, *Shakespeare for the People: Working-class Readers, 1800–1900* (Cambridge: Cambridge University Press, 2008), pp. 138–49.
9. Ben Brierely, *Home Memories and Recollections of a Life* (Manchester: Abel Heywood & Sons, 1886), p. 41; 'Kilbarchan', *Northern Star* (6 April 1850), p. 1. For more details on these productions, see Appendix 1, which lists all documented Chartist performances.
10. 'Nottingham', *Northern Star* (17 December 1842), p. 1; 'Leicester', *Northern Star* (3 December 1842), p. 1.
11. 'National Victim and Defence Committee', *Northern Star* (16 December 1848), p. 5.
12. 'London', *Northern Star* (27 September 1845), p. 5.
13. The series, titled 'Chartism from Shakespeare', ran from 25 April to 23 May 1840.

14 'Leicester', *Northern Star* (3 December 1842), p. 1; Cooper, *Life*, p. 229.
15 *Ibid.*, p. 228.
16 *Ibid.*
17 William Shakespeare, *Hamlet* (London: Simon & Schuster, 2012), p. 115 (2.2.567–68).
18 Robert Hall, *Voices of the People: Democracy and Chartist Political Identity, 1830–1870* (Monmouth: Merlin Press, 2007), p. 41.
19 On the cultural side of Chartist Life, see James Epstein, 'Some organisational and cultural aspects of the Chartist movement in Nottingham', in James Epstein and Dorothy Thompson (eds), *The Chartist Experience: Studies in Working-Class Radicalism and Culture, 1830–60* (London: Macmillan, 1982); Malcolm Chase, *Chartism: A New History* (Manchester: Manchester University Press, 2007); Paul Pickering, *Chartism and Chartists in Manchester and Salford* (London: Macmillan, 1995).
20 Jane Moody, *Illegitimate Theatre in London, 1770–1840* (Cambridge: Cambridge University Press, 2000).
21 On theatre and the Reform Bill, see Jacky Bratton, *New Readings in Theatre History* (Cambridge: Cambridge University Press, 2003) and Katherine Newey, 'Reform on the London stage', in Arthur Burns and Joanna Innes (eds), *Rethinking the Age of Reform: Britain 1780–1850* (Cambridge: Cambridge University Press, 2003).
22 Roberts, *Chartist Prisoners*, p. 76.
23 The Chartists, however, firmly rejected literacy qualifications for the vote. Gregory Vargo, *An Underground History of Early Victorian Fiction* (Cambridge: Cambridge University Press, 2018), pp. 133–34; Mike Sanders, 'From "technical" to "cultural" literacy: reading and writing within the British Chartist movement', in Ann-Catrine Edlund, T. G. Ashplant, Anna Kuismin (eds), *Reading and Writing from Below: Exploring the Margins of Modernity* (Umeå: Umeå University and the Royal Skyttean Society, 2016), p. 286.
24 Patrick Brantlinger, *The Reading Lesson: The Threat of Mass Literacy in Nineteenth-Century British Fiction* (Bloomington: Indiana University Press, 1998), p. 93.
25 James Vernon, *Politics and the People: A study in English Political Culture, c.1815–1867* (Cambridge: Cambridge University Press, 1993), p. 106.
26 Hall, *Voices of the People*, pp. 35–36.
27 Robert Lowery, *Robert Lowery: Radical and Chartist* (London: Europa, 1979), p. 109.
28 *Ibid.*, p. 10. On theatre's influence on Chartist oratory, see Janette Lisa Martin, 'Popular Political Oratory and Itinerant Lecturing in Yorkshire and the North East in the Age of Chartism, 1837–60' (PhD dissertation, University of York, 2010), pp. 196–99. For the theatrical nature of Chartist political spectacle, see Mike Sanders, 'The platform and the stage: the primary aesthetics of Chartism', in Peter Yeandle, Katherine Newey, and Jeffrey Richards (eds), *Politics, Performance and Popular Culture: Theatre and Society in Nineteenth-Century Britain* (Manchester: Manchester University Press, 2016); Vernon, *Politics*, pp. 232–33; Paul Pickering, 'Class without words: symbolic communication in the Chartist movement', *Past and Present*, 112 (August 1986), 144–62.
29 Timothy Randall, 'Chartist poetry and song', in Owen Ashton, Robert Fyson, and Stephen Roberts (eds), *The Chartist Legacy* (London: Merlin Press, 1999), p. 172. Anne Janowitz, *Lyric and Labour in the Romantic Tradition* (Cambridge: Cambridge

University Press, 1998) closely tracks the interplay between written and oral forms in Chartist poetry. On ways Chartist culture included the illiterate, see Robert Hall, 'Creating a people's history: political identity and history in Chartism, 1832–1848', in Ashton, Fyson, and Roberts (eds), *Chartist Legacy*; Robert Hall, 'At the dawn of the information age: reading and the working classes in Ashton-under-Lyne, 1830–1850', in James Connolly et al. (eds), *Print Culture Histories Beyond the Metropolis* (Toronto: University of Toronto Press, 2016), p. 245.

30 John Watkins, *John Frost: A Chartist Play in Five Acts* (London: n.p., 1841), p. 9 (p. 104). The number in parentheses refers to the present edition.
31 *Ibid.*, p. 20 (p. 119).
32 Gregory Vargo, 'Chartist drama: the performance of revolt', *Victorian Studies*, 61:1 (Fall 2018), 9–34, pp. 14–15.
33 Watkins, *John Frost*, p. 20 (p. 119).
34 'London', *Northern Star* (15 October 1842), p. 2.
35 'Burnley', *Northern Star* (22 February 1845), p. 5.
36 James Epstein, *Radical Expression: Political Language, Ritual, and Symbol in England, 1790–1850* (Oxford: Oxford University Press, 1994), pp. 147–65.
37 Ros Merkin, 'The Theatre of the Organised Working Class 1830–1930' (PhD dissertation, University of Warwick, 1993), pp. 7–8.
38 'Keighley', *Northern Star* (2 January 1841), p. 1.
39 'Coventry', *Northern Star* (9 April 1842), p. 1.
40 'London', *Northern Star* (14 August 1842), p. 4.
41 Many Chartist accounts add a second 't' to Emmet's name.
42 Richard Altick, *The English Common Reader: A Social History of the Mass Reading Public, 1800–1900* (Columbus: Ohio State University Press, 1957), p. 352.
43 'Emmett and the Men of 1798', *Poor Man's Guardian and Friend*, 4 (n.d.), p. 25. The speech appeared originally as 'The Speech of Robert Emmet, Esq.', *Poor Man's Guardian* (2 February 1832), pp. 267–69.
44 'Memoir of Robert Emmett', *Chartist Circular* (5 March–14 May 1842). 'Memoires of Celebrated Patriots. No. 2 – Robert Emmett', *English Chartist Circular* (n.d.), 1:11–1:21.
45 'Glasgow', *Northern Star* (1 April 1843), p. 1; 'Glasgow', *Northern Star* (22 April 1843), p. 1; 'To the Chartists of Scotland', *Northern Star* (29 April 1843), p. 5; 'To the Chartists of Scotland', *Northern Star* (13 May 1843), p. 4; 'Glasgow and Greenock', *Northern Star* (13 May 1843), p. 4.
46 'Gateshead', *Northern Liberator* (12 December 1840), p. 5; 'Examination of Mr. Wm. Beesley, at Burnley', *Northern Star* (17 September 1842), p. 6.
47 'Mr. O'Brien', *Northern Star* (4 September 1843), p. 1; Pickering, *Chartism and Chartists*, p. 153.
48 'Mr. Moncrieff and Boz', *Charter* (9 June 1839), p. 313.
49 'National Literature', *Labourer* (1847), 2: 279–88; 'National Literature. III. – Germany', *Labourer* (1848), 3: 232–43.
50 'Literary Review', *Labourer* (1847) 2: 94.
51 Mike Sanders, *The Poetry of Chartism* (Cambridge: Cambridge University Press, 2009), pp. 13–14.

52 Brierley, *Home Memories*, p. 39; Marc Baer, *Theatre and Disorder in Late Georgian London* (Oxford: Oxford University Press, 1992), p. 171.
53 Brierley, *Home Memories*, p. 41.
54 'More Horrors of the Whig Dungeons', *Northern Star* (17 October 1840), p. 7; Katrina Navickas, *Protest and the Politics of Space and Place, 1789–1848* (Manchester: Manchester University Press, 2016), pp. 189–216.
55 'Grand Chartist Tea Meeting', *Northern Star* (26 October 1839), p. 1.
56 'Notice', *Northern Star* (21 May 1842), p. 1; 'The Play the Thing', *Northern Star* (3 February 1849), p. 5.
57 Vargo, 'Chartist drama', p. 21.
58 Janowitz, *Lyric and Labour*, p. 138.
59 *Ibid.*, p. 159; Sanders, *Poetry of Chartism*, pp. 77–81.
60 Brierely, *Home Memories*, pp. 30–41; 'Hollingwood and Failsworth', *Northern Star* (24 December 1841), p. 1; 'Dramatic Entertainment for the Benefit of the Victim Fund', *Northern Star* (25 November 1843), p. 1; 'Chartism', *Manchester Courier and Lancashire General Advertiser* (9 January 1841), p. 3.
61 Shannon Jackson, *Social Works: Performing Art, Supporting Publics* (Abingdon: Routledge, 2011), p. 14.
62 'Kilbarchan', *Northern Star* (6 April 1850), p. 1.
63 Watkins, *John Frost*, p. 17 (p. 114).
64 *Ibid.*
65 *Ibid.*, p. 34 (p. 139).
66 Merkin, 'Theatre', p. 28.
67 Michael Sanders, 'Poetic agency: metonymy and metaphor in Chartist poetry 1838–1852', *Victorian Poetry*, 39:2 (Summer 2001), 111–36, p. 121.
68 Statistics for all figures are drawn from sources detailed in Appendix 1. The data include dramatic readings and performances of individual scenes. Figures count separate evenings of the same production as multiple performances, although almost all productions were staged only a single time in any given locale (or at least newspaper reports fail to record subsequent nights). While by no means definitive – and indeed likely missing dozens or more of performances not located in these sources – the figures nevertheless indicate certain trends. The ambiguity around *The Trial of Robert Emmet* reflects the fact that the *Star* ceased covering two competing touring productions, one of which had announced a plan to visit twenty-one or more locales. 'Glasgow', *Northern Star* (22 April 1843), p. 1; 'To the Chartists of Scotland', *Northern Star* (29 April 1843), p. 5; 'To Readers and Correspondents', *Northern Star* (13 May 1843), p. 5.
69 Other aspects of Chartist culture promoted a sense of radical history. See Hall, 'Creating a people's history'; Kate Bowan and Paul Pickering, '"Songs for the Millions": Chartist music and popular aural tradition', *Labour History Review*, 74:1 (2009), 44–63, p. 57; Sanders, *Poetry of Chartism*, p. 6; Rob Breton, *The Oppositional Aesthetics of Chartist Fiction: Reading against the Middle-Class Novel* (New York: Routledge, 2016), pp. 51–78. Rob Breton and Gregory Vargo (eds), 'Chartist Fiction Online', http://chartistfiction.hosting.nyu.edu/home (accessed 27 August 2019), lists over two hundred 'historical romances' appearing in Chartist papers.

70 *Memoir of Robert Emmett and the Irish Insurrection of 1803; with the Trial of Emmett for High Treason, His Memorable Speech, &c.* (London: Cleave, n.d.), p. 44 (pp. 179–80). The numbers in parentheses refer to the present edition (note that sections of Cleave's *Memoir* not in this edition are also sometimes quoted).
71 Robert Southey, *Wat Tyler: A Dramatic Poem in Three Acts* (London: Cleave, n.d.), p. 16 (p. 86). The number in parentheses refers to the present edition..
72 'Glasgow', *Northern Star* (1 April 1843), p. 1; 'Dundee Democratic School Soiree', *Northern Star* (29 December 1849), p. 1. For size of these venues, see Cooper, *Life*, p. 229; Christopher Richardson, *A City of Light* (Nottingham: Russel Press, 2013), pp. 119–22; Robert Hall, 'Work, class, and politics in Ashton-under-Lyne, 1830–1860' (PhD dissertation, Vanderbilt University, 1991), p. 150.
73 Heidi Holder, 'The East-End theatre', in Kerry Powell (ed.), *The Cambridge Companion to Victorian and Edwardian Theatre* (Cambridge: Cambridge University Press, 2004), p. 258; Jim Davis and Victor Emeljanow, *Reflecting the Audience: London Theatregoing, 1840–1880* (Iowa City: University of Iowa Press, 2001), p. 24.
74 'Chartism', *Manchester Courier and Lancashire General Advertiser* (9 January 1841), p. 3.
75 Robert Hall, 'Work, class, and politics', pp. 159–60.
76 'South Lancashire Delegates', *Northern Star* (17 October 1840), p. 2.
77 'The Irish in England', *Freeman's Journal* (21 December 1840), p. 2.
78 'Chartism', *Manchester Courier and Lancashire General Advertiser* (9 January 1841), p. 3.
79 'Hamilton', *Northern Star* (11 November 1843), p. 5; 'London', *Northern Star* (14 August 1841), p. 4; 'Nottingham', *Northern Star* (3 February 1844), p. 8.
80 'Darlington', *Northern Star* (31 October 1840), p. 2; 'East Bierley', *Northern Star* (27 February 1841), p. 1.
81 Nearly half of all benefits give no indication to what purpose profits were put. Many of these events likely funded organisational expenses as well.
82 'Local Intelligence', *Northern Liberator* (19 December 1840), p. 5; 'A New Move of the Chartists', *Preston Chronicle* (12 December 1840), p. 3; 'Keighley. – Chartist Festival', *Northern Star* (2 January 1841), p. 1; 'Dukenfield and Ashton-Under-Lyne', *Northern Star* (7 December 1850), p. 1.
83 'Donations', *Northern Star* (25 June 1842), p. 1; 'Balance-sheet of Provisional Committee', *Northern Star* (26 November 1842), p. 3; 'To the Chartists of Scotland', *Northern Star* (13 May 1843), p. 4. Figures for the London performance are ambiguous as outside debts are apparently debited against the benefit's profits.
84 *Ibid.*
85 Cooper, *Life*, pp. 228–29.
86 'Leicester', *Northern Star* (3 December 1842), p. 1.
87 Thomas Martin Wheeler, 'Sunshine and Shadow', *Northern Star* (26 May 1849), p. 3. The novel is also available in Ian Haywood (ed.), *Chartist Fiction* (Aldershot: Ashgate, 1999), vol. 1.
88 The Britannia may well have hosted Chartist benefits as well. See Jenna Gibbs, *Performing the Temple of Liberty: Slavery, Theater, and Popular Culture in London and Philadelphia, 1760–1850* (Baltimore: Johns Hopkins University Press, 2014), p. 218. Evidence also exists that when the Britannia lost its 'music and dance license' Chartists protested on its behalf. Gibbs, *Performing the Temple*, p. 218 and Clive

Barker, 'The Chartists, theatre, reform and research', *Theatre Quarterly*, 1:4 (Fall 1971), 3–10, pp. 8–9.
89 'Victoria Theatre', *Morning Advertiser* (16 January 1846), p. 3.
90 Gibbs, *Performing the Temple*, p. 218.
91 'The Whig Conspiracy Victims', *Northern Star* (14 October 1848), p. 5; 'Milton Street Theatre', *Northern Star* (21 October 1848), p. 8.
92 *Ibid.*
93 Marc Brodie, 'Free trade and cheap theatre: sources of politics for the nineteenth-century London poor', *Social History*, 28:3 (October 2003), 346–60, pp. 349–50.
94 Henry Mayhew, *London Labour and the London Poor* (London: Griffin and Company, 1861), vol. 1, p. 22.
95 *Ibid.*
96 Davis and Emeljanow, *Reflecting*, p. 48.
97 Anita Cowan, 'The relationship between theatre repertoire and theatre location: a study of the Pavilion Theatre', in Karelisa Hartigan (ed.), *All the World: Drama Past and Present* (Washington, DC: University Press of America, 1982), vol. 2, pp. 13, 17.
98 Quoted in Tracy Davis, 'Introduction: Repertoire', in Tracy Davis (ed.), *The Broadview Anthology of Nineteenth-Century British Performance* (Peterborough, Ontario: Broadview, 2012), p. 20.
99 Davis and Emeljanow, *Reflecting*, p. 37.
100 Chartist groups shared a particularly close relationship with the actor-manager John Douglass, who hosted two benefits at the Marylebone and four more after moving to the Standard. See, 'Royal Marylebone Theatre', *Northern Star* (6 February 1847), p. 3; 'Marylebone Theatre', *Northern Star* (27 February 1847), p. 3; 'Marylebone Theatre', *Northern Star* (6 March 1847), p. 3; 'Royal Standard Theatre, Shoreditch', *Northern Star* (14 October 1848), p. 5.
101 'The Widow and Fatherless Family', *Northern Star* (6 December 1845), p. 4.
102 'Dramatic Entertainment for the Benefit of the National Victim Fund', *Northern Star* (25 November 1843), p. 1.
103 'The Political Victim, Widow, and Orphan's Fund', *Northern Star* (21 October 1848), p. 7.
104 'Address', *Northern Star* (29 January 1842), p. 3. Such extra-diegetic prologues could also accompany Chartist amateur productions. For example, in Leeds a lecture on William Tell preceded a performance of a play of that title. 'Leeds', *Northern Star* (22 January 1842), p. 8.
105 'Victoria Theatre', *Morning Advertiser* (24 April 1846), p. 3.
106 'City of London Theatre', *Northern Star* (14 November 1846), p. 1.
107 The night featured George Colman's comedy *John Bull, or, an Englishman's Fire-Side* and the 'musical drama' *The Little Devil*. 'Royal Marylebone Theatre', *Northern Star* (28 November 1846), p. 4.
108 Farces and comedies, of course, also sometimes include class commentary. See, for instance, Walter Watt's *An Irish Engagement*, in which a servant impersonates and otherwise gets the better of upper-class characters. This farce played alongside John Baldwin Buckstone's revenge melodrama *Luke the Labourer* at a benefit for the Chartist prisoner John Shaw. Walter Watts, *An Irish Engagement: A Farce in one act*

(London: S. G. Fairbrother, n.d.); 'John Shaw's benefit at the City Theatre', *Northern Star* (6 July 1850), p. 8.
109 'Royal Albert Saloon', *Morning Advertiser* (12 May 1842), p. 2.
110 'Notice! Every Chartist in London to his Post', *Northern Star* (4 June 1842), p. 1.
111 On blackface performance in 1840s Britain, see Sarah Meer, 'Competing Representations: Douglass, the Ethiopian Serenaders, and Ethnic Exhibition in London', in Alan Rice and Martin Crawford (eds), *Liberating Sojourn: Frederick Douglass and Transatlantic Reform* (Athens, GA: University of Georgia Press, 1999).
112 'Metropolitan Delegates' Theatrical Benefit', *Northern Star* (1 May 1847), p. 3. For Chartist attitudes on race, see Patricia Hollis, 'Anti-Slavery and British Working-Class Radicalism in the Years of Reform', in Christine Bolt and Seymour Descher (eds), *Anti-Slavery, Religion, and Reform* (Hamden CT: Dawson, 1982); Kelly Mays, 'Slaves in Heaven, Laborers in Hell: Chartist Poets' Ambivalent Identification with the (Black) Slave', *Victorian Poetry*, 39:2 (Summer 2001), 137-63; Gregory Vargo, '"Outworks of the Citadel of Corruption": The Chartist Press Reports the Empire', *Victorian Studies*, 54:2 (Winter 2012), 227–53.
113 'Varieties', *Northern Star* (28 July 1849), p. 3; 'Dramatic Entertainment for the Benefit of the National Victim Fund', *Northern Star* (25 November 1843), p. 1. On Cuffay, see Martin Hoyles, *William Cuffay: The Life and Times of a Chartist Leader* (Hertford: Hansib, 2013).
114 Moody, *Illegitimate*, pp. 51–55.
115 Rosalind Crone, *Violent Victorians* (Manchester: Manchester University Press, 2012), p. 127; Monica Cohen, *Pirating Fictions: Ownership and Creativity in Nineteenth-Century Popular Culture* (Charlottesville: University of Virginia Press, 2017), p. 80.
116 Moody, *Illegitimate*, pp. 108, 124; Jane Moody, 'The theatrical revolution, 1776–1843', in Joseph Donohue (ed.), *The Cambridge History of British Theatre* (Cambridge: Cambridge University Press, 2004), p. 202.
117 Rowell George, *The Old Vic Theatre: A History* (Cambridge: Cambridge University Press, 1993), p. 24.
118 Tracy Davis, 'Introduction', p. 20.
119 Tracy Davis, *The Economics of the British Stage: 1800–1914* (Cambridge: Cambridge University Press, 2000), pp. 32–35.
120 Moody, *Illegitimate*, p. 42.
121 'Character of Trades' Unionists', *Poor Man's Guardian* (18 October 1834), p. 293.
122 'Royal Victoria Theatre', *Cleave's Gazette of Variety* (13 April 1839), p. 4; 'Glasgow Cotton Spinners', *Northern Star* (4 May 1839), p. 3; 'Victoria Theatre', *Charter* (29 September 1839), p. 568. Prominent Chartists, including John Cleave, Henry Hetherington, James Watson, and William Lovett sold tickets for one or both of these performances.
123 Playbill quoted in Chase, *Chartism*, p. 295. On the Victoria and radicalism, also see Brodie, 'Free trade'.
124 John Storey, *Culture and Power in Cultural Studies* (Edinburgh: Edinburgh University Press, 2010), pp. 45–46.
125 Brierley, *Home Memories*, p. 39.
126 Joseph Donohue, 'Actors and acting', in Powell (ed.), *Cambridge Companion*, p. 20;

Jackson Russell, 'Victorian and Edwardian stagecraft: techniques and issues', in Powell (ed.), *Cambridge Companion*, p. 56; Moody, 'Theatrical revolution', p. 208.

127 'The Longton Amateur Theatricals', *Northern Star* (1 February 1851), p. 5; Jeffrey Cox, 'Introduction', in Jeffrey Cox (ed.), *Seven Gothic Dramas 1789–1825* (Athens, OH: Ohio University Press, 1992), p. 16.

128 Mayhew, *London Labour*, vol. 1, p. 43.

129 Christopher Thomson, *The Autobiography of an Artisan* (London: J. Shaw and Sons, 1847), pp. 105, 185.

130 *Ibid.*, p. 105.

131 'Ashton', *Northern Star* (31 October 1840), p. 1.

132 '"Breath his name"', *Waterford Weekly Chronicle* (22 April 1843), p. 1.

133 'Winlaton', *Northern Star* (23 April 1842), p. 1. Even though relatively few accounts of Chartist performance mention music, many occurred at events, such as concerts or dances, where musicians played. Another staging of *John Frost* paired Watkins's play with a 'nautical burletta', so music likely accompanied both plays. 'Hamilton', *Northern Star* (11 November 1843), p. 5.

134 Michael Pisani, 'Music for the theatre: style and function in incidental music', in Powell (ed.), *Cambridge Companion*, p. 71.

135 David Karr, '"Thoughts that flash like lightning": Thomas Holcroft, radical theater, and the production of meaning in 1790s London', *Journal of British Studies*, 40:3 (July 2001), 324–56, pp. 326–28.

136 Mayhew, *London Labour*, vol.1, p. 20.

137 Charles Dickens, 'The Amusements of the People', *Household Words* (30 March 1850), pp. 14–15; George Augustus Sala, *Twice Round the Clock* (London: Houlston and Wright, 1859), p. 271.

138 Mayhew, *London Labour*, vol.1, p. 21.

139 Thomas Wright, *Some Habits and Customs of the Working Classes; By a Journey Man Engineer* (London: Tinsley Brother, 1867), p. 163.

140 Malcolm Chase, '"Love, bitter wrong, freedom, sad pity, and lust of power": politics and performance in 1820', in Peter Yeandle, Katherine Newey, and Jeffrey Richards (eds), *Politics, Performance, and Popular Culture*, p. 208; Moody, *Illegitimate Theatre*, p. 48.

141 Gibbs, *Performing the Temple*, p. 218.

142 *Ibid.*, pp. 225–26; John Russel Stephens, *The Censorship of English Drama 1824–1901* (Cambridge: Cambridge University Press, 1980), p. 59.

143 Patrick Geoghegan, *Robert Emmet, A Life* (Dublin: Gill and Macmillan, 2002), pp. 269–70.

144 William Cobbett, 'Aristocracy, Parsons, and Money-Mongers', *Cobbett's Political Register*, 88:10 (6 June 1835), pp. 592–97; Stephens, *Censorship*, p. 15.

145 *Ibid.*

146 W. E. Adams, *Memoirs of a Social Atom* (London: Hutchinson & Co., 1903), p. 196. For histories of Newport, see David Jones, *The Last Rising: The Newport Insurrection of 1839* (Cardiff: University of Wales Press, 2013); Chase, *Chartism*, pp. 110–16; Thompson, *Chartists*, pp. 77–87. In the most comprehensive history of the rising, Jones argues that Newport was likely planned as one of multiple risings and remained an attempt to spark a wider revolt after these had fallen through.

147 Dorothy Thompson, *The Chartists* (New York: Pantheon, 1984), p. 84; Chase, *Chartism*, p. 140; Jones, *Last Rising*, p. 214.
148 'Moral and Physical Force', *Charter* (1 December 1839), p. 1; Thompson, *Chartists*, p. 67; Helen Rogers, *Women and the People: Authority, Authorship and the Radical Tradition in Nineteenth-Century England* (Aldershot: Ashgate, 2000), p. 84; William Maehl, 'The dynamics of violence in Chartism: a case study in northeastern England', *Albion*, 7:2 (Summer 1975), 101–19, p. 101.
149 Watkins, *John Frost*, p. 6 (p. 99).
150 Chase, *Chartism*, pp. 119–20.
151 Vargo, 'Chartist drama', pp. 14–15.
152 Watkins, *John Frost*, p. 7 (p. 101); Sanders, *Poetry of Chartism*, p. 124.
153 Michael Sanders, 'Poetic agency', p. 111.
154 *Ibid.*, p. 119.
155 *Ibid.*, p. 121.
156 John Watkins, *Five Cardinal Points of the People's Charter, Separately Explained and Advocated* (London: John Watkins, n.d.), p. 2.
157 Merkin, 'Theatre', p. 28.
158 Watkins, *John Frost*, p. 9 (p. 104).
159 *Ibid.*, p. 32 (p. 137).
160 *Ibid.*, p. 21 (p. 120).
161 *Ibid.*, pp. 19, 24 (pp. 118, 124).
162 *Ibid.*, p. 24 (p. 124).
163 *Ibid.*, p. 32 (p. 136).
164 *Ibid.*, p. 5 (p. 99).
165 *Ibid*, p. 32 (p. 136).
166 Jones, *Last Rising*, pp. 193, 200.
167 Watkins, *John Frost*, p. 34 (p. 139).
168 *Ibid.*, p. 35 (p. 141).
169 *Ibid.*, p. 34 (p. 139).
170 *Ibid.*, p. 10 (p. 106).
171 *Ibid.*, p. 19 (p. 118).
172 *Ibid.*, p. 13 (p. 109).
173 *Memoir of Robert Emmett*, p. 41 (p. 177).
174 'The Irish in England', *Freeman's Journal* (21 December 1840), p. 2.
175 Southey, *Wat Tyler*, p. 3 (p. 61).
176 Ian Haywood, '"The renovating fury": Southey, Republicanism and Sensationalism', 'Romanticism on the Net' 32–33 (2003), DOI:10.7202/009256ar (accessed 15 January 2019).
177 Epstein, *Radical Expression*, p. 12.
178 William Lovett, 'Manifesto of the General Convention of the Industrious Classes', in Gregory Claeys (ed.), *The Chartist Movement in Britain 1838–1850* (London: Pickering, 2001), vol. 2, 137–43, p. 142.
179 Southey, *Wat Tyler*, p. 10 (p. 74).
180 *Ibid.*, p. 12 (p. 79).
181 *Ibid.*

182 *Ibid.*, p. 13 (p. 82).
183 *Ibid.*, p. 14 (p. 82).
184 *Ibid.*
185 Watkins, *John Frost*, p. 38 (p. 145).
186 *Ibid.*, p. 46 (p. 156).
187 Sanders, *Poetry of Chartism*, p. 6; Brian Maidment, *The Poorhouse Fugitives* (Manchester: Carcanet, 1987), p. 37. For a different view, see Simon Rennie, *The Poetry of Ernest Jones: Myth, Song, and the 'Mighty Mind'* (New York: Legenda, 2016), p. 67.
188 Sanders, *Poetry of Chartism*, p. 6.
189 Robert Sykes, 'Physical-force Chartism: the cotton district and the Chartist crisis of 1839', *International Review of Social History*, 30 (1985), 208–36, pp. 213–16; Hall, 'Work, class, and politics', p. 139.
190 Quoted in *Ibid.*, p. 156.
191 'Loyal National Repeal Association of Ireland', *Freeman's Journal* (22 December 1840), p. 2.
192 'The Irish in England', *Freeman's Journal* (21 December 1840), p. 2.
193 'Whig War Against the Working Classes', *Northern Star* (17 June 1848), p. 5; *Trial of Feargus O'Connor, ESQ., and Fifty-Eight Others, at Lancaster, on a Charge of Sedition, Conspiracy, Tumult, and Riot* (Manchester: Abel Heywood, 1843), p. 74.
194 'Mr. Vincent', *Northern Star* (20 October 1838), p. 6; 'The Queen v. O'Neill', *Northern Star* (19 August 1843), p. 6.
195 Antony Taylor, *London's Burning: Pulp Fiction, the Politics of Terrorism and the Destruction of the Capital in British Popular Culture, 1840–2005* (London: Continuum, 2012), p. 34.
196 'Whig "Reign of Terror" in Yorkshire', *Northern Star* (3 June 1848), p. 8.
197 Sanders, *Poetry of Chartism*, p. 136 and Thompson, *Chartists*, p. 145 suggest Emmet's rising was interpreted in this dual light.
198 *Memoir of Robert Emmett*, p. i.
199 'Emmett and the Men of 1798', *Poor Man's Guardian and Repealer's Friend*, 4 (n.d.), p. 28.
200 *Memoir of Robert Emmett*, p. 23.
201 'Emmett the Patriot', *Chartist Circular* (10 July 1841), p. 395.
202 Matthew Roberts, *Chartism, Commemoration and the Cult of the Radical Hero* (London: Routledge), p. 69 and passim.
203 'Nottingham Female Association', *Northern Star* (23 November 1839), p. 2.
204 'Persecution the Agent of Tyrants', *Chartist Circular* (26 September 1840), p. 213.
205 Sally Ledger, *Dickens and the Popular Radical Imagination* (Cambridge: Cambridge University Press, 2007), pp. 51–52.
206 Southey, *Wat Tyler*, p. 14 (p. 83).
207 *Ibid.*, p. 15 (p. 85).
208 'Ashton', *Northern Star* (31 October 1840), p. 1; 'Ashton-Under-Lyne', *Northern Star* (31 July 1841), p. 2.
209 *Memoir of Robert Emmett*, p. 36 (p. 174).
210 *Ibid.*, p. 44 (p. 180).

211 *Ibid.*, p. 40 (pp. 176-177).
212 *Ibid.*, p. 44 (p. 180). On the way Chartist performances of Emmet's trial mobilise counterfactual possibilities, suggesting how the past might have transpired differently, see Vargo, 'Chartist drama', pp. 26–28.
213 Edward Fitzball, *Hofer, the Tell of the Tyrol, an Historical Drama in Three Acts* (London: John Cumberland, n.d.), p. 40.
214 Knowles, *William Tell*, p. 51.
215 Rogers, *Women and the People*, p. 84.
216 Quoted in Chase, *Chartism*, p. 225.
217 Anna Clark, 'The rhetoric of Chartist domesticity: gender, language, and class in the 1830s and 1840s', *The Journal of British Studies*, 31:1 (January 1992), 62–88.
218 'Victoria Theatre', *Northern Star* (10 March 1849), p. 8.
219 Kerry Powell, *Women and Victorian Theatre* (Cambridge: Cambridge University Press, 2007), p. 35 makes an analogous argument about women in the commercial theatre.
220 Rogers, *Women and the People*, p. 81.
221 Thompson, *Chartists*, pp. 138, 147.
222 'Greenock', *Northern Star* (30 October 1841), p. 1; 'Manchester. – Female Chartists', *Northern Star* (24 September 1842), p. 8; D. Thompson, *Chartists*, pp. 126, 150; Pickering, *Chartism and Chartists*, p. 38; Dorothy Thompson, *Dignity of Chartism* (London: Verso, 2015), p. 45.
223 Richardson, *A City of Light*, pp. 135–42.
224 'Nottingham Female Political Union', *Nottingham Review* (26 October 1838), p. 4.
225 'The O'Connor Festival at Nottingham', *Northern Star* (20 November 1847), p. 7.
226 'Glasgow', *Northern Star* (24 April 1841), p. 1.
227 'Nottingham Female Association', *Northern Star* (23 November 1839), p. 2. Female fundraising often outstripped male efforts. At Todmorden, for example, female Chartists raised more than twice as much money for Peter McDouall as 'male Chartists'. See, 'Subscriptions Received by Mr. Cleave', *Northern Star* (28 January 1843), p. 1.
228 'Tea Party', *Northern Star* (2 January 1841), p. 1.
229 'Standard Theatre', *Northern Star* (6 October 1849), p. 7.
230 Navickas, *Protest*, p. 214; Christina Parolin, *Radical Space: Venues of Popular Politics in London, 1790–ca. 1845* (Acton: Australian National University E Press, 2010), pp. 173–75.
231 'The Incarcerated Victims', *Northern Star* (6 February 1841), p. 1; 'Finsbury', *Northern Star* (4 September 1841), p. 5; 'Enthusiastic Reception of Mr. Geo White, of Leeds, at Newcastle-upon-Tyne', *Northern Star* (5 December 1840), p. 1; 'Concert at Hanover Square in Aid of the Hungarian Cause', *Northern Star* (20 December 1851), p. 6.
232 'Polish and Hungarian Refugees', *Northern Star* (22 March 1851), p. 1.
233 John Home, *Douglas: a tragedy, in five acts* (London: Samuel French, n.d.), p. 9.
234 *Ibid.*
235 *Ibid.*, p. 54.

236 'City of London Theatre', *Northern Star* (14 November 1846), p. 1; Alex Lee, *I'll be No Submissive Wife, A Ballad* (New York: Firth & Hall, 1838), p. 7.
237 Knowles, *William Tell*, p. 64.
238 *Ibid.*, p. 82; 'Marylebone Theatre', *Northern Star* (6 March 1847), p. 3.
239 Watkins, *John Frost*, p. 11 (p. 107).
240 *Ibid.*, p. 13 (p. 109). Frost's disregard for his family's safety in Watkins's play is particularly striking in that it ran counter to much Chartist discourse that emphasised his familial commitments as evidence 'of his peaceable intentions' during the rising. See Sanders, *Poetry of Chartism*, pp. 100, 120 and Iota's fifth sonnet in Appendix 2.
241 'Kilbarchan', *Northern Star* (6 April 1850), p. 1.
242 William Shakespeare, *Othello* (London: Simon & Schuster, 2017), p. 245 (5.2.153).
243 *Ibid.*, p. 217 (4.3.104–108).
244 Shakespeare, *Hamlet*, p. 211 (4.5.92).
245 Thomas Otway, *Venice Preserved* (London: Thomas Hailes Lacy, n.d.), p. 21.
246 Ernest Jones, 'St. John's Eve: A Romantic Drama, in Three Acts', *The Labourer* (1848), vol. 4, p. 190 (p. 210). The number in parentheses refers to the present edition.
247 *Ibid.*, pp. 189, 238 (pp. 203, 223).
248 In correspondence about Watkins's not extant *Robin Hood*, Ebenezer Elliot complains of Watkins rendering Marian 'a brimstone virago'. John Watkins, *Life, poetry, and letters of Ebenezer Elliott, the Corn-law rhymer, with an abstract of his politics* (London, J. Mortimer, 1850), p. 160.
249 Watkins, *John Frost*, p. 11 (p. 107).
250 *Ibid.*, p. 27 (p. 129).
251 *Ibid.*, p. 46 (p. 156).
252 *Ibid.*
253 John Watkins, 'Address to the Women of England!', *English Chartist Circular* (n.d.), p. 49.
254 *Ibid.*, p. 50. On the concept of 'militant domesticity', see Barbara Taylor, *Eve and the New Jerusalem* (New York: Pantheon Books, 1983), passim. On this rhetoric in Chartism, see Anna Clark, *The Struggle for the Breeches: Gender and the Making of the British Working Class* (Berkeley: University of California Press, 1995), pp. 229–30.
255 Rogers, *Women and the People*, pp. 80, 101.
256 'Nottingham Female Political Union', *Northern Star* (8 December 1838), p. 6.
257 Watkins, *John Frost*, p. 34 (p. 140).
258 *Ibid.*
259 Sophia, 'Woman – Her Social and Political Influence', *English Chartist Circular* (n.d.), 1:16, p. 63.

1

Wat Tyler (1794/1817) – Robert Southey

Editor's introduction

On the occasions that Chartist groups performed Robert Southey's *Wat Tyler*, they mobilised a dense network of historical associations, invoking and overlaying at least three moments important in the history of radicalism.[1] First, the play's subject matter concerns the Great Rising of 1381, commonly referred to by the Chartists as Wat Tyler's rebellion. In 1381, some 50,000 commoners from Essex and Kent marched on London and succeeded in occupying the capital with the support of many Londoners. Although originally inspired by outrage over regressive poll taxes used to finance war with France, the rebels' programme, in the words of Frederick Engels, reached 'out beyond not only the present but also the future' in that it sought the abolition of serfdom and lordship and an egalitarian division of property.[2] As Southey recounts, the rebels forced King Richard II to sign charters ending serfdom in numerous English counties, to abolish the poll tax, and to grant amnesty. Although Richard annulled the charters and broke his other promises as soon as the rebellion was contained, the rising remained an example of an 'indigenous history of revolt' in popular memory.[3]

Second, the Chartists looked back to 1794 – the year in which Southey composed *Wat Tyler* – and more broadly to the era of the French Revolution. Southey's treatment of the Great Rising foregrounds aspects of the revolt resonant with this moment, including the egalitarian ideology of the rebels, the background of war with France, and the state's use of show trials. Two years before Southey wrote his play, Wat Tyler had emerged as a figure of ideological conflict when, in the second part of the *Rights of* Man, Thomas Paine defended

---

[1] Casie Legette, *Remaking Romanticism: The Radical Politics of the Excerpt* (London: Palgrave, 2017), pp. 74–75.
[2] Frederick Engels, *The Peasant War in Germany* (New York: International Publishers, 1966), p. 56; Alastair Dunn, *The Great Rising of 1381* (Stroud, Gloucestershire: Tempus, 2002), pp. 68–70.
[3] Antony Taylor, *London's Burning: Pulp Fiction, the Politics of Terrorism and the Destruction of the Capital in British Popular Culture, 1840–2005* (London: Continuum, 2012), p. 27.

him against the aspersions of Edmund Burke and other 'court sycophants'.[4] In the following decades, radicals and conservatives struggled over 'the legacy of 1381', celebrating the rising as an exemplary moment of popular democracy or using it to warn of the perils of revolution.[5] Chartist groups continued a Painite tradition of history from below by commemorating Wat Tyler in poetry, speeches, lectures, historical essays, and drama.[6]

Finally, performances of *Wat Tyler* evoked the period of political resurgence following the Napoleonic Wars. Southey's play was first published – without the author's knowledge or consent – in 1817, prompting a controversy that ensured the play's popularity for decades. In 1794, Southey had given the text in manuscript to the political prisoner Reverend William Winterbotham to arrange publication. When in the face of heightening governmental repression Winterbotham blanched at proceeding, Southey lost sight of the copy. By 1817, Southey had turned his back on the radicalism of his youth. Named Poet Laureate in 1813, he wrote regularly for the Tory *Quarterly Review*, denouncing democratic agitation and calling for the suppression of seditious journalism. Given his outspoken positions, reformers greeted with glee William Sherwood, Samuel Dunbar Neely, and Robert Jones's publication of *Wat Tyler* in February 1817. In Parliament, opposition MP William Smith made hay of Southey's hypocrisy by producing, from two coat pockets, copies of *Wat Tyler* and a *Quarterly Review* jeremiad against radical writing, then quoting the Poet Laureate against himself.[7] In the *Black Dwarf*, Thomas Wooler crowed, '[Southey] is a *friend* to *liberty*; and has merely gone over to the enemies' camp, to feed upon them, and report progress as *a spy*! ... Wonderful to say, the laureate is a *jacobin*, a *leveller*, and a *republican*! Do not complain any longer of the partiality of the court. They will choose the *Devil* next for a *royal chaplain*.'[8] William Hone's preface to his edition of the play quipped that 'WAT TYLER, alive, and in Smithfield, was not a more unpleasant object to Richard the Second ... than it is said that WAT TYLER, in print, is to Mr ROBERT SOUTHEY.'[9]

Southey's efforts to defend himself only fanned the flames. His widely

---

[4] Thomas Paine, *Rights of Man, Part the Second; Combining Principle and Practice* (London: W.T. Sherwin, 1817), p. 80.

[5] Dunn, *Great Rising*, p. 151; Stephen Basdeo, *The Life and Legend of a Rebel Leader: Wat Tyler* (Barnsley: Pen and Sword History, 2018), p. 84.

[6] Ibid., p. 115; 'The Insurrections of the Working Class', the *Labourer* (1848), 3:11–17; 'Institution of a Veteran Patriots' Fund and an Exiles' Widows and Children's Fund', *Northern Star* (20 September 1845), p. 1.

[7] Robert Southey, *The Life and Correspondence of Robert Southey* (London: Longman, Brown, Green, and Longmans, 1850), vol. 4, p. 256; Mark Storey, *Robert Southey: A Life* (London: Oxford University Press, 1997), p. 256.

[8] 'Political Literature', *Black Dwarf* (26 March 1817), p. 139.

[9] William Hone, 'Preface' in Robert Southey, *Wat Tyler; a Dramatic Poem* (London: William Hone, 1817), p. vi.

circulated open letter to Smith, which made light of the play as 'school-exercises' and reiterated his call to 'curb the seditious press', kept the matter before the public for months.[10] More disastrously still, Southey attempted to halt the play's circulation by asserting copyright over it in the Court of Chancery. In an ironic turn, Lord Eldon denied Southey's suit, ruling 'that a person cannot recover in damages for a work which is in its nature calculated to do an injury to the public'.[11] Now legally available for reprinting, Wat Tyler became a favourite of radical publishers, who produced cheap editions in rapid succession. The play's availability, its politics, and the controversy surrounding it made it one of the most widely read works of the Romantic period while enshrining its place in the radical canon for decades to come.[12] In 1832, Richard Carlile recalled how profits from Southey's 'excellent republican drama' funded wider exploits: 'I assisted in the cheapest edition, or in one at two-pence, sold above twenty thousand, and thereby made a profit to move on with other things.'[13] All told the play was said to sell 60,000 copies in the 1810s, 'twice or three times as many ... as all [Southey's] other works' combined.[14]

Wat Tyler's spectacular publication history has overshadowed interest in the play's performance. Indeed, because scholars have previously known of only one possible production in Britain – and that based on highly dubious evidence – the play has been treated as a closet drama.[15] Casie Legette's study of *Wat Tyler* within Chartist print culture goes further, arguing that radical periodicals transformed the text into lyric poetry by publishing excerpts without listing speakers or even the play's title.[16] Nevertheless, the Chartists did perform versions of *Wat Tyler* in whole or part on several occasions. Ben Brierley's Chartist 'Mutual Improvement Society' made 'Southey's "Wat Tyler" ... [their] first ambitious effort', staging the play in a Failsworth schoolroom that was itself associated

---

[10] Southey, *Life and Correspondence*, p. 384; 'The Critical Reception of Robert Southey's *Wat Tyler*', www.rc.umd.edu/editions/wattyler/contexts/reception.html. 2004, accessed 15 April 2019.

[11] Quoted in Southey, *Life and Correspondence*, p. 251.

[12] William St Clair, *The Reading Nation in the Romantic Period* (Cambridge: Cambridge University Press, 2004), p. 316.

[13] Richard Carlile, 'To the Editress of the *Isis*', *Isis* (7 July 1832), p. 343.

[14] St Clair, *Reading Nation*, p. 316; Southey, *Life and Correspondence*, p. 251.

[15] Evidence for this performance hinges on a letter to Southey that describes a supposed staging in Whittington. The communication, however, is patently satirical in that it is signed by the pseudonymous 'Jack Straw' (a rebel in the play) and praises '[Southey's] truly patriotic and enlightened poem' while noting that every 'soul in the theatre ... cordially lamented the sudden deterioration of [Southey's] principles'. Southey, *Life and Correspondence*, vol. 4, p. 237. See Ralph Anthony Manogue, 'A Critical Edition of Robert Southey's *Wat Tyler*' (PhD dissertation, New York University, 1971), pp. 211–13.

[16] Legette, *Remaking Romanticism*, pp. 71–72.

with radical activity in the 1790s.[17] In the Lancastrian town of Clitheroe, the 'Thespian company of Sabden ... (all Chartists of the right stamp) performed the drama of Wat Tyler' twice in November 1842, a time and place that would have affiliated the Great Rising with the massive strike wave of the preceding summer.[18] Indeed, the play facilitates this linkage by highlighting how the rebellion was also a strike: 'Who'll plough their fields', one character asks, 'who'll do their drudgery now, / And work like horses, to give them the harvest?'[19] Two planned performances at the Darlington Theatre to raise money for 'the Durham political prisoners' made contemporary connections still more explicit.[20] Wat Tyler remarks on John Ball's liberation: 'the people rise for liberty, / And their first deed should be to break the chains / That bind the virtuous.'[21] Finally, selections from *Wat Tyler* were performed at a Chartist grand 'ball and concert' in London and 'a tea and dancing party' in Coventry.[22] Where the play's revolutionary politics and use of extended speeches in place of dialogue rendered it unstageable at commercial venues, these attributes proved appealing in the context of Chartist amateur performance.

Of the above productions, Southey is mentioned by name in connection with only the one at Failsworth. One must, therefore, weigh the possibility that Chartist groups drew on alternative dramatisations of the Great Rising or Wat Tyler's life.[23] A number of factors, however, make Southey's text by far the most likely source of Chartist stagings.[24] First, the pirated play circulated widely

---

[17] Ben Brierley, *Home Memories and Recollections of a Life* (Manchester: Abel Heywood & Sons, 1886), p. 41; Katrina Navickas, *Protest and the Politics of Space and Place, 1789–1848* (Manchester: Manchester University Press, 2016), p. 209.

[18] 'Clitheroe', *Northern Star* (19 November 1842), p. 1.

[19] Robert Southey, *Wat Tyler: A Dramatic Poem in Three Acts* (London: Cleave, n.d.), p. 7 (p. 69).

[20] 'Darlington', *Northern Star* (31 October 1840), p. 2.

[21] Robert Southey, *Wat Tyler*, p. 7 (p. 69).

[22] 'To the Chartists of London', *Northern Star* (29 May 1841), p. 1; 'Coventry', *Northern Star* (9 April 1842), p. 1.

[23] In London, the exploits of Wat Tyler, Jack Straw, and John Ball served as the basis of street theatre and Bartholomew Fair shows from the mid-eighteenth to the mid-nineteenth century. See Taylor, *London's Burning*, p. 29; Dunn, *Great Rising*, p. 150. The Coburg Theatre (later renamed the Victoria) staged a play about Wat Tyler in 1825 and 1831 and produced a Christmas pantomime on the same subject nearly two decades later. See Jane Moody, *Illegitimate Theatre in London, 1770–1840* (Cambridge: Cambridge University Press, 2000), p. 141; Marc Brodie, 'Free trade and cheap theatre: Sources of politics for the nineteenth-century London poor', *Social History*, 28:3 (October 2003), 346–60, pp. 346–48. The Chartist playwright John Watkins also published his own *Wat Tyler*. Although Watkins's play is not extant, it was performed once in Whitby, Watkins's hometown. 'Whitby Theatre', *Yorkshire Gazette* (16 March 1839), p. 5; 'Register of Dramatic Doings', *Odd Fellow* (30 March 1839), p. 1.

[24] Another previously unknown production of *Wat Tyler* that identifies Southey by name occurred in Chartist friendly circles. John Cleave advertised and sold tickets for a May 1843 amateur performance, which also featured Sheridan Knowles's *Virginius, the Liberator of*

in working-class milieux throughout the Chartist period. The Manchester radical Abel Heywood sold 450 copies per week in the early 1850s.[25] The Chartist publisher John Cleave produced his own edition (the text used by this volume), which he advertised in the *Star* almost continuously between 1840 and 1842 and intermittently thereafter. Ads for Cleave's and other editions also appeared in the *Charter*, the *Northern Liberator*, the *Odd Fellow*, the *Southern Star*, and *Cleave's Gazette of Variety*, which also published illustrations of scenes from the plays (see Figure 1.1). Furthermore, Southey's version of the Great Rising demonstrably influenced Chartist ideas. Lectures and essays about the revolt featured such set pieces found in Southey as the molestation of Wat Tyler's daughter, the meeting at Smithfield, and Tyler's assassination by William Walworth.[26] Finally, other dramatic adaptations (which were frequently titled differently) treated the rebellion more ambiguously than Southey's play, representing 'the rebels as a drunken mob', praising the revolt's suppression, making the events the subject of burlesque, or omitting the radical preacher John Ball.[27] Chartist periodicals on the other hand excerpted Ball's climactic speech from Southey's text and Chartist speakers recited and commented upon it.[28] In substantial ways, then, the Chartists' Wat Tyler was Southey's hero; conversely, Chartist performances marked perhaps the only instantiations of one of the most notorious dramas of the Romantic era.

Rome; scenes from Byron's tragedy *Cain*; and an 'original' Owenite 'sketch ... in two scenes'. Although the event took place at a site with long associations with London radicalism, the London Literary Institution (formerly Richard Carlile's Rotunda), other than Cleave's participation there is no evidence to suggest the involvement of Chartist groups, so this performance is not included in Appendix 1 or the data in Tables 0.1–0.5. See 'Amateur Theatricals', *Cleave's Gazette of Variety* (6 May 1843), p. 4 and 'Rotunda Theatre', *Cleave's Gazette of Variety* (6 May 1843), p. 4.

[25] Richard Altick, *The English Common Reader: A Social History of the Mass Reading Public, 1800–1900* (Columbus: Ohio State University Press, 1957), p. 352.

[26] 'The Middle Classes', *Chartist Circular* (16 January 1841), p. 289; 'Mr Marriot', *Northern Star* (2 April 1842), p. 2; 'The Queen v. O'Neill', *Northern Star* (19 August 1843), p. 6; 'The Insurrections of the Working Class', *Labourer* (1848), vol. 3, p. 12.

[27] Moody, *Illegitimate Theatre*, pp. 141–45.

[28] 'The Rich Oppressor and his Slaves', *National Association Gazette* (25 June 1842), p. 210; 'Monday Evening', *Northern Star* (10 December 1842), p. 1.

Figure 1.1 Frontispiece illustrations for Cleave's edition of *Wat Tyler*. Taken from *Cleave's Penny Gazette of Variety and Amusement*, 10 March 1838, p. 1

WAT TYLER:

A Dramatic Poem, In Three Acts.

By Robert Southey, ESQ.
Poet Laureate to her Majesty.

London:
Cleave, Shoe Lane,
(One door from Fleet Street)

Dramatis Personae[1]

King Richard[2]
Archbishop of Canterbury[3]
Sir John Tresilian[4]
Walworth, *Lord Mayor*
Philpot
Wat Tyler[5]
John Ball[6]
Piers
Hob Carter

Notes for all plays draw on information from the *Oxford English Dictionary*, the *Oxford Dictionary of National Biography*, and *The Encyclopedia Britannica* as well as diverse other sources. For *Wat Tyler*, information about the Great Rising derives largely from R.B. Dobson, *The Peasants' Revolt of 1381* (London: Macmillan, 1970), an invaluable collection of medieval texts about the rising, and Alastair Dunn, *The Great Rising of 1381* (Stroud, Gloucestershire: Tempus, 2002).

[1] *Dramatis Personae*: as John Cleave's version of *Wat Tyler* omits a dramatis personae, the inserted list comes from an earlier edition by radical publisher William Hone: *Wat Tyler; A Dramatic Poem* (London: Hone, 1817). It follows the problematic convention of listing women second and separately. It also omits Tyler's wife, whom Southey fails to name and who speaks only one line.

[2] *King Richard*: Richard II; succeeded his grandfather Edward III in 1377 when he was only 10 years old; reigned until 1399 when deposed by Henry IV.

[3] *Archbishop of Canterbury*: Simon of Sudbury, newly appointed Chancellor, who helped impose the poll taxes.

[4] *Sir John Tresilian*: as Chief Justice of the King's Bench between 1381 and his execution in 1387, oversaw the trials and punishment of the defeated rebels. Southey mistakes his given name, which was Robert.

[5] *Wat Tyler*: a historical figure, although little is definitively known about his life other than his prominent role in the Great Rising. Chronicle sources agree that he came from Kent, and became a spokesperson for the rebels before being killed during a parlay with King Richard II.

[6] *John Ball*: also a historical figure; popular priest from York who preached in fields and market squares before being excommunicated and imprisoned for his egalitarian views.

Jack Straw[7]
Tom Miller

Alice, *Daughter to Wat Tyler*

Tax-gatherers, Herald, Soldiers, Mob, &c.

---

[7] *Jack Straw*: a historical figure but one about whom very little is known; sometimes confused with Wat Tyler in medieval chronicles. Straw featured prominently in later chapbooks and other street literature.

ACT I
SCENE I

A Blacksmith's Shop.

Wat Tyler at work within; a May-pole before the door.[8]

Alice, Piers, &c.
SONG.

   CHEERFUL on this holiday,
    Welcome we the merry May.
  On every sunny hillock spread,
  The pale primrose lifts her head;
  Rich with sweets, the western gale
  Sweeps along the cowslip'd dale.[9]
  Every bank, with violets gay,
  Smiles to welcome in the May.
  The linnet from the budding grove,[10]
  Chirps her vernal song of love.
  The copse resounds the throstle's notes
  On each wild gale, sweet music floats;
  And melody from every spray,
  Welcomes in the merry May.
   Cheerful on this holiday,
   Welcome we the merry May.

DANCE.
During the Dance, Tyler lays down his hammer, and sits mournfully down before the door.
Enter Hob Carter.
HOB. (*To Tyler.*) Why so sad neighbor? – do not these gay sports,

---

[8] *May-pole*: a tall pole decorated with flowers used in dances celebrating May Day.
[9] *cowslip'd*: covered with cowslips, a wild plant with yellow flowers.
[10] *linnet*: song-bird.

    This revelry of youth, recall the days
    When we too mingled in the revelry;
    And lightly tripping in the morris dance,[11]
    Welcomed the merry month?

TYLER.   Aye, we were young:
    No cares had quelled the hey-day of the blood:
    We sported deftly in the April morning,
      Nor marked the black-clouds gathering o'er our noon:
    Nor feared the storm of night.

HOB.   Beshrew me, Tyler,[12]
    But my heart joys to see the imps so cheerful!
    Young, hale, and happy, why should they destroy
    These blessings by reflection?

TYLER.   Look ye, neighbour –
    You have known me long.

HOB.   Since we were boys together,
    And played at barley-brake, and danced the morris:[13]
    Some five-and-twenty years!

TYLER. Was not *I* young, and hale, and happy?

HOB. Cheerful as the best.

TYLER. Have not I been a staid, hard-working man?
    Up with the lark at labour; sober, honest,
    Of an unblemished character?

HOB.   Who doubts it?
    There's never a man in Essex bears a better.

TYLER. And shall not these, tho' young, and hale, and happy,
    Look on with sorrow to the future hour?
    Shall not reflection poison all their pleasures?
    When I – the honest, staid, hard-working Tyler,
    Toil through the long course of the summer's day,
    Still toiling, yet still poor! when with hard labour
    Scarce can I furnish out my daily food,
    And age comes on to steal away my strength,
    And leave me poor and wretched! Why should this be?
    My youth was regular – my labour constant –
    I married an industrious, virtuous woman;
    Nor while I toiled and sweated at the anvil,
    Sat she neglectful of her spinning-wheel.

---

[11] *morris dance*: traditional English dance.
[12] *Beshrew*: mild oath; to invoke evil upon.
[13] *barley-brake*: traditional country game.

Hob! I have only six groats in the world,[14]
And they must soon by law be taken from me.
HOB. Curse on these taxes – one succeeds another –
Our ministers, panders of a king's will,
Drain all our wealth away, waste it in revels,
And lure, or force away our boys, who should be
The props of our old age! – to fill their armies
And feed the crows of France.[15] Year follows year,
And still we madly prosecute the war;
Draining our wealth, distressing our poor peasants,
Slaughtering our youths – and all to crown our chiefs
With Glory! – I detest the hell-sprung name.
TYLER. What matters me who wears the crown of France?
Whether a Richard or a Charles possess it?[16]
They reap the glory – they enjoy the spoil –
We pay – we bleed! The sun would shine as cheerly,
The rains of heaven as seasonably fall,
Though neither of these royal pests existed.
HOB. Nay, as for that, we poor men should fare better;
No legal robbers then should force away
The hard-earn'd wages of our honest toil.
The Parliament for ever cries *more money*,
The service of the state demands more money;
Just heaven! of what service is the state?
TYLER. Oh, 'tis of vast importance; who should pay for
The luxuries and riots of the court?
Who should support the flaunting courtier's pride,
Pay for their midnight revels, their rich garments,
Did not the state enforce? – Think ye, my friend,
That I, a humble blacksmith, here at Deptford,
Would part with these six groats – earned by hard toil,
All that I have! to massacre the Frenchman,
Murder as enemies men I never saw!
Did not the state compel me?

---

[14] *groats*: coins worth fourpence.
[15] *fill their armies ... of France*: the first of many references to the series of wars between England and France that marked the reigns of both Richard II and his predecessor Edward III. Southey's anti-militarism (directed against Britain's war with revolutionary France) would have resonated with Chartist opposition to the Opium and Afghanistan wars and to standing armies more broadly.
[16] *Charles*: Charles VI, the French monarch.

(*Tax-gatherers pass by.*)   There they go,
   Privileged ruffians! (*Piers & Alice advance to him.*)
ALICE. Did we not dance it well to-day, my father?
   You know I always loved these village sports,
   Even from my infancy, and yet methinks
   I never tripped along the mead so gaily.[17]
   You know they chose me queen, and your friend Piers[18]
   Wreathed me this cowslip garland for my head –
   Is it not simple? – You are sad, my father!
   You should have rested from your work to-day,
   And given a few hours up to merriment –
   But you are so serious!
TYLER.   Serious, my good girl!
   I may well be so: when I look at thee
   It makes me sad! thou art too fair a flower
   To bear the wintry wind of poverty.
PIERS. Yet I have often heard you speak of riches
   Even with contempt; they cannot purchase peace,
   Or innocence, or virtue – sounder sleep
   Waits on the weary ploughman's lowly bed,
   Than on the downy couch of luxury
   Lulls the rich slave of pride and indolence.
   I never wish for wealth! my arm is strong,
   And I can purchase by it a coarse meal,
   And hunger savours it.
TYLER.   Young man, thy mind
   Has yet to learn the hard lesson of experience.
   Thou art yet young: the blasting breath of want
   Has not yet froze the current of thy blood.
PIERS. Fare not the birds well, as from spray to spray,[19]
   Blithesome they bound – yet find their simple food
   Scattered abundantly?
TYLER. No fancied boundaries of mine and thine
   Restrain their wanderings: Nature gives enough
   For all; but Man, with arrogant selfishness,
   Proud of his heaps, hoards up superfluous stores

---

[17] *mead*: meadow.
[18] *queen*: the May Queen, a woman or girl chosen to preside over May Day festivities.
[19] *Fare not the birds*: see Matthew 6:26: 'Behold the fowls of the air: for they sow not, neither do they reap, nor gather into barns; yet your heavenly Father feedeth them. Are ye not much better than they?' (*King James Version*).

    Robbed from his weaker fellows, starves the poor,
    Or gives to pity what he owes to justice.
PIERS. So I have heard our good friend John Ball preach.
ALICE. My father, wherefore was John Ball imprisoned?[20]
    Was he not charitable, good, and pious?
    I have heard him say that all mankind are brethren,
    And that like brethren they should love each other;
    Was not that doctrine pious?
TYLER.   Rank sedition –
    High treason, every syllable, my child!
    The priests cry out on him for heresy,
    The nobles all detest him as a rebel,
    And this good man, this minister of Christ,
    This man, the friend and brother of mankind,
    Lingers in the dark dungeon! – My dear Alice,
    Retire awhile.   (*Exit Alice.*)
                Piers, I would speak to thee,
    Even with a father's love! you are much with me,
    And I believe do court my conversation;
    Thou coulds't not choose thee forth a truer friend;
    I would fain see thee happy, but I fear
    Thy very virtues will destroy thy peace.
    My daughter – she is young – not yet fifteen –
    Piers, thou art generous, and thy youthful heart
    Warm with affection; this close intimacy
    Will ere long grow to love.
PIERS.   Suppose it so;
    Were that an evil, Walter? – She is mild
    And cheerful, and industrious; now methinks
    With such a partner life would be most happy!
    Why would ye warn me then of wretchedness?
    Is there an evil that can harm our lot?
    I have been told the virtuous must be happy,
    And have believed it true; tell me, my friend,
    What shall disturb the virtuous?
TYLER. Poverty. A bitter foe.
PIERS.   Nay, you have often told me
    That happiness does not consist in riches.

---

[20] *John Ball imprisoned?*: The Chartist preacher J. R. Stephens was occasionally compared to John Ball, especially after his arrest in 1838. See 'The Progress of Liberty in England', *Northern Liberator* (25 April 1840), p. 3.

TYLER. It is most true; but tell me, my dear boy,
    Could'st thou be happy to behold thy wife
    Pining with want? the children of your loves[21]
    Clad in the squalid rags of wretchedness?
    And, when thy hard and unremitting toil
    Had earned with pain a scanty recompense,
    Could'st thou be patient when the law should rob thee,
    And leave thee without bread and pennyless?
PIERS. It is a dreadful picture.
TYLER.   'Tis a true one.
PIERS. But yet methinks our sober industry
    Might drive away the danger: 'tis but little
    That I could wish – food for our frugal meals,
    Raiment, however homely, and a bed
    To shield us from the night.
TYLER.   Thy honest reason
    Could wish no more: but were it not most wretched
    To want the coarse food for the frugal meal?
    And by the orders of your merciless lord,
    If you by chance were guilty of being poor,
    To be turned out adrift to the bleak world,
    Unhoused, unfriended? – Piers, I have not been idle,
    I never ate the bread of indolence –
    Could Alice be more thrifty than her mother?
    Yet with but one child, – and that one how good
    Thou knowest, – I scarcely can provide the wants
    Of nature: look at these wolves of the law,
    They come to drain me of my hard-earned wages.
    I have already paid the heavy tax
    Laid on the wool that clothes me – on my leather,
    On all the needful articles of life!
    And now three groats (and I worked hard to earn them)
    The parliament demands – and I must pay them,
    Forsooth, for liberty to wear my head. –[22]
        (*Enter Tax-gatherers.*)
COLLECTOR. Three groats a head for all your family.
PIERS. Why is this money gathered? 'tis a hard tax
    On the poor labourer! – it can never be
    That government should thus distress the people.

---

[21] *Pining*: wasting from physical or emotional suffering, in this context especially hunger.
[22] *liberty ... my head*: to live at all (a description of the poll-tax).

    Go to the rich for money – honest labour
    Ought to enjoy its fruits.
COLLECTOR.   The state wants money,
    War is expensive – 'tis a glorious war,
    A war of honour, and must be supported –
    Three groats a head.
TYLER.   There, three for my own head,
    Three for my wife's; what will the state tax next?
COLLECTOR. You have a daughter.
TYLER. She is below the age – not yet fifteen.
COLLECTOR. You would evade the tax.
TYLER.   Sir Officer,
    I have paid you fairly what the law demands.
      (*Alice and her mother enter the shop. The Tax-gatherers go to her. One of them lays hold of her. She screams. – Tyler goes in.*)
COLLECTOR. You say she's under age.
      (*Alice screams again. Tyler knocks out the Tax-gatherer's brains. His companions fly.*)
PIERS.   – A just revenge.
TYLER. – Most just indeed; but in the eye of the law
    'Tis murder: and the murderer's lot is mine.
      (*Piers goes out – Tyler sits down mournfully.*)
ALICE. – Fly, my dear father! let us leave this place
    Before they raise pursuit.
TYLER.   Nay, nay, my child,
    Flight would be useless – I have done my duty;
    I have punished the brute insolence of lust,
    And here will wait my doom.
WIFE.   Oh, let us fly,
    My husband, my dear husband!
ALICE.   Quit but this place,
    And we may yet be safe, and happy too.
TYLER. It would be useless, Alice, 'twould but lengthen
    A wretched life in fear.   (*Cry without*, Liberty, Liberty!)
      (*Enter Hob Carter, Mob, &c.*) (*Crying* – Liberty! Liberty! – No Poll-tax! No War!)
HOB. We have broke our chains, we will arise in anger,
    The mighty multitude shall trample down
    The handful that oppress them.
TYLER.   Have ye heard
    So soon then of my murder?
HOB.   Of your vengeance.

Piers ran throughout the village: told the news –
Cried out, to arms! – arm, arm for liberty;
For Liberty and Justice!
TYLER.   My good friends,
Heed well your danger, or be resolute!
Learn to laugh menaces and force to scorn,
Or leave me. I dare answer the bold deed –
Death must come once; return to your homes,
Protect my wife and child, and on my grave
Write why I died; perhaps the time may come
When honest Justice shall applaud the deed.
HOB. – Nay, nay, we are oppressed – and have too long
Knelt at our proud lords' feet; we have too long
Obeyed their orders, bowed to their caprices –
Sweated for them the wearying summer's day,
Wasted for them the wages of our toil;
Fought for them, conquered for them, bled for them.
Still to be trampled on, and still despised!
But we have broke our chains.
TOM MILLER.   Piers is gone on
Through all the neighbouring villages, to spread
The glorious tidings.
HOB.   He is hurried on
To Maidstone, to deliver good John Ball,
Our friend, our shepherd.   (*Mob increases.*)
TYLER.   Friends and Countrymen,
Will ye then rise to save an honest man
From the fierce clutches of the bloody law?
Oh, do not call to mind my private wrongs,
That the state drained my hard-earned pittance from me.
That, of his office proud, the foul Collector
Durst with lewd hand seize on my darling child,
Insult her maiden modesty, and force
A father's hand to vengeance; heed not this;
Think not, my countrymen, on private wrongs,
Remember what yourselves have long endured.
Think of the insults, wrongs, and contumelies,[23]
Ye bear from your proud lords – that your hard toil
Manures their fertile fields – you plough the earth,
You sow the corn, you reap the ripened harvest, –

---

[23] *contumelies*: contemptuous treatment.

They riot on the produce! – That, like beasts,
They sell you with their land – claim all the fruits[24]
Which the kindly earth produces, as their own,
The privilege, forsooth of noble birth!
On, on to freedom; feel but your own strength,
Be but resolved, and these destructive tyrants
Shall shrink before your vengeance.

HOB. On to London –
The tidings fly before us – the court trembles –
Liberty – Vengeance – Justice.

END OF THE FIRST ACT

---

[24] *sell you with their land*: as Southey recounts, the rising of 1381 had the abolition of serfdom as a central demand.
claim all the fruits: see 2 Timothy 2:6: 'The husbandman that laboureth must be first partaker of the fruits' (*King James Version*).

ACT II
SCENE I

Blackheath.[25]

Tyler, Hob Carter, &c.

SONG.

> 'When Adam delved and Eve span,
> Who was then the gentleman?'[26]
> Wretched is the infant's lot,
> Born within the straw-roofed cot;
> Be he generous, wise, or brave,
> He must only be a slave.
> Long, long labour, little rest,
> Still to toil to be oppressed;
> Drained by taxes of his store,
> Punished next for being poor;
> This is the poor wretch's lot,
> Born within the straw-roofed cot.
> While the peasant works, to sleep –
> What the peasant sows, to reap –
> On the couch of ease to lie,
> Rioting in revelry;
> Be he villain, be he fool,
> Still to hold despotic rule:
> Trampling on his slaves with scorn!
> This is to be nobly born.

---

[25] *Blackheath*: area just southeast of London in the fourteenth century (and now part of Greater London).

[26] *When Adam delved ... gentleman?*: a proverb that predated the rising and typified its radical egalitarianism. Radicals and Chartists gave this motto pride of place in accounts of the rising.

'When Adam delved and Eve span,
   Who was then the gentleman?'
JACK STRAW. The mob are up in London – the proud courtiers
   Begin to tremble.
TOM MILLER.   Aye, aye, 'tis time to tremble;
   Who'll plough their fields, who'll do their drudgery now,
   And work like horses to give them the harvest?
JACK STRAW. I only wonder we lay quiet so long.
   We had always the same strength, and we deserved
   The ills we met with for not using it.
HOB. Why do we fear those animals called lords?
   What is there in the name to frighten us?
   Is not my arm as mighty as a Baron's?
      (*Enter Piers and John Ball.*)
PIERS. (*To Tyler.*) Have I done well, my father? – I remember'd
   This good man lay in prison.
TYLER.   My dear child,
   Most well; the people rise for liberty,
   And their first deed should be to break the chains
   That bind the virtuous: – Oh, thou honest priest,
   How much hast thou endured![27]
JOHN BALL.   Why, aye, my friend!
   These squalid rags bespeak what I have suffered.
   I was reviled, insulted, left to languish
   In a damp dungeon; but I bore it cheerily –
   My heart was glad – for I have done my duty.
   I pitied my oppressors, and I sorrowed
   For the poor men of England.
TYLER.   They have felt
   Their strength: look round this heath; 'tis throng'd with men
   Ardent for freedom; mighty is the event
   That waits their fortune.
JOHN BALL.   I would fain address them.
TYLER. Do so, my friend, and teach to them their duty.
   Remind them of their long-withholden rights;
   What ho! there; silence!
PIERS.   Silence, there, my friends,
   This good man would address you.

---

[27] *the people rise ... endured*: for the Chartists, the liberation of Ball would have resonated with the purported aim of the Newport rising to free Henry Vincent as well as with efforts on behalf of other Chartist prisoners.

HOB.   Aye, aye, hear him –
    He is no mealy-mouthed court-orator,[28]
    To flatter vice, and pamper lordly pride.
JOHN BALL. Friends, brethren! for ye are my brethren all;
    Englishmen, met in arms to advocate
    The cause of freedom, hear me; pause awhile
    In the career of vengeance! – it is true[29]
    I am a priest, but, as these rags may speak,
    Not one who riots in the poor man's spoil,
    Or trades with his religion. I am one
    Who preach the law of Christ, and, in my life,
    Would practise what he taught. The Son of God
    Came not to you in power: humble in mien,
    Lowly in heart, the man of Nazareth
    Preach'd mercy, justice, love: 'Woe unto ye,
    Ye that are rich: if that ye would be saved
    Sell that ye have, and give unto the poor.'[30]
    So taught the Saviour; oh, my honest friends,
    Have ye not felt the strong indignant throb
    Of justice in your bosoms, to behold
    The lordly Baron feasting on your spoils?
    Have you not in your hearts arraigned the lot
    That gave him on the couch of luxury
    To pillow his head, and pass the festive day
    In sportive feasts, and ease, and revelry?
    Have you not often in your conscience asked
    Why is the difference, wherefore should that man,
    No worthier than myself, thus lord it over me,
    And bid me labour, and enjoy the fruits?
    The God within your breasts has argued thus;
    The voice of truth has murmur'd; came ye not
    As helpless to the world? Shines not the sun
    With equal ray on both? Do ye not feel
    The self-same winds of heaven as keenly parch ye?
    Abundant is the earth – the Sire of all,

---

[28] *mealy-mouthed*: indecisive, equivocating.

[29] *career*: course of action.

[30] *Woe ... unto the poor*: see Luke 6:24: 'But woe unto you that are rich! for ye have received your consolation', and Luke 18:22: 'Now when Jesus heard these things, he said unto him, Yet lackest thou one thing: sell all that thou hast, and distribute unto the poor, and thou shalt have treasure in heaven: and come, follow me' (*King James Version*).

Saw and pronounced that it was very good.[31]
Look round: the vernal fields smile with new flowers,
The budding orchard perfumes the sweet breeze,
And the green corn waves to the passing gale.
There is enough for all; but your proud Baron
Stands up, and, arrogant of strength exclaims,
'I am a Lord – by nature I am noble:
These fields are mine, for I was born to them,
I was born in the castle – you, poor wretches,
Whelp'd in the cottage are by birth my slaves.'[32]
Almighty God! such blasphemies are uttered;
Almighty God! such blasphemies believed!
TOM MILLER. This is something like a sermon.
JACK STRAW.   Where's the bishop
Would tell you truths like these?
HOB. There never was a bishop among all the apostles.
JOHN BALL. My brethren –
PIERS.   Silence, the good priest speaks.
JOHN BALL. My brethren, these are truths, and weighty ones –
Ye are all equal: nature made ye so.
Equality is your birthright; – when I gaze
On the proud palace, and behold one man
In the blood-purpled robes of royalty,
Feasting at ease, and lording over millions,
Then turn me to the hut of poverty,
And see the wretched labourer worn with toil,
Divide his scanty morsel with his infants,
I sicken, and indignant at the sight,
'Blush for the patience of humanity.'[33]
JACK STRAW. We will assert our rights.
TOM MILLER.   We'll trample down
These insolent oppressors.
JOHN BALL.   In good truth,

---

[31] *Saw ... was very good*: see Genesis 1:31: 'And God saw every thing that he had made, and, behold, it was very good' (*King James Version*).

[32] *Whelp'd*: birthed.

[33] *Equality is your birthright ... 'Blush for the patience of humanity'*: Southey draws frequently on the discourse of natural rights and equality found in Thomas Paine and Jean Jacques Rousseau. The quoted passage derives from James Mackintosh's 1791 *Vindiciae Gallicae*, which supported the French Revolution. In the 1817 parliamentary debate concerning the Seditious Meetings Bill, William Smith read this passage to embarrass Southey, who by 1817 had become a supporter of government censorship and the suppression of radicalism.

  Ye have cause for anger: but, my honest friends,
  Is it revenge or justice that ye seek?
MOB.   Justice, justice.
JOHN BALL. Oh, then remember mercy;
  And though your proud oppressors spare not you,
  Shew you excel them in humanity.
  They will use every art to disunite you,
  To conquer separately, by stratagem,
  Whom in a mass they fear – but be ye firm –
  Boldly demand your long-forgotten rights,
  Your sacred, your inalienable freedom –
  Be bold – be resolute – be merciful;
  And while you spurn the hated name of slaves,
  Shew you are men.
MOB.   Long live our honest priest.
JACK STRAW. He shall be made archbishop.
JOHN BALL. My brethren, I am plain John Ball, your friend,
  Your equal: by the law of Christ enjoined
  To serve you, not command.
JACK STRAW.   March we for London.
TYLER. Mark me, my friends – we rise for liberty –
  Justice shall be our guide: let no man dare
  To plunder in the tumult.
MOB. — Lead us on. Liberty; Justice.
   (*Exeunt, with cries of* Liberty! No Poll-tax! No War!)

SCENE II

 The Tower.

 King Richard, Archbishop of Canterbury, Sir John Tresilian, Walworth, Philpot,
  &c.

KING. What must we do? the danger grows more imminent.
  The mob increases –
PHILPOT.   Every moment brings
  Fresh tidings of our peril.
KING.   It were well
  To grant them what they ask.
ARCHBISHOP.   Aye, that my liege,
  Were politic. Go boldly forth to meet them,

Grant all they ask – however wild and ruinous –
Meantime, the troops you have already summoned,
Will gather round them. Then my Christian power
Absolves you of your promise.
WALWORTH. Were but their ringleaders cut off, the rabble
Would soon disperse.
PHILPOT. United in a mass,
There's nothing can resist them – once divide them
And they will fall an easy sacrifice.
ARCHBISHOP. Lull them by promises – bespeak them fair –
Go forth, my liege – spare not, if need requires
A solemn oath to ratify the treaty.
KING. I dread their fury.
ARCHBISHOP. 'Tis a needless dread,
There is divinity about your person;[34]
It is the sacred privilege of Kings,
Howe'er they act, to render no account
To man. The people have been taught this lesson,
Nor can they soon forget it.
KING. I will go –
I will submit to everything they ask;
My day of triumph will arrive at last. (*Shouts without.*)
   (*Enter Messenger.*)
MESSENGER. The mob are at the city gates.
ARCHBISHOP. Haste, haste,
Address them ere too late. I'll remain here,
For they detest me much. (*Shouts again.*)
   (*Enter another Messenger.*)
MESSENGER. The Londoners have opened the city gates,
The rebels are admitted.
KING. Fear then must give me courage; my lord mayor,
Come you with me. (*Exeunt. Shouts without.*)

---

[34] *divinity about your person*: an allusion to the divine right of kings.

SCENE III

Smithfield.[35]

Wat Tyler, John Ball, Piers, &c. Mob.

PIERS. So far triumphant are we: how these nobles,
   These petty tyrants, who so long oppressed us,
   Shrink at the first resistance.
HOB.   They were powerful
   Only because we fondly thought them so.
   Where is Jack Straw?
TYLER.   Jack Straw is gone to the Tower
   To seize the king, and so to end resistance.
JOHN BALL. It was well judged; fain would I spare the shedding
   Of human blood: gain we that royal puppet
   And all will follow fairly; deprived of him,
   The nobles lose their pretext, nor will dare
   Rebel against the people's majesty.
     (*Enter Herald.*)
HERALD. Richard the Second, by the grace of God,
   Of England, Ireland, France, and Scotland, King,
   And of the town of Berwick-upon-Tweed,[36]
   Would parley with Wat Tyler.
TYLER.   Let him know
   Wat Tyler is in Smithfield. (*Exit Herald.*) – I will parley
   With this young monarch; as he comes to me,
   Trusting my honour, on your lives I charge you
   Let none attempt to harm him.
JOHN BALL.   The faith of courts
   Is but a weak dependence. You are honest –
   And better is it even to die the victim
   Of credulous honesty, than live preserved
   By the cold policy that still suspects.
     (*Enter King, Walworth, Philpot, &c.*)
KING. I would speak to thee, Wat Tyler; bid the mob
   Retire awhile.

---

[35] *Smithfield*: centrally located London horse and cattle market. In the nineteenth century, Smithfield became a site of political mass meetings.

[36] *Berwick-upon-Tweed*: northernmost town in England, in the county of Northumberland.

PIERS.   Nay, do not go alone –
   Let me attend you.
TYLER.   Wherefore should I fear?
   Am I not armed with a just cause? – retire,
   And I will boldly plead the cause of Freedom. (*Advances.*)
KING. Tyler, why have you killed my officer?
   And led my honest subjects from their homes,
   Thus to rebel against the Lord's anointed?
TYLER. Because they were oppressed.
KING.   Was this the way
   To remedy the ill? – you should have tried
   By milder means – petitioned at the throne –
   The throne will always listen to petitions.
TYLER.   King of England,
   Petitioning for pity is most weak,
   The sovereign people ought to *demand justice*.
   I killed your officer, for his lewd hand
   Insulted a maid's modesty; your subjects
   I lead to rebel against the Lord's anointed,
   Because his ministers have made him odious;
   His yoke is heavy, and his burden grievous.[37]
   Why do we carry on this fatal war,
   To force upon the French a king they hate:
   Tearing our young men from their peaceful homes:
   Forcing his hard-earn'd fruits from the honest peasant;
   Distressing us to desolate our neighbours?
   Why is this ruinous poll-tax imposed,
   But to support your court's extravagance,
   And your mad title to the crown of France?
   Shall we sit tamely down beneath these evils
   Petitioning for pity?
                  King of England,
   Why are we sold like cattle in your markets –
   Deprived of every privilege of man?
   Must we lie tamely at our tyrant's feet,
   And, like your spaniels, lick the hand that beats us?
   You sit at ease in your gay palaces,
   The costly banquet courts your appetite,
   Sweet music soothes your slumbers: we the while,

---

[37] *His yoke … grievous*: ironic inversion of Matthew 11:30: 'For my yoke is easy, and my burden is light' *(King James Version)*.

Scarce by hard toil can earn a little food,
And sleep scarce sheltered from the cold night wind;
Whilst your wild projects wrest the little from us
Which might have cheered the wintry hour of age.
The parliament for ever asks more money;
We toil and sweat for money for your taxes:
Where is the benefit, what good reap we
From all the counsels of your government?
Think you that we should quarrel with the French?
What boots to us your victories, your glory?[38]
We pay, we fight, you profit at your ease.
Do you not claim the country as your own?
Do you not call the venison of the forest,
The birds of heaven, your own? – prohibiting us,
Even though in want of food, to seize the prey[39]
Which nature offers. King! is all this just?
Think you, we do not *feel* the wrongs we suffer?
The hour of retribution is at hand,
And tyrants tremble – mark me, King of England,

WALWORTH. (*Comes behind him, and stabs him.*)[40]
Insolent rebel, threatening the king!
PIERS. Vengeance, vengeance!
HOB. Seize the king.
KING. I must be bold. (*Advancing.*)
                      My friends and loving subjects,
I will grant you all you ask; you shall be free –
The tax shall be repealed – all, all you wish.
Your leader menaced me, he deserved his fate.
Quiet your angers: on my royal word
Your grievances shall all be done away;
Your vassalage abolished. A free pardon
Allowed to all: so help me God, it shall be.
JOHN BALL. Revenge, my brethren, beseems not Christians:
Send us these terms, signed with your seal of state.
We will await in peace: deceive us not –
Act justly, so to excuse your late foul deed.

---

[38] *boots*: benefits.

[39] *the venison ... the prey*: laws punishing poaching with severe penalties remained a cause célèbre through the Chartist era.

[40] *Walworth ... stabs him*: for his role in killing Wat Tyler, London's Mayor was infamous in Chartist accounts of the Great Rising, often as an example of middle-class perfidy. See, 'Persecution the Agent of Tyrants', *Chartist Circular* (26 September 1840), p. 213.

KING. The charter shall be drawn out: on mine honour
   All shall be justly done.

                    END OF THE SECOND ACT

ACT III
SCENE I

Smithfield.

Piers, John Ball.

PIERS. *(To John Ball.)* You look disturbed, my father.
JOHN BALL.   Piers, I am so.
    Jack Straw has forced the Tower: seized the Archbishop,
    And beheaded him.[41]
PIERS.   The curse of insurrection.
JOHN BALL. Aye, Piers, our nobles level down their vassals,
    Keep them at endless labour, like their brutes,
    Degrading every faculty by servitude:
    Repressing all the energy of mind.
    We must not wonder, then, that, like wild beasts,
    When they have burst their chains, with brutal rage
    They revenge them on their tyrants.
PIERS.   This Archbishop,
    He was oppressive to his humble vassals:
    Proud, haughty, avaricious –
JOHN BALL.   A true high priest;
    Preaching humility with his mitre on.[42]
    Praising up alms and christian charity,
    Even whilst his unforgiving hand distressed
    His honest tenants.
PIERS.   He deserved his fate, then.
JOHN BALL. Justice can never link with cruelty.
    Is there among the catalogue of crimes
    A sin so black that only Death can expiate?

---

[41] *forced the Tower ... beheaded him*: Southey draws upon historical events for this episode as for the meeting at Smithfield and Tyler's killing.

[42] *mitre*: bishop's headdress.

Will reason never rouse her from her slumbers,
And darting through the veil her eagle eye,
See in the sable garments of the law[43]
Revenge concealed? This high priest has been haughty,
He has oppressed his vassals: tell me, Piers,
Does his death remedy the ills he caused?
Were it not better to repress his power
Of doing wrong – that so his future life
Might remedy the evils of the past,
And benefit mankind?

PIERS. But must not vice be punished?

JOHN BALL. Is not punishment revenge?
The momentary violence of anger
May be excused: the indignant heart will throb
Against oppression, and the outstretched arm
Resent its injured feelings: the Collector
Insulted Alice, and roused the keen emotions
Of a fond father. Tyler murdered him.

PIERS. Murdered! – a most harsh word.

JOHN BALL. Yes, murdered him:
His mangled feelings prompted the bad act,
And nature will almost commend the deed
That Justice blames: but will the awakened feelings
Plead with their heart-removing eloquence
For the calm deliberate murder of Revenge?
Would you, Piers, in your calmer hour of reason,
Condemn an erring brother to be slain?
Cut him at once from all the joys of life,
All hopes of reformation – to revenge
The deed his punishment cannot recall?
My blood boiled in me at the fate of Tyler,
Yet I revenged not.

PIERS. Oh, my christian father,
They would not argue thus humanely on us,
Were we within their power.

JOHN BALL. I know they would not;
But we must pity them that they are vicious,
Nor imitate their vice.

PIERS. Alas, poor Tyler!
I do repent me much that I stood back,

---

[43] *sable*: fur from the sable, a species of marten.

    When he advanced, fearless in rectitude,
    To meet these royal assassins.
JOHN BALL.   Not for myself,
    Though I have lost an honest, virtuous friend,
    Mourn I the death of Tyler: he was one
    Gifted with the strong energy of mind,
    Quick to perceive the right, and prompt to act
    When Justice needed: he would listen to me
    With due attention, yet not yielding lightly
    What had to him seemed good; severe in virtue,
    He awed the ruder people, whom he led,
    By his stern rectitude.
PIERS.   Witness that day
    When they destroy'd the palace of the Gaunt;[44]
    And hurled the wealth his avarice had amassed,
    Amid the fire: the people, fierce in zeal,
    Threw in the flames a wretch whose selfish hand
    Purloin'd amid the tumult.
JOHN BALL.   I lament
    The death of Tyler for my country's sake.
    I shudder lest posterity enslaved,
    Should rue his murder. Who shall now control
    The giddy multitude, blind to their own good,
    And listening with avidity to the tale
    Of courtly falsehood.
PIERS.   The king must perform
    His plighted promise.[45]
        (*Cry without* – The Charter; – the Charter.)
        (*Enter Mob and Herald.*)
TOM MILLER. Read it out – read it out.
HOB. Aye, aye, let's hear the Charter.
HERALD. Richard Plantagenet, by the grace of God, King of England, Ireland, France, Scotland, and the town of Berwick-upon-Tweed, to all whom it may concern, – These presents:[46] Whereas our loving subjects have complained

---

[44] *palace of the Gaunt*: Uncle of Richard II, John of Gaunt was closely identified with the imposition of the Poll Tax of 1381. He was especially hated for this role as well as for his attempts to assert the royal court's authority and restrict Londoners' rights. The destruction of his palace the Savoy was a famous episode in the Great Rising. Southey follows medieval chroniclers who emphasise that the rebels did not allow members to loot the destroyed palace.
[45] *plighted*: pledged.
[46] *presents*: a legal phrase denoting the present document.

to us of the heavy burdens they endure, particularly from our late enacted
poll-tax; and whereas they have risen in arms against our officers, and
demanded the abolition of personal slavery, vassalage and manorial rights;
we, ever ready in our sovereign mercy to listen to the petitions of our loving
subjects, do annul all these grievances.

MOB. Huzza! long live the king.

HERALD. (*Continues.*) And do of our royal mercy grant a free pardon to all
who may have been anyways concerned in the late insurrections. All this
shall be faithfully performed on our royal word, so help us God. – God save
the King.

   (*Loud and repeated shouts.*)

HERALD. Now then depart in quiet to your homes.

JOHN BALL. Nay, my good friend, the people will remain
  Embodied peaceably, till parliament
  Confirm the royal charter: tell your king so:
  We will await the Charter's confirmation,
  Meanwhile comporting ourselves orderly,
  As peaceful citizens, not risen in tumult,
  But to redress their evils.   (*Exit Herald, &c.*)

HOB.   'Twas well ordered.
  I place but little trust in courtly faith.

JOHN BALL. We must remain embodied; else the king
  Will plunge again in royal luxury;
  And when the storm of danger is past over,
  Forget his promises.

HOB.   Aye, like an aguish sinner,[47]
  He'll promise to repent, when the fit's on him,
  When well recovered, laugh at his own terrors.

PIERS. Oh I am grieved that we must gain so little.
  Why are not all these empty ranks abolished,
  King, slave, and lord, 'ennobled into MAN.'
  Are we not equal all; – have you not told me
  Equality is the sacred right of man,[48]
  Inalienable, though by force withheld?

JOHN BALL. Even so: but, Piers, my frail and fallible judgement
  Knows hardly to decide if it be right,
  Peaceably to return, content with little,
  With this half restitution of our rights,
  Or boldly to proceed, through blood and slaughter,

---

[47] *aguish*: afflicted; affected with fever.
[48] '*Equality ... right of man*': again Southey echoes Paine and Rousseau.

    Till we should all be equal and all happy.
    I chose the milder way: – perhaps I erred!
PIERS. I fear me, by the mass, the unsteady people
    Are flocking homewards – how the multitude
    Diminishes.
JOHN BALL. Go thou, my son, and stay them.
    Carter, do you exert your influence,
    All depends upon their stay: my mind is troubled
    And I would fain compose my thoughts for action.
        (*Exeunt Hob and Piers.*)
    Father of mercies! I do fear me much
    That I have erred. Thou gav'st my ardent mind
    To pierce the mists of superstitious falsehood; –
    Gav'st me to know the truth. I should have urged it
    Through every opposition; now, perhaps,
    The seemly voice of pity has deceived me,
    And all this mighty movement ends in ruin.
    I fear me I have been like the weak leech,[49]
    Who, sparing to cut deep, with cruel mercy
    Mangles his patient without curing him. (*Great tumult.*)
    What means this tumult? hark! the clang of arms.
    God of eternal justice – the false monarch
    Has broke his plighted vow.
        (*Enter Piers, wounded.*)
PIERS. Fly, fly, my father – the perjured king – fly, fly!
JOHN BALL. Nay, nay, my child; I dare abide my fate.
    Let me bind up thy wounds.
PIERS.   'Tis useless succour.
    They seek thy life; fly, fly, my honoured father.
    Fain would I die in peace to hope thee safe.
    I shall soon join thee, Tyler: – they are murdering[50]
    Our unsuspecting brethren: half unarmed,
    Trusting too fondly to the tyrant's vows,
    They were dispersing: – the streets swim with blood.
    Oh, save thyself.
        (*Enter soldiers.*)

---

[49] *weak leech*: poor doctor, after the medical use of leeches.

[50] *Fain would ... they are murdering*: One of few instances where significant differences separate Sherwood's version of 1817 (and the many following unauthorised versions) and Southey's edition of 1837. Whereas Cleave usually follows the 1837 edition, here he uses Sherwood's text. The 1837 variant reads: 'And let me have the hope to sweeten death / That thou at least hast 'scaped. They are murdering'.

1ˢᵀ SOLDIER. This is that old seditious heretic.
2ᴺᴰ SOLDIER. And here the young spawn of rebellion:
    My orders ar'nt to spare him.   (*Stabs Piers.*)
    Come, you old stirrer-up of insurrection,
    You bell-wether of the mob – you ar'n't to die[51]
    So easily.   (*Leading him off.*)
        (*Mob fly across the stage – the troops pursue them – tumult increases – loud cries and shouts.*)

SCENE II

    Westminster Hall.[52]

    King, Walworth, Philpot, Sir John Tresilian, &c.

WALWORTH. My liege, 'twas wisely ordered, to destroy
    The dunghill rabble, but take prisoner
    That old seditious priest: his strange wild notions
    Of this equality, when well exposed,
    Will create ridicule, and shame the people
    Of their late tumults.
SIR JOHN TRESILIAN. Aye, there's nothing like
    A fair, free, open trial, where the king
    Can choose his jury and appoint his judges.
KING. Walworth, I must thank you for my deliverance,
    'Twas a bold deed to stab him in the parley.
    Kneel down, and rise a knight, Sir William Walworth.[53]
    (*Enter Messenger.*)
MESSENGER. I left them hotly at it. Smithfield smoked
    With the rebels' blood! your troops fought loyally,
    There's not a man of them will lend an ear to pity.
WALWORTH. Is John Ball secured?
MESSENGER.   They have seized him.
    (*Enter Guards, with John Ball.*)
1ˢᵀ GUARD. We've brought the old villain.

---

[51] *bell-wether*: leader, from the leading sheep in a flock, on whose neck a bell is hung.
[52] *Westminster Hall*: Centre of government and prime residence of the King.
[53] *thank you ... rise a knight, Sir William Walworth*: The Chartists sometimes repeated the erroneous idea (also found in Richard Carlile) that London's city shield featured 'Walworth's bloody dagger'. 'The Epitah', *Northern Star* (8 January 1848), p. 3.

2ND GUARD. An old mischief-maker –
Why there's fifteen hundred of the mob are killed
All through his preaching.
SIR JOHN TRESILIAN. Prisoner, are you the arch-rebel, John Ball?
JOHN BALL. I am John Ball; but I am not a rebel.
Take ye the name, who, arrogant in strength,
Rebelled against the people's sovereignty.
SIR JOHN TRESILIAN. John Ball, you are accused of stirring up
The poor deluded people to rebellion;
Not having the fear of God and of the king
Before your eyes; of preaching up strange notions,
Heretical and treasonous; such as saying
That kings have not a right from Heaven to govern;
That all mankind are equal; and that ranks
And the distinctions of society,
Aye, and the sacred rights of property,
Are evil and oppressive: plead you guilty
To this most heavy charge?
JOHN BALL. If it be guilt,
To preach what you are pleased to call strange notions,
That all mankind as brethren must be equal;
That privileged orders of society
Are evil and oppressive; that the right
Of property is a juggle to deceive
The poor whom you oppress; I plead me guilty.
SIR JOHN TRESILIAN. It is against the custom of this court
That the prisoner should plead guilty.
JOHN BALL. Why then put you
The needless question? Sir Judge let me save
The vain and empty insult of a trial.
What I have done, that I dare justify.
SIR JOHN TRESILIAN. Did you not tell the mob they were oppressed;
And preach upon the equality of man;
With evil intent thereby to stir them up
To tumult and rebellion?
JOHN BALL. That I told them
That all mankind are equal, is most true:
Ye came as helpless infants to the world;
Ye feel alike the infirmities of nature;
And at last moulder into common clay.
Why then these vain distinctions? – bears not the earth
Food in abundance? – must your granaries

O'erflow with plenty while the poor man starves?
Sir Judge, why sit you there, clad in your furs;
Why are your cellars stored with choicest wines?
Your larders hung with dainties, while your vassal,
As virtuous, and as able too by nature,
Though by your selfish tyranny deprived
Of mind's improvement, shivers in his rags,
And starves amid the plenty he creates.
I have said this is wrong, and I repeat it –
And there will be a time when this great truth
Shall be confessed – be felt by all mankind.
The electric truth shall run from man to man,
And the blood-cemented pyramid of greatness
Shall fall before the flash.
SIR JOHN TRESILIAN.   Audacious rebel;
How darest thou insult this sacred court,
Blaspheming all the dignities of rank?
How could the Government be carried on
Without the sacred orders of the king
And the nobility.
JOHN BALL.   Tell me, Sir Judge,
What does the government avail the peasant?
Would not he plough his field, and sow the corn,
Aye, and in peace enjoy the harvest too;
Would not the sun shine and the dews descend,
Though neither King nor Parliament existed;
Do your court politics aught matter him;
Would he be warring even unto death
With his French neighbours? Charles and Richard contend.
The people fight and suffer: – think ye, Sirs,
If neither country had been cursed with a chief,
The peasants would have quarreled?
KING.   This is treason!
The patience of the court has been insulted –
Condemn the foul-mouthed, contumacious rebel.[54]
SIR JOHN TRESILIAN. John Ball, whereas you are accused before us,
Of stirring up the people to rebellion,
And preaching to them strange and dangerous doctrines;
And whereas your behaviour to the court
Has been most insolent and contumacious;

---

[54] *contumacious*: insubordinate.

>   Insulting Majesty – and since you have pleaded
>   Guilty to all these charges; I condemn you
>   To death: you shall be hanged by the neck,
>   But not till you are dead – your bowels opened –
>   Your heart torn out, and burnt before your face –
>   Your traitorous head be severed from your body –
>   Your body quartered, and exposed upon
>   The city gates – a terrible example –
>   And the Lord God have mercy on your soul.
>
> JOHN BALL. Why, be it so. I can smile at your vengeance,
>   For I am arm'd with rectitude of soul.
>   The truth, which all my life I have divulged,
>   And am now doomed in torments to expire for,
>   Shall still survive – the destined hour must come,
>   When it shall blaze with sun-surpassing splendour,
>   And the dark mists of prejudice and falsehood
>   Fade in its strong effulgence. Flattery's incense
>   No more shall shadow round the gore-dyed throne;
>   That altar of oppression, fed with rites
>   More savage than the priests of Moloch taught,[55]
>   Shall be consumed amid the fire of Justice;
>   The rays of truth shall emanate around,
>   And the whole world be lighted.
>
> KING.   Drag him hence –
>   Away with him to death; order the troops
>   Now to give quarter, and make prisoners –
>   Let the blood-reeking sword of war be sheathed,
>   That the law may take vengeance on the rebels.

THE END.

---

[55] *Moloch*: Canaanite god; in biblical sources, associated with the practice of child sacrifice.

2

John Frost: A Chartist play, In Five Acts (1841) – John Watkins

Editor's introduction

John Watkins's 1841 play *John Frost* is exceptional as the only Chartist literary work that grappled with the Newport rising as a sequence of unfolding events, rather than (as in poetry about the incident), a subject for mourning, reflection, and remembrance. What transpired in early November 1839 represented a decisive moment in the history of Chartism. Following a period of increased militancy in the movement and corresponding repression by the government, some 9,000 armed miners and ironworkers descended on the Welsh town of Newport in the early morning hours of 4 November 1839. Among them was John Frost, a prosperous tradesman and Newport's former deputy mayor, who upon joining the Chartist cause had quickly risen through the ranks to serve as president of the Chartist National Convention the preceding spring and summer. Although the marchers' aims remain the subject of debate, they likely sought to precipitate revolution. A confrontation with soldiers at the Westgate hotel, however, led to the rising's unravelling in the face of at least twenty-two casualties. Treason trials for three leaders – Frost, Zephaniah Williams, and William Jones – followed. The three escaped hanging when their death sentences were commuted, but they were transported for life to Van Diemen's Land (modern-day Tasmania).

Although the return from exile of the rising's leaders remained a central demand of the movement, Newport's failure prompted many Chartists to reconsider support for strategies involving political violence. In this context, Watkins's play functioned as a polemical intervention in debates about physical force (as discussed in more detail in this volume's introduction). While Newport poetry might honour 'The fallen brave! – fall'n in a glorious cause', it simultaneously distanced itself from the 'mistaken ... way' the marchers pursued or attributed violence not to the main body of Chartists but to the 'drunk insanity' of a few 'amongst the mass'.[1] Other poems called on the Chartists to

---

[1] Iota, 'Sonnet Devoted to Chartism', *Northern Star* (9 May 1840), p. 7; Iota, 'Sonnets Devoted to Chartism', *Northern Star* (1 August 1840), p. 3. Iota's sonnet sequence on the Newport

exert moral pressure by 'petition[ing] again and again' so that 'she who adorns Britain's throne / Shall freedom restore' to the Newport prisoners.² Watkins's play, on the other hand, celebrated the rising as a legitimate response to tyranny, advocated further armed struggle, and derided other means of seeking redress.³

Beyond the rising itself, *John Frost* takes up issues rarely addressed in Chartist literature. In particular, it evokes the movement's political culture in ways much Chartist fiction and poetry neglects. To highlight this emphasis, Watkins changed his play's title from 'John Frost, or the Insurrection at Newport' to 'John Frost: a Chartist Play'.⁴ As the introduction declares, 'This drama was designed not so much to illustrate the characters in it, nor the insurrection at Newport, on which the plot turns, as Chartism itself.'⁵ The play depicts political meetings in Acts 2 and 4, providing studies of movement life curiously absent in much Chartist literature. The outdoor location of the Chartist gathering in Act 2 and the way the police surveil and disrupt the meeting in Act 4 instantiate the drastic pressures brought to bear upon the campaign, highlighting how participants' choices occur in a context shaped by Chartism's opponents. These scenes also allow Watkins to represent the participatory democracy Chartist gatherings modelled. Finally, the meetings explore the interclass nature of the movement. Where Chartist historical fiction frequently leaves the hero's class identity 'conspicuously indistinct', Watkins emphasises the costs respectable society exacts on his renegade protagonist.⁶ More surprisingly, the play suggests (if fleetingly) that Frost's privileged, middle-class position leaves him ill-fitted to head the movement. Significantly, Watkins renders Shell, a working-class militant, the rising's true leader. When faced with the possibility of bloodshed, Frost urges the Chartists to return home, Shell warns, 'he shall [come]! … / And if he does not … we'll drag him forth / … He shan't desert us now when most we want him.'⁷

Besides engaging in arguments within Chartism, Watkins's play intervened in ongoing debates about the place of theatre in broader cultural life. As described in this volume's introduction, a theatrical monopoly restricted

---

rising appears in Appendix 2. For a detailed study of the poetic response to Newport, see Mike Sanders, *The Poetry of Chartism: Aesthetics, Politics, History* (Cambridge: Cambridge University Press, 2009), pp. 87–128.

² 'The Mountain Minstrel's Appeal', *Northern Star* (6 June 1840), p. 7.

³ The play, however, registers a certain ambivalence towards violence. See Gregory Vargo, 'Chartist drama: The performance of revolt', *Victorian Studies*, 61:1 (Fall 2018), 9–34, pp. 14–15.

⁴ 'Prologue to a New Drama, Entitled "John Frost, or the Insurrection at Newport"', *Northern Star* (5 December 1840), p. 3; John Watkins, *John Frost: A Chartist Play in Five Acts* (London: n.p., 1841), p. 1 (p. 95).

⁵ *Ibid*, p. 5 (p. 98).

⁶ Rob Breton, *The Oppositional Aesthetics of Chartist Fiction: Reading Against the Middle-Class Novel* (New York: Routledge, 2016), p. 54.

⁷ Watkins, *John Frost*, p. 34 (p. 140).

the performance of the 'legitimate' genres of tragedy and comedy to select theatres possessing royal patents. In this context, Watkins's decision to write a five-act verse play about a condemned traitor became a polemical gesture, to which he called attention in his subtitle. Although a letter to Watkins from the 'Corn-Law rhymer' Ebenezer Elliot complains of Watkins's blank verse in his earlier *Wat Tyler* – 'not because it is bad ... but because your prose is infinitely better' – verse lines in *John Frost* lend Chartism a cultural dignity while affiliating Frost's struggles and defeat with the tragic heroes of Shakespeare.[8] The play's antiquated orthography and archaic expressions (such as 'ye' for 'you') similarly elevate the subject matter. Anachronistic language simultaneously evokes the lost freedom of ancient English democracy, to which the preface alludes, and helps establish a 'millenarian register' appropriate to the revolutionary struggle the play concerns.[9] As Watkins's prose writings make clear, he had himself studied Shakespeare's tragedies; allusions to *Romeo and Juliet*, *Macbeth*, *King Lear*, *Julius Caesar*, and *Othello* pepper his essays and letters. The play's portrait of the Chartist hero draws specifically on *Macbeth* (in Frost's hesitation to act) and *King Lear* (in the protagonist's confusion and abandonment following the rising).

Watkins leaned on personal experience in imagining the consequences John Frost might have confronted for his decision to join a working-class movement. Born in 1808, Watkins grew up in a wealthy family in Aislaby Hall near the Yorkshire coastal town of Whitby. He was apprenticed to local solicitors but 'renounced the *"lawyer* and all his works"' – as he put it in an autobiographical account – resolving not to '[live] by the "system" ... but ... independent of it, or in opposition to it'.[10] Like his play's hero, Watkins was recruited by 'the working men of [his home town] ... to come forward and be their leader. [He] acceded to their request and drew them up rules for an association.'[11] The group's efforts to procure a room met with harassment (another incident *John Frost* adapts), so it gathered on the Whitby pier where Watkins lectured and conducted Chartist church services.[12] The new activist encountered more serious problems as he began to agitate in wider circles. A speech at Stockton led to Watkins's arrest, though he was released without being charged.[13] He also faced ostracism at home, a fact he repeatedly emphasised in his self-presentation as one who had abandoned class

---

[8] John Watkins, *Life, poetry, and letters of Ebenezer Elliott, the Corn-law rhymer, with an abstract of his politics* (London: J. Mortimer, 1850), p. 134.
[9] Simon Rennie, *The Poetry of Ernest Jones: Myth, Song, and the 'Mighty Mind'* (New York: Legenda, 2016), p. 73.
[10] 'Narrative of John Watkin's Imprisonment', *Northern Liberator* (4 April 1840), p. 6.
[11] *Ibid.*
[12] Malcom Chase, 'John Watkins', in Keith Gildart and David Howell (eds), *Dictionary of Labour Biography* (Basingstoke: Palgrave, 2005), vol. 12, pp. 298–99.
[13] John Watkins, *Five Cardinal Points of the People's Charter, Separately Explained and Advocated* (London: John Watkins, n.d.), p. 15.

privilege for democratic principle (and which he dramatised in his protagonist's dysfunctional family life).[14] After Watkins's move to London in March 1840, his brother wrote to inform him of his father's resolve not to 'support [him] in such a system' while a sister (likely the inspiration for Mrs Frost) denounced his 'open rebellion and defiance to the laws of [his] Maker and the laws of society'.[15]

In London, Watkins found success as a writer and speaker but struggled financially, especially after becoming embroiled in a series of disputes with fellow Chartists. By 1841, he worked as a full-time lecturer and contributed a regular column to the *Northern Star*, for which he also wrote a substantial amount of poetry and the occasional short story (under the pseudonyms 'Chartius' and 'Junius Rusticus').[16] During this time, Watkins also composed several plays and essays. The latter were influential, particularly the 'Address to the Women of England', which supported the enfranchisement of single (though not married) women and defended women's right to participate in politics even as it celebrated the home as the 'proper sphere of woman'.[17] Watkins himself married in the winter of 1841–42, crossing class barriers to wed a stonemason's daughter, whom Malcolm Chase hypothesises he met through his political activities, which involved lectures at the stonemasons' union.[18]

Despite Watkins's growing prominence, his combative temperament and extreme politics involved him in a number of controversies. In particular, *John Frost* – dealing with the sensitive subject of the Newport rising – led to public breaks with prominent Chartists. In the post-Newport environment, where openly advocating physical force involved serious risk, Watkins struggled to find a publisher for his polemical work. As he recounted in a letter to the *Star*, the Chartist publishers James Watson and John Cleave both blanched at accepting the manuscript: 'When ... I offered the drama of John Frost for publication. – "Oh," said one, "go to another." – and that other said – "go back to the other." I was thus to be bandied about like a shuttlecock.'[19] Forced to 'put his own name upon the title-page because no one else dared let his stand there', Watkins produced a self-published edition. He encountered further difficulties, however, when it came to selling copies. Chartist booksellers 'not only rejected but ...

---

[14] Sanders, *Poetry of Chartism*, pp. 154–55.
[15] Watkins, *John Frost*, p. 6 (p. 98); John Watkins, 'John Watkins to the People in Answer of Feargus O'Connor', in *Feargus O'Connor: Attack and Defense* (London: Garland, 1986), p. 16.
[16] Malcom Chase, 'John Watkins', p. 299; Malcolm Chase, *Chartism: A New History* (Manchester: Manchester University Press, 2007), p. 123. A series of four tales began in the *Star* on 6 August 1842 with 'Lady Alice Lisle. – A Tale of the Law', p. 7.
[17] John Watkins, 'Address to the Women of England!', *English Chartist Circular* (May 1841), p. 49.
[18] Malcom Chase, 'John Watkins', p. 302.
[19] 'John Watkins, to his Brother Chartists', *Northern Star* (5 June 1841), p. 5; Watkins, 'John Watkins to the People', p. 6.

denounced' the play.[20] Lacking other ways to distribute his writing, Watkins borrowed £100 to establish his own bookstore, a 'Chartist depot for the true vend of Chartism'.[21] The venture met little success, however, probably due in part to Watkins's decision to stock 'no books but Chartist ones – none of your Joe Miller's Jest books, those crackling thorns under the pot'.[22] Watkins would eventually complain, 'God Almighty never intended me to be a bookseller, and God knows I never intended it myself.'[23] In his own account, as his financial woes deepened he sold his possessions to support himself 'till at last [he] had nothing left to sell or pawn'.[24] 'Anxiety, ill fare, privation, [and] destitution' followed.[25] By late 1843, he '[subsisted] on casual charity, helped by gleanings in potatoe fields' while expecting 'to be turned out into the street' for arrears in rent.[26]

During these struggles, Watkins courted further controversy. Where his attacks on prominent publishers spoke of 'grubs' that might be 'killed by a little Chartist quick-lime', he advocated literal violence against William Lovett and other moderates who had precipitated a schism in Chartism in 1840–41. In a series of speeches, Watkins defended 'the justice of assassinating' these figures. 'If Frost was a traitor to government', he reasoned, 'he was true to us, and if [being hung and quartered] was to be his fate, shall traitors to the people – the worst of traitors – be tenderly dealt with – nay, courted, caressed? No, ... let us prevent their future treasons.'[27] After finally turning against his long-time ally, the important Chartist leader and publisher Feargus O'Connor, Watkins found himself isolated in the movement.[28] He would ultimately drift away from Chartism, a decision hastened by an inheritance upon his father's death that 'render[ed] [him] independent ... of popular support'.[29]

Neither Watkins's chequered career nor his play's incendiary politics deterred Chartist groups from performing it. It was staged in full on at least five occasions: once in Winlaton and twice each in Nottingham and Hamilton, Scotland. The

---

[20] Watkins, *John Frost*, p. 6 (p. 99); 'To the Subscribers to the Watkins' Testimonial Fund', *Northern Star* (5 November 1842), p. 7.

[21] Watkins, 'John Watkins to the People', p. 6; 'Books Published by John Watkins', *Northern Star* (3 July 1841), p. 2; 'To All Chartists, Whether in Town or Country', *Northern Star* (5 June 1841), p. 5.

[22] 'John Watkins, to his Brother Chartists', *Northern Star* (5 June 1841), p. 5.

[23] 'To the Subscribers to the Watkins' Testimonial Fund', *Northern Star* (5 November 1842), p. 7.

[24] Watkins, 'John Watkins to the People', p. 15.

[25] Ibid.

[26] Ibid., p. 19.

[27] William Lovett, *The Life and Struggles of William Lovett, in his Pursuit of Bread, Knowledge, and Freedom* (London: Trübner, 1876), p. 251.

[28] Watkins, 'John Watkins to the People'.

[29] Ibid., p. 19.

latter performances occurred on 3–4 November 1843, thus commemorating the rising's fourth anniversary with Watkins's play.[30] Additionally, scenes from *John Frost* were recited or acted at gatherings in Ashton and London. As chair of the fundraising committee for the recently freed journalist Bronterre O'Brien, Watkins himself helped organise the London concert where two scenes were performed as part of a benefit on O'Brien's behalf.[31] As with all Chartist drama, other productions probably went unrecorded. In any event, after *The Trial of Robert Emmet*, *John Frost* ranks with *William Tell* and Southey's *Wat Tyler* as one of the plays the Chartists staged most frequently.

Besides *John Frost*, Watkins wrote several other dramas in the late 1830s and early 1840s, including at least four during the years he played a part in radical politics. He completed *Wat Tyler, or the Poll-Tax Rebellion* by March 1839 when it was performed at the Whitby theatre – apparently Watkins's only play other than *John Frost* to see the stage.[32] In 1840, he wrote (along with *John Frost*) the *Yorkshire Tragedy*, *Robin Hood*, and *The Poor Law Martyrs*.[33] He published the latter play as well as *Wat Tyler* in 1841, though neither appear to be extant.[34]

After the playwright stopped actively participating in Chartism, he also composed *Griselda, or, Love and Patience*; *Oliver Cromwell, the Protector*; *Isolda*; and *Runnymede; or Magna Charta*.[35] When the *Star* came across copies of *Griselda* and *Runnymede*, Watkins received comeuppance for years of polemical attacks, including against the *Star*'s publisher O'Connor. The paper recommended *Runnymede* as 'a valuable opiate, should any one require artificial aid in courting the embraces of sleep' and it damned *Griselda* with faint praise even as it excerpted a passage for its 'Feast of the Poets' feature on May Day 1847.[36] Two other popular newspapers reviewed *Griselda* more kindly. The *Leeds Times* praised its 'beautiful poetry', 'striking characters', and 'considerable dramatic power' while *Lloyd's Weekly Newspaper* deemed the work 'of very considerable merit'.[37]

---

[30] 'Hamilton', *Northern Star* (11 November 1843), p. 5.
[31] 'London', *Northern Star* (14 August 1841), p. 4.
[32] 'Whitby Theatre', *Yorkshire Gazette* (16 March 1839), p. 5.
[33] Watkins, *Life, poetry, and letters of Ebenezer Elliott*, pp. 149–62.
[34] 'Books Published by John Watkins', *Northern Star* (3 July 1841), p. 2.
[35] John Watkins, *Griselda, or, Love and Patience: a Play in Five Acts* (London: W. Strange, 1846); John Watkins, *Oliver Cromwell, the Protector; an Historical Tragedy, in Five Acts* (London: C. Mitchell, 1848); 'John Watkins, the Poet', *Theatrical Journal* (21 April 1860), p. 110. *Griselda* and *Oliver Cromwell* are the only Watkins plays other than *John Frost* known to be extant.
[36] 'Feast of the Poets. Part II', *Northern Star* (1 May 1847), p. 3; '*Runnymede; or Magna Charta*. A Historical Tragedy. By John Watkins', *Northern Star* (2 October 1847), p. 1.
[37] 'Griselda; or, Love and Patience', *Leeds Times* (27 June 1846), p. 6; 'Griselda; or, Love and Patience', *Lloyd's Weekly Newspaper* (28 June 1846), p. 8. Like Watkins's other plays (besides *John Frost* and *Wat Tyler*), *Griselda* never seems to have been performed.

Unfortunately, no substantial reviews of any other of Watkins's dramas (including *John Frost*) appear to have been published. In correspondence with the playwright, however, Ebenezer Elliot commented on several of Watkins's early plays, making observations that resonate with *John Frost*. Elliot strongly objected to Watkins's portrait of the title character of *Robin Hood* as well as the play's melodramatic tendencies but found in it 'lines that would not discredit Wordsworth – passages sweetly idiomatic, which remind me of our Elizabethan poets'.[38] Elliot was deeply affected by the *Yorkshire Tragedy*, regarding it such 'an impressive commentary on the time' as to read it to his family and try to arrange a reading for friends.[39] On the other hand, he criticised the epilogue to *The Poor Law Martyrs* – 'dull and dead as a stone' – and complained of the over-reliance on 'single speeches' and 'the idle trick of soliloquy' to advance its 'action' (a critique he lodged against *Robin Hood* as well).[40] Yet if the latter criticism might strike modern readers of *John Frost* as apt, one should remember the performance context Watkins anticipated. Regularly encountering speeches as part of Chartist life, activist audiences had a strong appetite for drama that included political oratory, as the popularity of *The Trial of Robert Emmet* and Southey's *Wat Tyler* testified.

---

[38] Watkins, *Life, poetry, and letters of Ebenezer Elliott*, pp. 159–60.
[39] Ibid., p. 154.
[40] Ibid., p. 155.

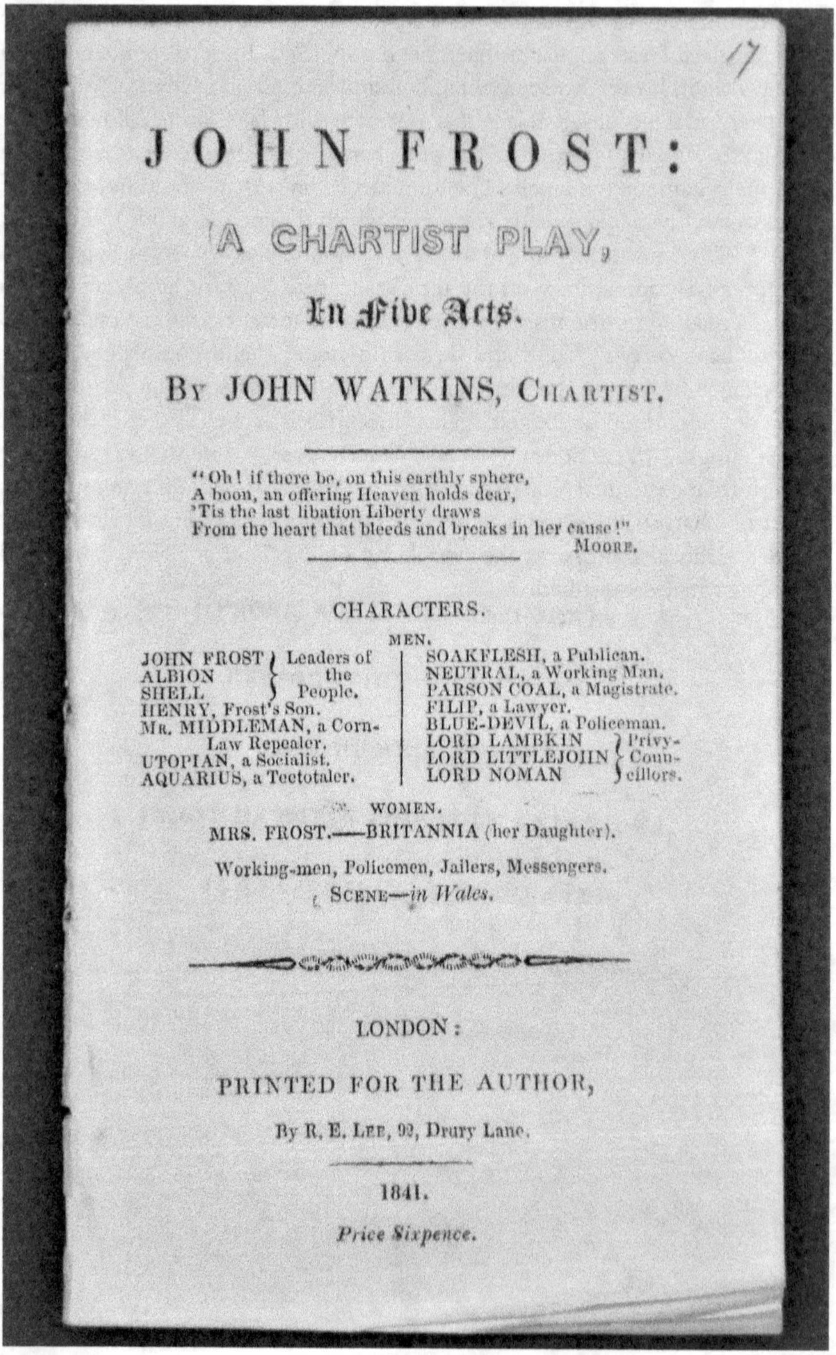

Figure 2.1 Title page of John Watkins's *John Frost, A Chartist Play in Five Acts*

JOHN FROST:
A Chartist Play, In Five Acts.[1]

By John Watkins, Chartist.

Oh! if there be, on this earthly sphere,
A boon, an offering Heaven holds dear,
'Tis the last libation Liberty draws
From the heart that bleeds and breaks in her cause![2]
    MOORE.

CHARACTERS.
MEN.

JOHN FROST ⎫
ALBION[3] ⎬ Leaders of the People.
SHELL[4]   ⎭
HENRY, Frost's Son.
Mr MIDDLEMAN, a Corn-Law Repealer.[5]

BLUE-DEVIL, a Policeman.
LORD LAMBKIN ⎫
LORD   ⎬ Privy-
LITTLEJOHN ⎨ Councillors.
LORD NOMAN ⎭

---

[1] *John Frost: A Chartist Play, in Five Acts*: an excerpt of the play published in the *Northern Star* appeared under a different title: *John Frost, or the Insurrection at Newport*. 'Prologue to a New Drama, Entitled "John Frost, or the Insurrection at Newport"', *Northern Star* (5 December 1840), p. 3.

[2] *Oh! if there be ... / her cause*: from Thomas Moore's 'Paradise and the Peri', in *Lalla Rookh* (1817).

[3] *Albion*: the nation (or island) of England or Britain. As indicated in Watkins's introduction, Albion is a figure for Henry Vincent, a Chartist writer and organiser in western England and Wales. Vincent strongly supported the right of the Chartists to use physical force, although his position changed significantly following a year-long incarceration that began May 1839.

[4] *Shell*: George Shell, cabinet-maker from Pontypool, Wales; his death in the rising at the young age of 19 made him the most famous Chartist martyr. See Appendix 2.

[5] *Corn-Law Repealer*: supporter of the repeal of tariffs on the import of grain, which was an important cause to middle-class reformers in the 1830s and 1840s until repeal was passed in 1846. Although many Chartists supported repeal, they were sceptical it would ameliorate other social problems without democratic reform. The Chartists were also hostile to many of the proponents of repeal for their embrace of orthodox political economy on other questions.

UTOPIAN, a Socialist.[6] NEUTRAL, a Working Man.
AQUARIUS, a Teetotaler.[7] PARSON COAL, a Magistrate.
SOAKFLESH, a Publican. FILIP, a Lawyer.[8]

WOMEN.

MRS FROST.——BRITANNIA (her Daughter)[9]

Working-men, Policemen, Jailers, Messengers.

Scene—*in Wales.*

London:
PRINTED FOR THE AUTHOR,
By R.E. Lee, 92, Drury Lane.

1841.

Price Sixpence.

---

[6] *A Socialist*: a member of Owenite socialism or Owenism, which enjoyed a broad base and took many forms in the 1820s and later, including experimental communities, cooperative stores, labour exchanges, and the National Union of the Working Classes; also associated with free thought (religious scepticism) and feminism. Although the Chartists did not programmatically support socialism, there was overlap between Owenites and Chartists at the local level.

[7] *Teetotaler*: one who promotes abstaining from alcohol. Several Chartists, including Watkins, supported teetotalism.

[8] *Filip, a Lawyer*: pun on the various meanings of fillip: a trivial addition; a gesture made by the straightening of a finger curled against the thumb; a blow; something that excites.

[9] *Britannia*: allegorical figure for Britain, typically depicted as a woman wearing a helmet and holding a shield and trident.

TO THE
'FROST, WILLIAMS AND JONES
RESTORATION COMMITTEE',
THIS HUMBLE EFFORT
IN AID OF THEIR FRIENDLY EXERTIONS,
IS RESPECTFULLY DEDICATED,
BY THEIR FELLOW-CHARTIST,
THE AUTHOR.[10]

---

[10] *Frost ... Restoration Committee*: as the name implies, this Chartist group sought the pardon of the Newport prisoners, which would have granted them the right to return to Britain.

Introduction

And more true joy Marcellus exiled feels
Than Caesar with a senate at his heels.[11]
                    POPE.

THIS DRAMA was designed not so much to illustrate the characters in it, nor the insurrection at Newport, on which the plot turns, as Chartism itself. Nevertheless, the writer has selected the chief Chartist victim as his hero, and so far as one not personally known to him could know him, he has endeavoured to paint a true portrait of him, likewise of Shell. Albion was originally meant as a sketch of Vincent.[12] Melbourne, Russell, and Normanby are caricatured; but a Socialist, a Teetotaler, a Corn Law Repealer, a Parson Magistrate, and others, are all brought in as representatives of their peculiar classes.[13] The Mrs Frost of the play is not, however, the real Mrs Frost, nor intended for her – the character is altogether fictitious; or, rather, it was partly drawn from a near relative of the author.[14] In short, the whole piece is a *composition*, in the artistic sense of the word; made up of characters, incidents, and events, taken separately from the history of Chartism, and dovetailed together. I chose the dramatic form, because I agree with my friend Elliott that the Theatre (yet what theatre will bring this piece on the stage while the present government-censorship exists?)

---

[11] *And more true joy ... / at his heels*: Alexander Pope, *Essay on Man* (IV.257–58) (1732–34).

[12] *Albion ... sketch of Vincent*: see Footnote 3.

[13] *Melbourne*: William Lamb, Viscount Melbourne (1779–1848); Whig politician; served as Prime Minister, 1835–41.
Russell: Lord John Russell (1792–1878); MP for Stroud; Whig leader in the House of Commons and architect of the Reform Bill of 1832; Prime Minister, 1846–52. Watkins's name for him plays on his diminutive stature.
Normanby: Constantine Phipps, Marquess of Normanby (1797–1863); served as Home Secretary 1839–41.

[14] *near relative of the author*: Watkins describes his father's, brother's, and sister's rejection of him following his embrace of Chartism. His sister seems the most likely source for Mrs Frost; Watkins excerpts letters from her that include criticism of his activism on religious grounds. See John Watkins, 'John Watkins to the People in Answer of Feargus O'Connor', in *Feargus O'Connor: Attack and Defense* (London: Garland, 1986), p. 16.

might be made 'the most powerful of State organs'.¹⁵ The author limited himself to an act a day in writing it, as he found it necessary to rein himself in.

The Play is dedicated to the 'Frost, Williams and Jones Restoration Committee', to shew them that though I refused to accede to their request to become an honorary member of their body, it was not from indifference to the fate of Frost, but from a conviction of the uselessness as well as mean-spiritedness of petitioning those who had banished him. What I would not stoop to do for myself, I would not do for him.

This Play has been written some time, but could not find a publisher. The chief Chartist publisher in London shrank from the responsibility, and that is the reason why the author has taken it upon himself.¹⁶ He has put his own name upon the title-page because no one else dared let his stand there. This must plead his excuse for the inconvenience which consequently results to himself and to purchasers. Honours and profits he seeks not – those he possessed he sacrificed to the cause – and he has refused those which have been offered to him.¹⁷ He seeks but the diffusion of Chartist opinions and sentiments, convinced as he is that they tend to promote the interests of truth, justice, and humanity.

London, 22, Chadwell-street, Myddleton-square, April 6ᵗʰ, 1841.

---

[15] *Elliott*: Ebenezer Elliott (1781–1849); factory owner and English poet, known as the 'Corn-Law Rhymer' for his support for the repeal of the Corn Laws; father of Watkins's second wife from 1849.
what theatre ... government-censorship: The Stage Licensing Act of 1737, which remained in place until 1843, restricted the performance of comedies and tragedies to theatres with a royal patent while requiring these submit scripts to the Lord Chamberlain. Unlicensed theatres were also subject to surveillance from local magistrates.

[16] *chief Chartist publisher*: probably John Cleave or James Watson; Watkins complained that both refused to publish the play. See, Watkins, 'John Watkins to the People', p. 6. Watkins likely also approached and was refused by a third important Chartist publisher, Henry Hetherington.

[17] *sacrificed to the cause*: of an affluent background, Watkins lost parental support upon his decision to join the Chartists; he lived in poverty for a time but came into a substantial inheritance in 1844.

Prologue

       THE plund'ring Picts and wand'ring Scots invade[18]
Our Rome-deserted Isle – sea-Saxon aid[19]
Drives back the horde – the northern locust pest,
But next drives us from our green ocean nest;
And we to bleak and barren hills must fly,
Where Snowdon's summits scale the cloudy sky –[20]
All inaccessible save to wild birds,
Or beasts of prey, or clamb'ring mountain-herds.
But, worse than Picts and Saxons, Normans come[21]
And will not leave us e'en that rugged home.
We now indeed are conquer'd, and must bear
The yoke of bondage yet without despair.
Aye they may chain the body; but, in mind,
We still are free as first of British kind, –
Tameless and struggling like the caged-up dove
That ever pants for Freedom – its first love!
Tyrants may train us up in servile sin
And torture us to quench the light within;
But, stronger, fiercer, in our warm Welch hearts
Burns freedom's flame, and such a glow imparts
As makes us break the despot's galling chain,

---

[18] *Picts*: Celtic people who inhabited what is now northern and eastern Scotland.
Scots: Gaelic people inhabiting Ireland and the west of Scotland in the early medieval period.
[19] *sea-Saxon*: Germanic people who conquered and inhabited southern Britain in the fifth and sixth centuries CE.
[20] *Snowdon's summits*: highest mountain in Wales.
[21] *Normans*: Scandinavian and Frankish people inhabiting Normandy, who invaded England in 1066. Ideas of a 'Norman yoke' supplanting ancient British democracy were common in radical politics.

And bid him try his bootless rack again.[22]
Born with our life this love of liberty,
'Tis nature, instinct, and can never die.
Our foes may task us – bury us in mines,
And make us slave where knowledge never shines;
Nay, though they whip us till we drop and die,
Still, Freedom! Freedom! to the last we'll cry.
The very sound of that inspiring word
Lifts us to life, and seems to give a sword.
They cannot starve us to submission – no!
We spurn the *food* that's offered by a foe.
Extremest misery nor bends nor breaks
The heart that, not for self, but Freedom aches.
All foes are conquer'd when we conquer fear,
As did bold Shell, who braved a bloody bier.[23]
To gain his rights he took the manliest course –
The plain straightforward argument of force!
Vengeance! is now our cry. Remember Shell!
We'll live like him – at least, we'll die as well.
Silurian Frosts again shall lead us on,[24]
And Freedom's baffled battle yet be won!

---

[22] *bootless rack*: ineffective tortures.
[23] *Shell*: see Footnote 4.
    bier: a frame for carrying a corpse to the grave.
[24] *Silurian*: related to the Silures, ancient British people of south-eastern Wales.

Epilogue[25]

THANKS to the system we Britons live under,
Old England so merry is now a world's wonder.
There's Vick with her thousands on thousands a year,
'Tis the money we pay her that makes her so *dear*.
Then the sausage young Prince, 'come from Germany',[26]
Who did us the honour Queen's husband to be,
Fill his pockets and kite with ev'ry good thing,[27]
And he'll get us a prince to be one day our king.
There's the good Bishops next, whose church is a cradle,
Where they rock poor John Bull till his brains are quite addle.
Who sing psalms for lullabies like pious old nurses,
And bless us devoutly to tithe all our purses.
The Lords they come next who swear, ''pon their honour',
That none can be guilty but men like O'Connor.
They do what they like, that is, drink, drab, and swear —[28]
All they wish for is theirs, as our wants do declare.
The Tories that knock at the Government door
Which never shall open to them any more,
And Whigs who love office as dear as their skin,
Supported by Rads. lest the Tories jump in.[29]

---

[25] *Epilogue*: Watkins's original publication places the epilogue before the body of the play, which this version retains.

[26] *the sausage young Prince*: Prince Albert of Saxe-Coburg and Gotha; married Queen Victoria on 10 February 1840, near the time the Newport prisoners would have been executed if their sentences had not been commuted.

[27] *kite with*: use fraudulently.

[28] *O'Connor*: Feargus O'Connor (1796?-1855); important Chartist leader and publisher of the leading movement newspaper the *Northern Star*.
drink, drab, and swear: a variation on this phrase appears in *Hamlet* 2.1.27; *drab*: to associate with prostitutes or other women of dubious sexual morals.

[29] *Rads*: Radicals; members of the parliamentary group including Daniel O'Connell, which helped the Whigs form a government in 1835; distinct from the working-class movement

All tremble to hear the loud crack of the whip.
Which the Chartists now flourish to make the things skip;
For Britons are roused, see the lion awakes,
He roars out the Charter! – his huge mane he shakes,[30]
And scatters the vermin that fed while he slept,
By a lash of his tail the land will be swept.
Then down go the prisons and bastiles I'm sure,[31]
Those palaces built by rich men for poor.
No longer shall Britons be starved into fear,
And made to bear burthens that beasts should not bear.
No more be it said of the British so brave
They're the best in the world to dupe and enslave.

---

of Chartism and sometimes described by Chartists as 'sham Radicals' (the implicit perspective here).

[30] *his huge mane he shakes*: play on the allegorical figure of the British lion and likely allusion to Percy Bysshe Shelley's 'The Mask of Anarchy', a poem popular in Chartist culture.

[31] *bastiles*: common name (and the typical spelling) for the workhouses of the Poor Laws, especially after the 1834 New Poor Law was enacted.

ACT I
SCENE I

A Library Room.

FROST. (*solus*) Freedom, ye slaves; oh! when will man be free?
   Are free-born Britons slaves of foreigners?
   Robb'd of the rights their fathers did bequeath,
   Have they not spirit to regain their own?
   Will they, like beasts, drudge on their native land,
   While tyrants lord it o'er them at their ease?
   Oh! will they yet toil on, and pine and die
   Famished, forlorn, in sight of food and joy, –
   Mocked by the rulers that usurp their all?
   Who gave one man the power to rule another?
   'Twas man himself – man's brother is his master;
   Nor rules except to gorge on right, his prey!
   Man toils not for himself, but for his wronger:
   Himself, and all that's his, he lost, renounced, –
   He sold his birthright to become a slave –[32]
   Raising his equal – disparaging himself.
   He must obey and suffer! Must he? why?
   Because his power is will'd unto another.
   Oh! shameful step, to sell his unborn sons.
   But since all thus conspired against themselves
   To give to one the power of all o'er each,
   Can't all resume their gift – with it, their power?
   Can't we regain ourselves? Aye, with a will!
   Combined for freedom, we at once were free;
   Then, 'stead of all being sacrificed to one,
   That one would be the servant, friend of all,

---

[32] *He sold his birthright*: see Genesis 25:24–34 in which Esau, the son of Isaac, sells his birthright to his brother Jacob for a pot of stew.

And Man the sovereign – not the sovereign's slave!
Alas! the people now have many masters;
And though they work for all, they cannot eat.
Revolt, ye slaves! rebel against your lords!
Be men, and own one God alone for Lord.
The few usurp your rights, engrossing all
The blessings God would bounteously dispense,
And what your labour for yourselves might earn.
God's promised blessings were for men, not slaves; –
We forfeit them when we forego our Charter.
I am no willing slave; but I'm a slave
Because my fellows are – involved with them:
But were they free, so then should I be free,
And then God's covenant would be renewed.
I'll rouse my brethren to obtain their rights; –
We will be free, or die in the attempt!
    (*Enter Henry.*)
HENRY. Father,
    A letter for you from some men at door.
FROST. A hand more used to toil than write; what's here?
    (*Reading*) 'Sir, knowing that you sympathise with the oppressed, we call on you to aid us in uniting to regain our rights. We are but few at present, but, if you will come forward to instruct us, we shall presently grow numerous.'
Begin they now, indeed, to feel their fetters?
Can their numb'd flesh be galled? 'tis well! 'tis good!
Shame shall afflict their souls, as want their bodies;
They shall know all they feel – shall know the cause –
And know the wealth of those that make them poor.
Admit them, Ned.
HENRY. Nay, but their shoes and clothes are ragg'd and dirty,
    They are not fit to come into our parlour.
FROST. These are their working-clothes, they work for us;
    Or might have our fine clothes, and parlours too.
    (*Enter Mrs Frost.*)
MRS FROST. Who are those ragged wretches at the door?
    Come they a begging? – send them off to work.
FROST. Came they for bread, we should not give a stone;
    For fish, a serpent; your cold taunts are these.
    But not for bodily, but mental food
    They come; they seek instruction and shall find.
MRS FROST. Instruction! none they want except for mischief,

>   And none they need for that – their nature prompts.
>   They know to work, but are not willing to 't.
>   They want to live in idleness and sin,
>   Upon industry's careful pains and gains.
>
> FROST. Their betters do so, till employment fails,
>   And then the workman starves.
>
> MRS FROST. There's work enough if they would seek for it.
>
> FROST. No, all is done; and, now they are not needed,
>   They must die off, or quit their native land,
>   That drones may revel on their labour's produce.
>   And shall the idler feast upon their store,
>   And spurn away the plundered working men?
>
> MRS FROST. Aye, send them to the treadmill, or the work-house;[33]
>   Or, if they are dissatisfied with that,
>   Let them quit the country – they can be spared.
>   Go tell them, Ned, we don't serve vagabonds.
>
> FROST. Stay, Ned.
>   Would you employ our son in tasks like that?
>   Make him a dog, to bark the poor away?
>   They have their feelings stronger than our own;
>   For they, alas, are made to feel much more!
>   Shall they be told by us they have supplied,
>   That, now we have enough, they may go die?
>   Such is the meed that tyrants give to slaves;[34]
>   But I will teach them other things than this.
>
> MRS FROST. Aye, teach them to rebel! Much they will gain
>   By rising 'gainst their betters, and the law.
>   The soldiers will be sent to cut them down,
>   And teach them to submit to Providence.
>
> FROST. Thus tyrants make God partner in their crimes;
>   But God will yet lay proud oppressors low.
>
> MRS FROST. It is their drunkenness brings them to want,
>   And justly for their sins they suffer woe.
>
> FROST. The glutton wastes what hunger begs in vain;
>   The poor man's wife and children likewise want;

---

[33] *treadmill*: instrument of discipline used in prisons and workhouses involving a horizontal wheel with stairs to climb in an exhausting exercise.
work-house: establishment that provided poor relief to inmates. Workhouses became widely regarded as punitive and carceral after passage of the New Poor Law of 1834, which sought to deter people from claiming relief by separating families in workhouses, demanding degrading labour of paupers, and enforcing other unpopular measures.

[34] *meed*: reward.

All are expos'd to ev'ry earthly woe:
Are they sole sinners, that should suffer solely,
Or chiefest sinners in the sight of God?
Are richest men, who sin with gross impunity,
Spoiling the poorest, and denying them, –
Are they alone the favourites of heaven?
Your ignorance speaks, and that is your excuse;
Your ignorance, that breeds your prejudice –
Your pride and scorn, so full of prejudice –
Unfemininely chilling, callous, cruel!
Be candid or be silent. – Admit them, Ned.
MRS FROST. I'll leave the house, if they come in.
FROST. Unpitying woman! Stay, I'll go to them. (*Exit.*)
MRS FROST. Thy father, Ned, is willfully resolv'd
  To league himself with idle, wicked men,
  Against thy mother, sister, thee, and all –
  To bring disgrace and ruin on his house!
HENRY. If I'd known that, I'd not have brought the letter,
  But set them off at first.
MRS FROST. To make the son an evil messenger
  To his own father, *that* is like such villains.
  Never again, my boy, aid such designs,
  But burn the note they give thee to betray.
    (*Enter Brittania.*)
BRITANNIA. Mother, what want those workmen with my father?
MRS FROST. They want to make him scorn'd, despis'd as they;
  And he, so simple, sinks down to their wish.
BRITANNIA. Nay, but I heard them ask him to instruct
  And guide them on the road to their just rights.
MRS FROST. His road to ruin! What said he?
BRITANNIA. That he could show them freedom's path to plenty;
  But 't would depend more on themselves than him,
  If they reach'd home at last.
MRS FROST. Home? ——a gaol!
BRITANNIA. I think my father would not teach them wrong.
MRS FROST. He has no call to teach them anything.
  Let them grope out their wicked way themselves.
  Freedom, forsooth! A meteor o'er a bog!
  Will he act jack-a-lantern for such wretches?[35]
  Sooner they'll lead him wrong, than he them right;

---

[35] *jack-a-lantern*: a lure into danger.

    Nor can he lead, but he must go with them,
    And be identified in all they do.
BRITANNIA. But sure, my mother, 'tis our due to God
    To succor the oppress'd, and help the poor.
    What do we live for else? Why have we means?
MRS FROST. God will befriend them, if he *be* their friend.
BRITANNIA. He tries our love by trusting them to us.
MRS FROST. I do not say your father should oppress,
    But be content with *not* oppressing them.
    Let *him* mind his own business – *them* mind theirs.
    Why should he fly in face of all his friends,
    To please a mob, for their most stinking praise?
    Who else would be so foolish? None. I'm sure.
    They know this, and 'tis therefore they come here.
BRITANNIA. I heard him tell them to seek some one else,
    More qualified – more able than himself:
    They said they had applied to two before;
    But one was worldly, and one fear'd the world!
MRS FROST. Did not this caution warn him to refuse?
BRITANNIA. It seemed to kindle him the more: he said,
    'Then I alone will aid you if I can.'
MRS FROST. He knows not what he does: to side with them,
    What is it but to show to foe and friend –
    One is too bad, one not so good as he?
    He'll make himself a mark for both to hate;
    And we, too, shall be scorn'd on his account.
BRITANNIA. 'Tis his humanity – 'tis charity,
    And, sure, he should be more respected for't.
MRS FROST. Charity! It should begin at home, then.[36]
BRITANNIA. But should go forth when home is not in want.
MRS FROST. There's no respectable, no decent person,
    That would be seen in such vile company.
BRITANNIA. I'm sure my father knows how to descend,
    And yet keep his own dignity unstain'd.
    He will descend – not to sink down to them,
    But to enlighten them and lift them up.
MRS FROST. Better we ne'er had rank'd above such wretches,
    Than now be lowered down to their vile level;
    He will be hated by the world which strives
    To keep down those he seeks to raise in spite.

---

[36] *Charity! It should begin at home*: proverb.

BRITANNIA. If that's the sole alternative, my mother,
   He chooses best who chooses not the world.
     (Re-enter Frost.)
MRS FROST. Keep off him, Henry – come not near him;
   He has been mixing with vile lees and dregs,[37]
   And will contaminate us all with filth.
   Faugh! what a beggar's smell he has brought in.
     (Exit Mrs Frost and Henry.)
FROST. Hear you your mother, what she says, Britannia?
BRITANNIA. Yes, father, but why give her this pain?
   You know her prejudices.
FROST. Yes, and I know 'tis they give her this pain,
   Not I, I fain would cure her of them;
   For while she feeds her pride and hatred thus,
   She must be miserable, passion-plagued.
   She thinks 'tis fashionable, most genteel,
   To scorn the humble, and respect the proud –
   Nothing can be more vulgar; nothing shews
   More poverty of mind, however rich
   In all externals such an one may be.
   Had I indulged this feeling, I had not
   Made her my wife; for she was poor as these,
   And 'tis her origin she scorns in them,
   Thinking to hide – but makes it more appear.
   True greatness loves the lowly, scorns the proud,
   And knows that goodness is its surest proof.
BRITANNIA. I do confess, I'm more your child, than hers –
   My father's spirit, not my mother's, reigns
   In my poor heart with love for my dear country,
   More than for my poor self, or aught, save Heaven.
   Yet fain I'd mediate between you both;
   For sure *our* peace is precious as *their* freedom.
FROST. Peace? War! peace is not, cannot, shall not be
   Until Britannia's slaves have food and freedom.
   By Heaven, I'd put away the wife that thwarts me,
   Doom my own son to death, nay thee, my daughter,[38]
   And sacrifice myself, for my poor country.

---

[37] *lees*: residue from wine or other liquid.
[38] *Doom my own son to death*: possible allusion to Lucius Junius Brutus, Roman consul who condemned his sons to death for their role in attempting to overthrow the Roman republic; in radical rhetoric, Brutus exemplified civic sacrifice and virtue.

BRITANNIA. What shall redeem her, and emancipate?
FROST. The Charter! girl, the Charter! freedom's law;
   'Tis that must heal the wounds our tyrants make
   In hearts more honest, minds more skill'd than theirs.
   'Tis that must do away the branded curse
   Which now marks British brows and makes us beasts.
   A life of freedom! or, a death of glory.
     (*Enter Albion.*)
   Albion, you're come in time, my daughter here,
   Thinks honesty should beg and merit starve,
   That lordly thieves may die of gluttony.
BRITANNIA. Nay, father, now you are unjust to me;
   But virtue, thwarted, cankers into gall
   And frowns on friends, mistaking all for foes.
FROST. Your mother thinks so, then – forgive me, child;
   I'm somewhat sterner than a sire should be.
ALBION. I met bold Shell with others, as I came;
   They said they had been here, to ask your aid,
   Which you have promised them – I come to thank you.
   Now there is hope that slaves will pull down tyrants.
FROST. No longer dupes, no longer they'd be slaves,
   Victims no longer; we must teach them truth:
   Open their eyes to see themselves and others,
   To know what they should be, feel what they are;
   For, with this sense, they would get courage too,
   To save their country by enfranchisement.
   I go to draw up rules; remain you here –
   I'll come with them, anon.   (*Exit.*)
BRITANNIA. My father's soul is steel'd – he gives up home,
   His family, himself, and strives for others
   With greater zeal than e'er he strove for us.
ALBION. He is a patriot, and such men sometimes
   Forget the father; all things but their country,
   As though they were identified with it
   And felt the wrongs of all men in themselves.
   Thus man doth cease to be himself, as 'twere,
   And lives by sympathy in all that suffer.
   I, too, have felt this burning godlike zeal
   Which pity's sighs fan into flaming rage;
   Yet I've a rival flame within, more soft,
   Which melts what *that* has hardened, and my heart,
   Glowing with love, would pour itself in thine –

Myself, my country, all forgot, but thee!
Thou all – thou more than all – Britannia.
BRITANNIA. Alas, 'tis now no time to think of love:
My grief goes with my father, and my fear
Attends my mother; thus divided, torn,
I have no heart to give – 'tis cleft and gone
Till these divisions heal'd do make it whole –
And then again it may be mine, for thee.
ALBION. But mine is thine – thine and my country's, love.
Ye, both are one, at least to me ye are;
For seems to me, I strive for her in thee.
BRITANNIA. Nay, while thy heart thus gives itself to both,
Neither can have it wholly – which of us
Would'st thou give up? which, for the other's sake? (*A pause.*)
Thou hesitat'st – that is enough – love her –
Gain her her rights, save her from ruin, Albion,
Obtain the Charter, make thyself a man –
Thou now art but a slave, and would'st thou wed
To make thy wife a slave, thy children too?
Thou can'st not love me! free thyself and me,
And then with such a heart as brides should own,
A merry heart, not loaded as 'tis now, –
A heart whose chains would fall when fell my country's,
With such a heart, I then might love thee Albion,
And know no bonds save those of holy wedlock. (*Exit.*)
ALBION. Stay! hear me! she's gone – oh! how proud she look'd
How nobly beautiful! – it shall be so,
And here I vow, my country first I'll free;
Or ere I wed; then wed with liberty.
   (*Re-enter Frost.*)
FROST. Here are the rules, not more than twelve, short, simple,
But let them follow these – let them unite,
And soon they will obtain peace, plenty, freedom.
ALBION. Perish the coward that withholds his hand!
FROST. 'Tis numbers and intelligence does all –
If they will think, and hope, and strive, and act,
And not lie down in sluggish apathy,
Lost in the lethargy of dull despair,
The mere machines and instruments of others –
ALBION. They shall not sleep, nor sink – we'll rouse them up,
With strokes of fire shall reach their inmost souls
And quicken what of life is yet left there.

'Tis something that they now begin to ask –
That their enquiring minds look up for knowledge.
FROST. Rein in thy ardour to keep pace with them
And do not overrun them in thy haste;
Or they will be discourag'd by thy zeal,
Deeming it rash and too unsafe to follow,
Then thou wilt lose thyself – not lead them on.
March slow; the surer then! nor falter back;
But, like a steady tide, advancing still,
Turn tyranny itself to patriotism.
ALBION. I will, or pull, or push the people on.
    (*Re-enter Mrs Frost.*)
MRS FROST. I hope that Albion is not led away
By those new doctrines of disorder'd rule.
ALBION. Oh, ma'am, we mean to put the state in order –
Bad managers have made it spoil itself.
MRS FROST. Surely you rev'rence Government.
ALBION. Not ours, good ma'am, I do despise, detest it.
It gives its countenance to vice and folly,
And doth discourage talent and true merit.
It does the very thing it should not do,
Is the reverse of what it ought to be, –
Too bad to mend, what must be done with it?
MRS FROST. You've kept bad company of late, I see;
I thought, young sir, you had more self-respect.
ALBION. I do respect myself, and that's the reason
Why I not bow to this vile government.
With all my soul I hate it, and despise
The mean supporters of its horrid baseness.
When vice is thron'd, the virtuous must rebel,
Since none but fools and knaves will be her subjects.
MRS FROST. You'll not succeed – you cannot overthrow
A government upheld by power divine.
ALBION. By Satan say – a system worthy him!
God and our rights! – Down with the hellish engine!
The people will no longer prop the proud.
What are the great but bubbles on the sea?
FROST. Consider, Mary, our fictitious lords
Would be mere nothings, did we count them such.
Let you and I assume the dignities
Of Duke and Duchess, why we should be laugh'd at:

And did the people laugh at all such puppets,[39]
Instead of swearing fealty, paying homage,
And giving them the power they could not take,
Their coronets would seem but caps of fools,
And in good sooth they are.
ALBION. Aye, why should one man be more privileg'd
Than others are, as though all strength and skill
Were his and they had none at all?
FROST. 'Tis most unjust, most insolent to those
Who oft possess more real claims to rank.
MRS FROST. You cannot get the world to think with you;
Nor must you think to master it with words.
FROST. The world grows old and should grow wiser now.
Meanwhile, let time declare this truth for me –
Frost was a man that walk'd not with the world.
ALBION. Albion another that dared cross its way.
MRS FROST. I have not patience with such stuff & nonsense. (*Exit.*)
ALBION. I'm sorry Mrs Frost should go in anger.
FROST. She's better than she was – her heart is right,
And will, erelong, bring round her mind to it.
Come, we will go and speak to our poor patriots.
ALBION. With all my heart – oh, for a tongue of flame
To kindle stern enthusiasm up,
And throne great Liberty where despots sit.

(*Exeunt.*)

END OF ACT THE FIRST.

---

[39] *our fictitious lords / ... did the people laugh at all such puppets*: echoes consistent rhetoric in Thomas Paine's *Rights of Man*, including the condemnation of the 'puppet-shew of state and aristocracy'. Thomas Paine, *Rights of Man, Part the Second; Combining Principle and Practice* (London: W. T. Sherwin, 1817), p. 18.

ACT II
SCENE I

An open Place.

Enter Shell and a number of working-men.

SHELL. The base, bloody, and brutal whigs do know[40]
    Our cause is just – they cannot answer us, –
    So what do they but try to stop our mouths.
    Those gagging whigs won't let us have a room,[41]
    A place to meet in to discuss our griefs.
    They persecute us, prejudice our friends,
    And threat with ruin all who else would serve us.
    Here in the open air, expos'd to storms, –
    Here only we can meet; but meet we will,
    In spite of wind and weather, or the whigs.
1 WORK. It was not so when we shouted for them; but now that we stand up for ourselves, they'd knock us down.[42]
2 WORK. Faith, they're a queer crew – they promise Reform and give us a law

---

[40] *whigs*: major parliamentary party associated with the interests of the manufacturing class in the 1830s and 1840s. Although the Whigs supported limited franchise reform, they alienated working-class radicals over a number of issues, including their failure to pursue the further expansion of the franchise following passage of the Reform Bill of 1832; their commitment to social austerity, particularly the New Poor Law; their support for Irish coercion; and their willingness to restrict civil liberties in the face of the Chartist agitation. Note that Watkins inconsistently capitalises 'Whig' (and less frequently 'Tory'). As this choice appears intentional – the speech of certain characters leaves these terms lower-case – the text is not emended.

[41] *won't let us have a room*: in Newport and throughout Britain, the Chartists confronted legal obstacles as well as discrimination and harassment that made meeting difficult. Watkins details his experience with such challenges in 'Narrative of John Watkins's Imprisonment', *Northern Liberator* (4 April 1840), p. 6.

[42] *when we shouted for them*: the Whigs encouraged popular demonstrations and used the threat of civil disturbance to help win passage of the Reform Bill of 1832.

of Hell with devils to enforce it, – they promise retrenchment and lay on
more taxes – they promise peace and go to war.[43]
3 WORK. Curse 'em, they do it all to spite us.
SHELL. And now they want us, like so many bulls,
To bellow out for further boons for them;
And, when we say, let us have something too;
Oh, then, say they – 'you know not what you want –
It can't be had – it is impracticable.'
Aye, truth and justice are so to those whigs;
But not to us – we'll set them an example.
We'll get what we do want without their aid,
Yea, spite of their most vile hostility,
The Charter! whole! and nothing else but it!
    (Enter Frost.)
FROST. Aye, the Charter, my good fellows! the Charter!
Three cheers again for your own little Charter!
That be the darling of your hearts – the apple
Of your eyes – 'tis freedom's opening plant,
Fann'd by men's groans – watered by women's tears,
Nourished at root by martyrs' holy blood
And blooming in the sunshine of God's smile.
Oh! it shall flourish fair, a British oak,
The tree of Liberty to shade our sons,
'Neath which they'll sit, none making them afraid,
While, we, in Heaven, shall hear them bless our names.
1 WORK. I wish our fathers had reared such a tree for us.
2 WORK. Aye, but they have left us nought but slavery.
3 WORK. When I make my will I'll leave my children one legacy – all I can
leave them; one only, but they'll not want another, and that's liberty.
ALL. So will we all.
FROST. My friends, the Charter is our testament:
Let each man sign his name to that – the Charter!
Those Whigs are like the ivy round the oak:
They seem to garland it, but suck its strength –

---

[43] *they promise Reform and give us a law of Hell*: the dialogue alludes to widespread disappointment with the Reform Bill of 1832. 'Law of Hell' most likely refers to the New Poor Law of 1834, which cut relief while making it more punitive.
devils to enforce it: likely the Assistant Poor Law Commissioners who oversaw the implementation of the New Poor Law. The Police Act of 1839, which allowed counties to form police forces, was also widely criticised.
go to war: Britain began two major wars in 1839, the Anglo-Afghan War and the Opium War (with China). The Chartists consistently condemned both.

They make it seem to flourish while they blast it;
And Tories would conserve the wasting worms.
Touch not, taste not the fruit the factions offer;[44]
'Tis but to tempt your credulous desires,
And make you lose the paradise you'd gain.
They look with sourest hatred on your hopes,
And reach an apple full of bitterest curses.
Be wary of their wiles – despise their threats –
And, with the Charter, beat the villains back
Who'd make your love of freedom fatal to you.

SHELL. Aye, they tempt us to betray us.

FROST. Are there any Scotsmen here?

SCOTSMAN. Yes, I am one.

FROST. And wherefore left ye your far home?

SCOTSMAN. To seek a living here; but, in good faith, I may e'en travel back again. Auld Scotland now is not so poor as her proud neebor.

FROST. Are there any Irishmen here?

IRISHMAN. Faith, here's a few too many of us.

FROST. And what brought you across the sea?

IRISHMAN. I'faith, the devil drove us, like our pigs to market.

FROST. Get the Charter; Scots nor Irish then need leave
Their fathers' bones to come and die with us.

SHELL. Aye, then they need not underbid us Welch,
And turn us out of work at quarter wages.
But quarter loaves are better far than none,
And that is all our choice. We curse these men,
But 'tis the system we should curse, not them;
The cursed system, which doth curse us all.

FROST. How do those live that have no work?

SHELL. They beg from those that scarce can feed themselves;
Or else go to the parish, or the prison,
Or wander forth in search of work and food,
While robbers live on what they stole from them.

FROST. But what comes of their families?

SHELL. What pleases Providence, their sole dependence.
There is no rest for them, by night nor day, –
Sorrow and suff'ring will not let them sleep.
Hunger, 'tis said, will break stone walls for food,

---

[44] See Genesis 3:3, 'But of the fruit of the tree which is in the midst of the garden, God hath said, Ye shall not eat of it, neither shall ye touch it, lest ye die' *(King James Version)*. The remainder of Frost's speech plays on this episode from Genesis.

>   And they break laws, or die, or kill themselves.
>   Then worms are fed on those that died for want.
> FROST. What! old grey-headed men and women, too,
>   Who all their lives have labour'd for the state,
>   And brought up sons whose hearts are dried by famine –
>   Daughters that cannot suckle their own babes, –
>   Must cold and hunger be their end at last?
>   'Tis not for England's honour this should be;
>   Our glorious Queen should be ashamed of this.
>   What are you, man? – why weep you so?
> WEAVER. I was a member of a Trades' Union, sir; our masters wanted to lower our wages; we struck, and bound each other by an oath not to give in; I administered the oath, was informed of, seized, tried, and transported.[45] I have but newly returned, to find my wife in the workhouse, my children in the streets. Sir, my wife was as good a woman as ever lived – a skilful, industrious, cheerful woman, sir: – she's now in a madhouse, for she attempted to kill our children![46] Misery had turned her head, sir.
> FROST. Merry England, the glory and the envy
>   Of surrounding nations!
> MINER. I have work, but my wages are so small – only a penny a day for each of us, – that, when I give my earnings to my wife, she does not know what to do with them; she dares not lay the money out; and I have sometimes to carry in a loaf with me, which she cuts up and gives to our little ones, bit by bit, but never takes a morsel herself. She is a perfect skeleton, sir! I shall lose her, I see I shall!
> SHELL. A too common case, sir; we grow harden'd
>   By seeing such sights so often.
> FROST. You look faint and feverish, my man.
> GRINDER. I'm a grinder, and the dust is killing me. An old man at thirty, you see, sir.[47]
> FROST. Why not use the preserver?[48]
> GRINDER. Alack, sir, if we all did that, too many of us would live, and there would not be work for us all. Better die of the dust, than starve.
> FROST. Where lost you your leg, good man?

---

[45] *a member of a Trades' Union ... I administered the oath, was ... transported*: alludes to a radical cause célèbre, the 1834 prosecution and penal transportation of six farm labourers from Tolpuddle (Dorset) for administering union oaths.

[46] *to kill our children*: both the Chartist press and other papers including *The Times* gave extensive coverage to cases of infanticide that poverty and the New Poor Law of 1834 were thought to have precipitated.

[47] *a grinder*: one who grinds coal as part of the mining process.

[48] *preserver*: meaning untraced but context suggests a mask for coal dust.

SOLDIER. In the glorious wars, where my brother lost an arm. We fought for our country, and swept away her enemies; and we now – sweep the streets!
FROST. You are all discontented, I suppose?
ALL. Yes.
FROST. Are there any parsons, or lawyers, among you?
MEN. No – not one.
FROST. They're contented, I supposed; quite satisfied! –
   'Tis I, they say, stir you to discontent.
   They think ye have no feeling of your pains,
   Nor hope of better life – they've none for you;
   And those who pity you are hated for't –
   Called rebels, traitors, if they take your part.
   Yet, though they make me feel worse woe than yours,
   I'll not oppress you, nor let them oppress.
   I will not coldly see you suffer thus;
   But die if this curs'd system can't be chang'd:
   'Tis culpable to live and witness it.
   No man that honours God, or human nature,
   Can bear to live where such things must be seen.
   Our Government, that most infernal engine,
   Deals woe, disease, and death on all around,
   While devils, in the centre, dance with joy.
   My friends, here is our National Petition,[49]
   Wherein your wants, your woes, your wrongs are writ,
   The cause set forth, and quick redress implor'd.
   Let each man sign it, then it shall be sent
   From the poor people to their parliament.
SHELL. I write my name in black, for I'm a slave;[50]
   But I will write it red, or I'll be free.
   I'd rather it were blotted from life's book,
   As it deserves to be, and surely will,
   If I should die a slave and shame my maker
   Who meant me for a man and made me one.
   Good God! how many epitaphs might stand –
   'Here lived and died a slave in British land!'

---

[49] *National Petition*: petition calling for the Charter, a programme of democratic reforms, which the remainder of the scene adumbrates.

[50] *my name in black, for I'm a slave*: example of Chartist rhetoric linking political or wage 'slavery' with chattel slavery. Slavery was abolished in British colonies in 1838.

FROST. While we live slaves our Maker owns us not;
   We lose his image; but, let us be free!
   And, though we die for't, we shall fly to Heaven.
SHELL. Next time I write, I'll dip my pen in blood –
   The blood of tyrants, and a pike my pen.
FROST. I trust the pen will now prevent the pike.
1 WORK. I cannot write, but I can read.
FROST. They have but fed and cloth'd and taught thee half.
   The royal dogs are better tended to,
   Yes, better housed than are the paying people.
   Our nursing mother is the queen of monkeys.[51]
SHELL. Aye, perish the people! live the queen's monkeys.
2 WORK. I can neither read nor write; but I can work, and, maybe, fight.
FROST. More shame for Government that makes a crime
   Of ignorance, and send it to the gaol,
   The only school for unlearn'd poverty.
SHELL. Three cheers for our petition.
FROST. I wish the Government could hear you.
SHELL. We'll make it hear, for hunger makes us howl.
   Three cheers, my men; three for the Charter, friends,
   And may no frosty spirit nip its bud.
FROST. Thou dost not hint at me in that?
SHELL. Oh, no, good sir, you have a heart so warm,
   'Twould thaw this icy world as doth the sun.
   Three cheers for Mr Frost.
FROST. Thank you, my friends – if I can do you good,
   I'll thank the God of Heaven that gives me power.
   Now go in peace, and pray that God may turn
   Your tyrants' hearts to listen to our prayers.
   Shell, with the sound of ocean in thy soul,
   For ever thundering in the tyrant's ear,
   Assemble those true men again next week
   To hear the fate of their petition.
SHELL. Its fate is ours and theirs. (*Exit, with men.*)
   (*Enter Mr Middleman.*)
MIDDLEMAN. Why, Mr Frost, I am surprised at you.
   A gentleman, and a magistrate to boot,
   To know no better than to join a crew
   Of mere riff-raff, the scum of all the town,

---

[51] *queen of monkeys*: Queen Victoria; reference untraced, though contemporary satirical poems refer to the royal family keeping monkeys and other animals at Windsor castle.

And think to get what never can be got,
    Nor ought not if it could; you should know better,
    Although these fellows don't. What is't you want?
FROST. The Charter!
MIDDLEMAN. What's that?
FROST. And do you come, thus full at me with censure,
    For what you know not, nor why, nor wherefore?
    Had you considered first, you would have found
    It was a rightful cause that drew me forth.
    Why should you think I am a foe to peace,
    And fond of outrage? *Know* before you blame.
MIDDLEMAN. 'Tis Universal Suffrage that you seek.[52]
FROST. Yes, Universal Suffering claims it.
MIDDLEMAN. Mere humbug, ruin, folly, nonsense all,
    You'll not succeed; you'll only fling us back
    And stop the course of rational reform.
FROST. God and our rights, we cry; it *is* a right,
    And all who love what's just will join for it;
    Aye, though the Heavens themselves should fall.
MIDDLEMAN. All gammon – *you* have the franchise.[53]
FROST. Yes, but others, more needing it than I,
    Have not, and I would help them to obtain it.
    They starve.
MIDDLEMAN. And they deserve to starve for choosing you.
    Why need *you* prate? you're not a working man.
FROST. The more I'm bound to tender those that are;
    But wish, for their sake, they had chose a better.
    I'll second *you* if you will take my post.
MIDDLEMAN. Nay, I want no such notoriety.
FROST. I go among them, not so much to teach,
    As to be taught; I learn from them, far more
    Than I can teach – I learn what they experience,
    And find them honest and intelligent.
    They know more than you think – feel more than know,
    And are the foremost in true freedom's field.
MIDDLEMAN. They are not fit for freedom; liberty

---

[52] *'Tis Universal Suffrage*: a central demand of Chartism and one of the six points of the Charter. However, the Chartists sought universal manhood suffrage, only in rare instances advocating suffrage for women. Watkins supported the enfranchisement of unmarried women, but not of married women. See, John Watkins, 'Address to the Women of England!', *English Chartist Circular* (May 1841), p. 49.

[53] *gammon*: nonsense or falsehood.

Would be licentiousness in them, and ruin.
  If they get uppermost all else must down;
  The tyranny of mobs is worst of all.
FROST. Nay, but the Charter doth so fix the franchise,
  Constituencies would be more wholesome then.
  Mob-men excluded, others would but get
  The necessary power, not to destroy,
  But to controul the selfish power of class.
  A juster equilibrio they'd give
  To all the classes for the good of each.
MIDDLEMAN. Not to the suffrage should I so object,
  As to the clause for Annual Parliaments.
  'Twill cause a change of members ev'ry year.
FROST. Why our septennial members are return'd![54]
MIDDLEMAN. Well, but the clause for payment of the members,[55]
  I must object to that.
FROST. Better be paid to serve us, than to rob.
MIDDLEMAN. At least your clause against all property[56]
  May wake a just alarm.
FROST. Your fears are groundless, prove and find them so.
  The people always strive for what is just.
  Right is the good of all – wrong, of a few.
MIDDLEMAN. You ask too much – why can't you be content
  With what is to be got? get that, then more.
FROST. They ask but for their own, and ask of those
  Who do usurp it – who can give the whole,
  Soon as a part, and rights should not be doled.
  They think us dogs, to silence us with sops.
  The factions deal but fractions of our due;
  But we will have the whole – the whole at once.
MIDDLEMAN. You'll get your heads broke, *that's* all you will get.
  Why don't you join us for repeal and ballot?[57]

---

[54] *septennial members*: MPs serving seven-year terms as established by the Septennial Act of 1715. Annual elections was one of the six points of the Charter.

[55] *payment of the members*: another demand of the Charter; meant to allow working men to serve in Parliament.

[56] *against all property*: another point of the Charter called for the abolition of the property qualification for Members of Parliament; Middleman, however, might also articulate the common perception that Chartism sought the redistribution of property.

[57] *join ... repeal and ballot*: the repeal of the Corn Laws (see Footnote 5) and support for a secret ballot, the latter being one of the six points of the Charter.

FROST. You say, if we join'd you these would be got,
    That proves, if you join'd us, ours would be got.
    You do but speculate for your own selves –
    We for you, for us, and all, to end the chapter.
MIDDLEMAN. Aye, England, then, might close accounts at once
    And shut up shop – a bankrupt in the world.
    I'd sooner join the tories than you Chartists –
    I wish that Government would hang you all.
                                (Exit, in a rage.)
FROST. Ye cry, more gold! the people cry, more food!
    'Tis vain to argue with your willful malice;
    We get nought from you but non-plus'd abuse;
    For since you cannot dupe, you would destroy.
    (Enter Utopian.)
UTOPIAN. Ah, Mr Frost, do you desire to better
    The sad condition of the human tribe?
    'Tis not in Government – 'tis not in law,
    But love, to bless the family of man,
    Society must be reform'd – that is,
    We must reform ourselves – nought else can do't.
    The old world must be morally renew'd.[58]
FROST. Alas, I fear you could not root out hate
    With all your love – you mean well; but in vain.
    The seeds of vice would still spring, as of old,
    To choke your happiness and break your bands,
    Since no perfection can be found below.
UTOPIAN. Vice would be check'd, not foster'd as 'tis now,
    Virtue would meet with fair play, not oppression.
FROST. Suppose Utopia could be realiz'd,
    The Charter first must clear the ground for it,
    Else Government would hover like a hawk
    To pounce on all the tender breeding virtues.
    Let Universal Suffrage be the plan,
    The ground of Universal Socialism.
UTOPIAN. I am a Chartist, too.
FROST. Scarcely, I think; for nothing but the Charter
    Would then employ your mind till it was got.
    You'd make the Charter your first step – your pivot.

---

[58] *The old world must be morally renew'd*: reference to the Owenite journal the *New Moral World* and more broadly to Owenism's stress on social, rather than political, reform.

Besides you socialists are too, too social,
If you give up your wives and property.[59]
UTOPIAN. We are belied, as you are – you, they say,
Would level all, and we, have all in common:
But 'tis not so; nor wives, nor property
Would we make common – they were neither then!
To alter character by circumstance
And change men's fortune by their conduct – these
Are our chief aims; our means, tuition.
    (Enter Aquarius.)
FROST. Good day, Aquarius! your friend and I,
Are just discussing the respective merits
Of Socialism and of Chartism.
AQUARIUS. Both may be good – teetotalism's best –
The woes of poverty arise from drink.
FROST. Say, rather, drink comes of its woes.
AQUARIUS. 'Tis drink robs men of food, and clothes, and reason;
Drives them to death, or murther of their friends.
FROST. When wages are too low and bread too high,
Not much can then be earn'd for drink – men fast.
They then *abstain*, because they can't *obtain*;
They've nought to save, or spend – they want to get.
AQUARIUS. Perhaps, they wasted what they earn'd before.
FROST. Perhaps! demoraliz'd by Government,
That patronizes vice and ignorance.
First change the cursed cause of brutal sin,
And Circe's cup will then be dash'd to earth.[60]
Let us, my friends, unite in triple league –
A Suffrage-Abstinent Society.
Our aim is mutual – let our means be so.
Yonder is Albion – he will tell us more.   (*Exeunt.*)

END OF ACT THE SECOND.

---

[59] *give up your wives*: Owenism's criticism of sexual inequality and especially marriage as a patriarchal institution left it open to charges that it supported free love or other forms of sexual licence.

[60] *Circe's cup*: In Homer's *Odyssey*, Circe is an enchantress of the island of Aeaea. When Odysseus and his men visit her home, she turns his crew into swine by having them drink a potion from an enchanted cup.

ACT III
SCENE I

A Council-Chamber.

Lord Noman surveying himself in a glass.
Enter Littlejohn.

LITTLEJOHN. Where's Lambkin?
NOMAN. He has not come yet, the court detains him.
   I s'pose he's tickling Vick to make her laugh,
   For that's the way he courts her smiling mother.
LITTLEJOHN. He plays the fool; but we must play the senators.
   Egad, I'm dry – I've talked myself to death.
   A little *eau de vie* may give me life.[61]   (*Drinks.*)
NOMAN. Why, what's being done in the House today?
LITTLEJOHN. The most ridiculous thing you can conceive.
   Great Tom of Lincoln, no, of Birmingham,[62]
   Brought in the so-much-talk'd-of-you-know-what.
   Egad! 'twas roll'd up like a cylinder,
   The members stared aghast awhile, and then,
   Burst into laughter fit to shake the house.
NOMAN. I should have thought, so large a roll of names,
   So huge a blunderbuss would have astonish'd.
LITTLEJOHN. Nay, 'twas its size – its most ludicrous size[63]
   That made them laugh – I was right glad to see it.
   More joyful then they all, yet did not laugh.
NOMAN. I wonder you could help it – I should not.
LITTLEJOHN. Nor could e'en those that roll'd the monster in.

---

[61] *eau de vie*: brandy.
[62] *Great Tom ... of Birmingham*: Thomas Attwood, radical MP for Birmingham; presented the first Chartist petition on 7 May 1839.
[63] *ludicrous size*: containing almost 1.3 million signatures, the petition ran to three-miles length and was carried into Parliament by a dozen men.

NOMAN. How many names might it contain?
LITTLEJOHN. A million and a quarter – had so many
   Been parcell'd in a thousand small petitions
   And poured upon us from all parts and sides,
   I cannot tell what mischief had been done;
   Such hand-grenades had routed us, I fear;
   But this huge bomb fell dead and could not burst,
   And now it sleeps in peace beneath the table.
NOMAN. I'm glad you got the laugh upon our side
   And wish I had been there to join in it.
   A sneering laugh can beat all argument,
   And, *entre nous*, they have the right with them.[64]
LITTLEJOHN. The more it doth behove us to be cunning.
   Give me the management of members *in*,
   I care not for the people *out* – not I!
   But, come, let's celebrate our victory.
NOMAN. A at the end, then 'tis Victoria.[65]
LITTLEJOHN. Here's may the people 'tition us again,
   That we may sneeze and laugh our fill once more.
   Come, my dear lord, they fast and pray, give thanks.
   'Tis Governmental wine – we, in the pale,
   We ministers have an exclusive right.
NOMAN. I ate too much today, I cannot drink,
   I dread the doctor and blue devils much.[66]
LITTLEJOHN. You long, lank fellows, always are great gluttons.
NOMAN. 'Tis true I love a French goose-liver pie.
LITTLEJOHN. Beware, my lord, you live not over high.
NOMAN. Don't frighten me, do I not take emetics?
LITTLEJOHN. Yes, till they've lost the power to make you sick.
NOMAN. I'll think no more of eating, but of dress.
LITTLEJOHN. You'll charm the fair, and make your danger less.
NOMAN. I'll set the fashion of a new surtout.[67]
LITTLEJOHN. 'Twill be called Noman's fashion if you do.
   (*Enter Lambkin.*)
LAMBKIN. How now, my lord, what grave debate have you,
   What serious council for the nation's weal?
   Discussing griefs, or wine and walnuts, eh?

---

[64] *entre nous*: amongst ourselves (French).
[65] *A at the end*: a play on words: adding an 'a' to 'victory' produces 'Victoria'.
[66] *blue devils*: low spirits or melancholy.
[67] *surtout*: great-coat or overcoat.

LITTLEJOHN. Nay, we have waited for your help, my lord.
LAMBKIN. With all my heart 'tis yours.
        (*Sings*) 'Then shall not we
        Merry men be,
        Who form the Cabinet.'——
LITTLEJOHN. Trinity! I'm best at this, my lord.
LAMBKIN. Oh! I know you're a bit of a poet;
  Don Carlos to wit.
LITTLEJOHN. You too patronize the muses, or muse;
  Mrs Norton to wit.[68]
LAMBKIN. Aye, and our friend Noman was once an actor.
  Faith, we all follow the fine art – finesse.
LITTLEJOHN. How does your pretty actress; what's her name?
NOMAN. Matilda, I gave it to my racing-mare.
LITTLEJOHN. Because she'd led you a fine gallop, ha!
  But come, lord marquis, thank me for your title.
LAMBKIN. He did deserve it for his lady's sake,
  To whose most necessary services
  We owe our privy places.
LITTLEJOHN. Jordens, they say, should crown bedchamber lords;
  Phipps found the way to honour up back-stairs.
LAMBKIN. Why his nobility was love-begot:
  He boasts the bar of bastard royalty.
NOMAN. Go to, my lord, no lady at the court
  Is of more use than you, you wagtail pet lamb!
  And, for a monkey, what ails Jacko here?
LAMBKIN. Lord Littlejohn, you went too far, I ween,[69]
  When you advised and licensed free debate;
  'Tis carried here to most unpleasant lengths,
  And 's ten times more annoying out of doors.
LITTLEJOHN. Why, we're liberals, you know; libertines.
  'Tis politic sometimes to seem most honest,
  The better to deceive the honest people.
  You know, if we can *seem*, we need not *be*;
  Besides 'tis diff'rent, speaking out of doors
  And in the House, you know.

---

[68] *Mrs Norton*: Caroline Norton (1808–1877), feminist poet, novelist, and polemicist; authored pamphlets on female property and custody rights after a marital separation in 1836, in which she was accused of adultery. Norton lost custody of her children and property as a result of the separation.

[69] *ween*: believe.

LAMBKIN. Aye, there you err'd as far the other way,
   When you declared Reform should not go on.
LITTLEJOHN. Confound it! there's no speaking *in* or *out*,
   But that our words are caught up by wrong ears.
   I meant the liberty of speech for friends,
   And foes have used it: on the other hand,
   Friends are displeased at what I meant for foes.
NOMAN. Now I avoid to give offence at all;
   And as offences needs must come, why, then
   I shift the burthen off to other shoulders.
LAMBKIN. And yet, my lord, you let the bishops use you.
NOMAN. Aye, but I soon backed out from that position.
LAMBKIN. Because, my lord, you found it rather awkward
   As prosecutor for religion's sake.
   Now I conceit myself the best of all,
   For I keep clear from blame, and please myself.
NOMAN. You are a jester, privileged as such;
   But well, I ween, we should promise fair,
   No matter for performance – all is right.
   A promise from a lord need not be kept;
   The honour of the promise is enough.
   Thanks to John Bull, he loves a lord at heart.[70]
LITTLEJOHN. And so he does, we've but to please his fancy;
   But these cursed Chartists pluck our borrowed plumes,
   And, not content with words, they ask for deeds.
NOMAN. I fear them most; how shall we keep them down?
   I doubt they've too much sense to be deceived.
LITTLEJOHN. We'll bribe the press to call them odious names.
NOMAN. Aye, that's the easiest, most effectual thing,
   And, best of all, 'tis done with their own money.
LITTLEJOHN. I'll not stick at a trifle; in the House
   I'll raise a horror that shall thrill the nation.
NOMAN. As how, my noble lord?
LITTLEJOHN. I'll burke 'em. I'll fling a pike, and say 'tis theirs.[71]
NOMAN. Faith, that will counteract their grand petition.
   But how shall we fob off our own supporters,
   That clamour now against our Corn Law Rents.[72]

---

[70] *John Bull*: typical Englishman, or Englishmen collectively.
[71] *burke 'em*: murder, after infamous murderer William Burke, who sold corpses for dissection.
[72] *Corn Law Rents*: tariffs on imported grain, which had the effect of increasing the profitability of domestic farming and thus the value of land.

LAMBKIN. Leave them to me, I can cajole them best;
   I'll give them hopes; then they will keep us in.
   They fear alike the Tories and the people,
   And so, betwixt them both, you know —
NOMAN. We lick the platter clean.[73]
   Hurrah! my lords, our lease is not yet out:
   We still may grease our carriage wheels with sweat,
   And sauce our meat with poor men's blood and marrow,
   Hear the sweet music of their sighs and groans,
   Feed on their famine, and enjoy their woes,
   Clothe with their nakedness, starve them to slaves,
   And laugh at their petitions: hurrah! hurrah!
LITTLEJOHN. National, forsooth! and did they think we should
   Prefer the nation to ourselves? ha! ha!
LAMBKIN. So breaks our council up. I'm for the court.
NOMAN. I for Newmarket.[74]
LITTLEJOHN. I to St. Stephen's Chapel.[75]   (*Exeunt.*)

SCENE II

Frost's Parlour.

Frost, Mrs Frost, and Henry.

MRS FROST. I told you it would come to this: was't likely
   That they would suffer you to go uncheck'd?
   You said you would unseat Lord Littlejohn –
   He has unseated you. Struck from the bench,[76]
   You will be brought before it next; mind that!
FROST. I care not for his lordship's little spite;
   'Tis worthy of him; it is like himself.
   He first appointed me a magistrate,
   When I was useful to him in reform;

---

[73] *lick the platter clean*: proverbial, from nursery rhyme 'Jack Sprat'.

[74] *Newmarket*: town in Suffolk known for horseracing.

[75] *St. Stephen's Chapel*: chamber of the House of Commons from 1547 to 1834; after destruction by fire in 1834 replaced by St. Stephen's Hall. Littlejohn goes to Parliament.

[76] *Struck from the bench*: Frost had been elected Justice of the Peace in 1836, and his position as magistrate enhanced his local and national reputation in Chartism, particularly after he exchanged letters with the Home Secretary John Russell, who threatened Frost with the loss of his office for his Chartist activities. Frost was removed from office on 21 March 1839.

    I still go forward, he is sliding back,
    And now, of course, he deprecates my zeal.
MRS FROST. Aye, you'd give power unto a blackguard crew
    Whom he would fain keep down; ere long, you'll find
    What folly 'tis, to think that government
    Can be o'erthrown by such a low-lifed set.
HENRY. Mother, my schoolfellows call me a Chartist;
    What is a Chartist?
MRS FROST. There, you hear, poor little Henry, too, he
    Must be disgraced and flouted for your folly:
    He, poor fellow, must be interdicted,
    And all of us proscribed by all the town;
    And all for such a crew as you bring hither.
    What recompense can they make for our ruin?
FROST. My conscience tells me 'tis my Christian duty
    To do and suffer all in this good cause.
MRS FROST. Your conscience! you have no conscience; – conscience
    Would tell you not to sacrifice my peace.
    Good Parson Coal said I was to be pitied,
    And so I am; he has some feeling in him,
    But you have none – you don't consider us (*weeps*).
FROST. Oh! all you people, little do you know
    What I must brave and suffer in your cause.
    Can you be wanting to yourselves, when I
    Endure so much in patience for your sakes?
    She, who should heal with balmy sympathy
    The wounds my spirit must sustain abroad,
    Pierced by the evil eyes of friends turned foes, –
    She rankles them with venom of her own;
    And there's no peace for me abroad; no rest at home.
    I tell you, wife, your scoffs, and taunts, and jeers,
    But goad me on with zeal made furious, mad,
    To fight for justice, vengeance – vengeance, justice –
    Justice for others – vengeance for myself.
MRS FROST. Was ever woman worser used than I?
    Fast as I build, he labours to destroy;
    And all for what? To gain a mob's applause.
FROST. You are but one, yet selfishly prefer
    Your vainest whims to all men's future good;
    And you mistake, if you think aught on earth
    Could pay my pains; no, my hope rests in Heaven!
MRS FROST. This is the worst of all, to think that God
    Can sanction such rebellion 'gainst Himself.

Come, Henry, your father cares not for us;
A shocking pattern he sets you, God knows.
If no one but himself was hurt by this,
'Twould be no matter, for he merits it;
But we are implicated in the curse;
The innocent must suffer with the guilty.

HENRY. Father, don't be a Chartist; don't, dear father!
It makes my mother cry, and boys call me.

(*Exeunt Mrs Frost and Henry.*)

FROST. Poor boy! they know not what they say; they're taught
To deem their best friends foes, their worst foes friends;
But they'll know better when they grow up men (*pauses*).
Oh! do not soften me – but harden me;
Harden my heart and temper it to steel;
It should be steel to bear the strokes it feels.
Let not a woman's tears melt my firm purpose;
I must not think of wife and child, or self;
But of the millions that, with want and woe,
Drag on, from day to day, a life of death.
Oh! curse the Government that causes this,
That indurates the heart of man to man.[77]
Oh! why was one so weak, forlorn, as I,
Set on so stern, so resolute a task?
I must go through, though every nerve may quiver.

(*Enter Britannia.*)

BRITANNIA. My father weeping! let me dry those tears.
What! does this blow from Government distress you?
Think what 'tis for, and smile upon the stroke.

FROST. Bless thee, Britannia, heaven bless thee, girl!
Not for myself I weep, but for my country.
They may degrade me, but they can't disgrace;
Disgrace recoils from me and sticks on them.
The cause I suffer for makes me amends,
Supports and comforts me in all I do.
Hast thou seen Albion?

BRITANNIA. We parted even now; I sent him forth
To animate the patriots.

FROST. Prompted by thee, his zeal may go too far.
And, 'stead of helping, he may fall a victim,

---

[77] *indurates*: hardens.

    And then become a burthen to the poor.
    He told thee our petition was thrown out?[78]
BRITANNIA. Yes, and he's gone to tell it to the people.
    I would the Charter were obtained, my father;
    For our success would change the minds of men,
    And we should all be safe and honoured then.
FROST. Aye, since 'tis might they rev'rence, and not right,
    Success would turn the most stiffneck'd to us.
    (Enter Mrs Frost and Parson Coal.)
MRS FROST. Good Mr Coal has come to speak to you, –
    God grant his words may have the wished effect.
COAL. I'm sorry, sir, and never did I think
    Duty would send me here for your reproof;
    But, as your pastor, I am bound to warn,
    Nay, to admonish you from your sad course.
FROST. I'm sorry, sir, that our opinions differ:
    I think your duty should lead *you* to do
    What *I* am forced to do, instead of you.
    A Christian minister should foremost be
    To step between the oppressor and oppress'd;
    To shield the poor man and to succour him;
    For thus true prophets did in holy times
    When only lying prophets took the side
    Of pomp and power against the weak and helpless.
COAL. You do forget I am a magistrate.
FROST. Nay, I perceive the magistrate alone.
COAL. I bear the sword of justice.
FROST. Mind that your sword cut not the cross away.
    Vengeance is mine, saith God – He leaves us mercy.[79]
    But we take vengeance, and to God leave mercy.
COAL. 'Tis writ – be subject to the higher powers;
    The powers that be are all ordained of God.[80]
    'Twas meant the sword should not be borne in vain.
    What did the rebel, Korah, gain by strife?[81]

---

[78] *our petition was thrown out*: On 12 July 1839, the petition was defeated 235 votes to 46.
[79] *Vengeance is mine, saith God*: see Romans 12:19, 'Dearly beloved, avenge not yourselves, but rather give place unto wrath: for it is written, Vengeance is mine; I will repay, saith the Lord' (*King James Version*).
[80] *subject ... are all ordained of God*: see Romans 13:1, 'Let every soul be subject unto the higher powers. For there is no power but of God: the powers that be are ordained of God' (*King James Version*).
[81] *What did the rebel, Korah, gain by strife?*: see Numbers 16:1–40. Korah revolts against Moses.

FROST. I know not but that Korah's claim was just
    Though answered by the usual argument;
    For justice oft mistakes its rightful office,
    And visits on the victim punishment
    Due to his wronger, often found in judgment.
    Can rich men ne'er do ill? the poor do well?
    Why should the weaker be presum'd the worst –
    The stronger party always deem'd the juster?
    The present powers that be are evil powers,
    And such are not ordained of Heaven, but hell.
COAL. Their power is proof they are ordain'd of God –
    Whence else can power proceed?
FROST. Their power came from the people, given for good,[82]
    But sore abused; witness the people's woes,
    That came from them, and their own luxuries.
    If they hold power from God, what need of armies?
    But neither God nor people dare they trust.
    The people's voice is God's and cries against them.
COAL. This is rank blasphemy, sedition, treason.
FROST. Aye, so you say, but 'tis not for all that:
    What if I prove your doctrine such; not mine.
    Truth is sedition where vile despots rule,
    And justice treason. Truth, too, is blasphemy
    To bigots who love superstition better.
    But is not God the God of truth and justice?
COAL. What strange, what wicked thoughts are these! why, sir,
    You are much worse than I suspected you.
    You are an atheist, as well as rebel;
    But such crimes go together, vile yoke-fellows.
    Woe to those sad, those sinful, shocking times
    When magistrates themselves aid and abet
    Those they should quell, and turn against the good!
    Ah, what avails God's providence to man.
    Whose lines had fall'n more pleasantly than yours?
    Come of an ancient, noble family,
    Endow'd by nature, and by fortune, too,
    Bless'd with a virtuous wife and lovely children,

    As punishment, he is swallowed alive by the earth while his followers are immolated by fire sent from heaven.

[82] *power came from the people*: see Thomas Paine, *Rights of Man*, Part 2, chapter 4.

Rais'd to the bench, a man of influence,[83]
Your business thriving, yourself respected –[84]
And all these blessings most ungratefully
You do forget, nay use them 'gainst the giver –
What can befal you, but to forfeit all?
And for whose sake? a murderous crew of thieves.
FROST. Aye such the names you ever give the poor
Who seek those rights the rich deprive them of.
'Tis you, ye parsons, are the plunderers,
And worst of all, you'd murder those you've robb'd,
If they demand to have the spoil disgorged;
'Twas such as you, when Christ was on the earth,
Cried 'Crucify Him!' and would so again.
You poison'd Socrates, and now you starve[85]
The poor, and punishment is all your pity.
COAL. Madam, your husband's mad; I pity him:
But most I pity you and this poor boy.
Remove him, ma'am, remove him, in good time,
Lest he imbibe his father's shocking spirit.
MRS FROST. It's a hard case, sir, a very hard case.
I've said what I could say – done what I could
To turn him from the path he is pursuing;
But all in vain; it breaks my heart to think on't.
COAL. Deluded man! admit that Christ was poor,
That his Apostles laboured with the poor;
The church was then but in its infancy,
And what might suit it then, suits not it now.
FROST. Did Christ intend his precepts to be changed,
And his example to be none at all?
His golden rule was meant to bind all time,[86]
A motto round the Heavens, for earth to read.
He did not live in want and die in pain,

---

[83] *Rais'd to the bench*: as a Justice of the Peace. See Footnote 76.
[84] *Your business thriving, yourself respected*: formerly a draper, from 1831 Frost dedicated himself solely to politics and held several offices in Newport, rising as high as the town's deputy mayor.
[85] *poison'd Socrates*: in 399 BCE Socrates was condemned to death for corrupting the youth of Athens and denying the city's deities; the death sentence was carried out by Socrates drinking poisonous hemlock.
[86] *His golden rule*: see Matthew 7:12 (In the *King James Bible*: 'Therefore all things whatsoever ye would that men should do to you, do ye even so to them'); this maxim was referred to as the 'golden rule' by the late seventeenth century.

> That, on his fate, a system might be founded
> Just like, or worse, than that he died to alter.
> Shall worldly priests, in his most injured name,
> Thrive by the very things he did denounce?[87]
> Good parson, Coal, you have two good fat livings;
> Christ had not one, nor where to lay his head.
> You preach against the poor, whom he preached for,
> And all because the church now flourishes.

COAL. As to my two fat livings, as you call 'em,
> They evidence the merit that did win 'em,
> And are, to me, a source of worthy pride,
> As well as comfort, nor shall what you say
> Make me take shame for two such noble proofs
> Of what the church considers I deserve.

FROST. Not always wealth is shower'd on worthy men;
> More often on the undeserving now.
> There's many better Christians poor as Christ.

COAL. You grow personal, Mr Frost – personal!
> I'll leave you, sir, and doubt not you'll be brought
> Before me soon, where once you sat beside.
> I shall not scruple then to do my duty;
> And not, perhaps, so much in vain as now. –
> We cannot help it, ma'am; a wilful man,
> On whom reproof and admonition fail!

(Exeunt Mrs Frost and Coal.)

FROST. This parson Coal would leave the poor to Heaven,[88]
> But takes good care to help himself on earth.
> The suff'rings of the poor are deem'd deserv'd,
> God's visitation on them for their sins!
> He revels in his wealth, which, I suppose
> He deems God's special bounty for his virtues.
> I've heard this very Coal, when dining out,
> Gobble with mouth o'erfull of luscious meat,
> Half chok'd with haste to vent his angry spite
> On naked wretches, begging for a crust.
> Aye, such as he are shook with pious horror

---

[87] *Shall worldly priests ... he did denounce*: see Matthew 21:12–17, in which Jesus throws the money lenders out of the temple.

[88] *would leave the poor to Heaven*: play on a Beatitude from Jesus's Sermon on the Mount; see Luke 6:20: 'And he lifted up his eyes on his disciples, and said, Blessed be ye poor: for yours is the kingdom of God' (*King James Version*).

When poverty complains of grinding laws.
　　　They preach contentment up, content themselves –
　　　But not with hunger, cold, and nakedness.
BRITANNIA. I've heard he lib'rally contributes coals,
　　　In winter time, to such as go to church;
　　　And also that he lib'rally subscribes
　　　All lists of charity.
FROST. Christ came to free the enslav'd poor; he took
　　　No tithe from them, nor publish'd his good deeds.
　　　What signifies relief to single wants?
　　　While the great gen'ral cause is kept in action,
　　　'Twill keep us doing by undoing all.
　　　A radical reform alone can cure;
　　　But oh, my child, most truly said the sage,
　　　That he who marries gives a bond to fate,
　　　And children are an hostage to the state.
　　　I must divorce my wife to wed my country,
　　　And sacrifice my tend'rest hopes to her.
BRITANNIA. Be it so, my father; we die to save her. (*Exeunt.*)

　　　　　　　　END OF ACT III.

ACT IV
SCENE I

An Open Place.

Enter Shell and Working-men.

SHELL. They mock our prayers – insult our want and woe,
    The sensual, selfish, sordid causers of it!
    What shall we do? – I know what I will do –
    Send no more papers begging of my own,
    To get no answer but a curse or scoff –
    Spurn'd from the door of our own House by Thieves,[89]
    Who revel on the booty that's within!
    I'll take a pike, next time, for my petition;
    And knock so loud with it, the door shall fly;
    Then woe to those who scoff'd our prayers before!
1 WORK. Aye, we'll make them glad to jump out at window.
SHELL. Petitions do no good, but harm; as this –
    They are acknowledgments of unjust power,
    As if usurp'd and fraudful force were legal.
    We have the odds, and God, upon our side.
1 WORK. Let slaves and cowards go a begging next,
    And get a beggar's answer – 'We can't serve you!'
SHELL. 'Tis not alone our rights will serve us now;
    Contention cries for satisfaction – vengeance!
    Nor simple death will serve, but tortures too.
MEN. Aye, vengeance! blood! The longer they deny,
    The stronger be our cry.
SHELL. Here's Albion coming; clear the way for Albion!
      (*Enter Albion.*)
ALBION. They laugh at you – they mock your miseries –
    Make mirth and profit of your helplessness.

---

[89] *own House*: the House of Commons.

SHELL. 'Tis no laughing matter to us, I trow,
  And shall not be to them next time, mayhap.
ALBION. Methinks I hear their laugh, their fiendish laugh!
  It tingles in my veins – it fires my blood!
  Oh, would the laughers were before me now!
  I'd look them dead with light'ning of my eye!
  Just Heaven, where was thy thunder? Sleeps it, God?
  Oh, at our cries awake it, let it fall!
SHELL. We'll launch it forth – our hands shall deal the bolt!
  We are not passive, non-resisting slaves.
ALBION. Too long, too long you've been so; this it is
  Makes your oppressors laugh at your sad cries.
  Laugh! 'tis well: let them laugh on: laughs do more
  To rouse your wrath than e'en the woes they laugh at.
  Laugh louder, tyrants! we will weep no more;
  We will laugh too. Vengeance! no cry but vengeance!
  We'll be revenged; and not so much for wrongs –
  For all that guilt has made the guiltless suffer,
  As for their laugh of triumph in it all.
  They might have caused our woes unwittingly,
  Might not have known of them: we told them all,
  And humbly sued for peaceful mitigation:
  They heard us, and they laughed! 'twas best of sport!
  This their redress of our long suff'ring –
  This the reward of our most patient hopes;
  Well, well; we merit all! Are we not slaves?
  The fault is not in them; 'tis fit they spurn us;
  What better worth are we than their contempt?
  How can they help but make us laughing-stocks?
  Why, they should tax our noses, ears and lips;
  Tax us, and leave us nought to pay the tax,
  Then tread the blood from out our hearts, like wine;
  Yea, quaff it, as they now drink our fast tears:
  We shall deserve it all if we submit.
SHELL. Aye, so we shall, and may expect it next.
1 WORK. Here's a policeman among us – a spy?
ALBION. I care not for him; I but speak the truth.
  A policeman! what comes he here to do?
  What wants the spy? And must our sighs be counted –
  Our groans be noted – our tears told to tyrants?
  Words, too – words which come hot from honest hearts,
  The truthful exclamations of despair,

Must all be taken down as evidence –
Not of our wrongs, our griefs, and suff'rings,
But of our discontent, sworn to, forsooth?
Content! aye, we must be content with wrongs,
Pleased with anxiety and pain, or punished
For want of cheerfulness – that's law for slaves,
Since slaves must smile, when tyrants choose to strike,
Must thank the blow, or smart for feeling it.
A policeman, call ye the monster-man?
Yes, for ye are not men; and one of ye
That same policeman was, who now, for pelf,[90]
Turns round, a tyrant's tool, to watch the woes
Himself did feel; and now betrays his brethren,
Because they feel them still; their woes their crimes;
Informs against the wretchedness he felt,
And is rewarded by your tax-wrung toils.
'Tis seething kids in their own mother's milk!
SHELL. Down with the bloody police! Down with them!
The traitors are more hateful than our tyrants.
ALBION. Nay, raise yourselves, and get them better work.
But, should they touch you, wrest their staves from them,
And break them on their heads. To arms, my men!
Meet force with force – repel their force with force,
Control them with the weapons that they bring,
And beat the villains and their masters too.
To arms! to arms! no more petitions – pikes!
They laugh at us, and hound their dogs to bite us –
That's all their mercy for our miseries.
They laugh! aye, we'll laugh too – laugh at their shrieks
When on our pikes we carry them impal'd.
Laugh at their writhing – laugh to see them bleed –
Their blood shall flow as fast as did our tears.
Oh, how we'll laugh! I can't laugh now – I weep –
But soon I'll laugh as loud as they at us.

(*The police make an onslaught and drive away the people. They seize Albion.*)

BLUE. You are my prisoner.[91]

---

[90] *pelf*: money.

[91] *You are my prisoner*: Henry Vincent was arrested in London on 8 May 1839 on a charge of riotous assembly and committed to Monmouth Gaol shortly thereafter. In August, he was found guilty and sentenced to a year in prison.

ALBION. What warrant have you to disturb a meeting
   Assembled to discuss their grievances?
BLUE. You've spoken treason, urg'd the mob to arm –
   Incited them to break the Queen's good peace.
ALBION. 'Tis you have broke the peace and people's heads,
   Ye peace preservers!
BLUE. We have our orders from the magistrates
   Not to allow assemblages like these.[92]
ALBION. 'Tis we have cause of fear, not they – off, hirelings!
   Go tell your masters, next time they do this,
   We'll make them answerable for our hurts.
BLUE. Come sir, to prison, quietly, or else,
   I'll knock you down and shackle you; come, sir.
ALBION. I'll answer what I've said, and they shall answer
   For what they've done.   (*Exeunt.*)
   (*Re-enter Shell with a crowd armed with guns and pikes.*)
SHELL. They've bruis'd our backs, broken our heads and arms,
   Because we were defenceless, they have dragg'd
   Our friend to gaol for advocating us.
   This is the way they cure the griefs they cause.
   The bloody cowards dare not meet us now,
   Now we are arm'd to meet them on their terms.
   If we can't rescue Albion let us die;[93]
   For there will be no longer hope on earth,
   And Hell itself can't match the heartless fiends
   Which Government has sent to cure our woes.
   Aye, this indeed is an effectual way!
   They'd better come and massacre us all.
   Where's Frost? he is our only leader now.
   Run for him some one – let him come at once.
1 WORK. We'll be reveng'd on these accurs'd police.[94]
2 WORK. I left my children crying for a crust,
   And went back bleeding to them.

---

[92] *Not to allow assemblages*: from spring 1839, restrictions had been placed on the right to hold meetings throughout Britain, including Wales.

[93] *If we can't rescue Albion*: at the trial of the Newport prisoners, the defence claimed the march on Newport was a protest of Vincent's imprisonment or an attempt to liberate him (though Vincent was held at Monmouth, not Newport).

[94] *We'll be revenged ... accursed police*: here Watkins uses verse lines for workers' speech for the first time in the play, perhaps suggesting that their participation in the rebellion elevates them.

3 WORK. And I, mine stopp'd their cry in fear for me.
  My wife herself gave me this pike and said,
  Kill the police if we all die for it.
SHELL. Aye, they have shut themselves in their stronghold;
  But we will burn it down to have them out.[95]
    (Enter a Messenger.)
MESSENGER. Frost says you must go home, he will not come.
SHELL. Won't he? he shall! go tell him we are waiting,
  And if he does not come, we'll drag him forth,[96]
  Nor spare his house, nor him, nor aught that's his.
    (Exit Messenger.)
  He shan't desert us now when most we want him.
  Our blood is rous'd, 'tis up, away with all.
  The Charter's self – we want but this – Revenge!
  Blood calls for blood, calls with a voice so loud,
  It will be heard and answer'd first – blood! blood!
    (Enter Middleman.)
  Seize the shopocrat – make him a prisoner.
MIDDLEMAN. Why this violence? why this restraint on me?
SHELL. You are a whig, sir – so is the Devil, too,
  And you like him go seeking up and down
  Whom to devour, whom of the working-men.
MIDDLEMAN. Is this your boasted love of liberty?
SHELL. We'll seize on all until our friend's releas'd,
  Make hostages of all.
    (Enter Frost.)
MIDDLEMAN. Your men here, Mr Frost, keep me by force;
  I beg you'll be my liberator, sir.
FROST. I hate your politics; but you may go.
SHELL. Had not our friend been your friend too;
  You'd not got off so easily. Good sir,
  Bethink you they'd not let you off so well.
    (Exit Middleman.)
FROST. Oh go, my friends, go home in peace, go home;
  Defer your vengeance till another day.
  Disperse, I say – part peaceably – come do;
  Or you will have the soldiers on you next.

---

[95] *in their stronghold / ... burn it down*: the climactic confrontation of the Newport rising occurred at the Westgate hotel, to which town officials had retreated and in which Chartist prisoners were being temporarily held.

[96] *if he does not come ... drag him forth*: Frost was a willing participant in the rising, so Watkins invents his hesitation, perhaps to support calls for his pardon.

SHELL. We care not, let them come, let devils come
   All hot from hell, burning with flaming brimstone,
   We'll be reveng'd – we will have blood for blood.
   So lead us on, we'll rescue Albion first,
   And then have at the brutes that broke our bones.
   We'll fire the town and all that's in't destroy;
   But we will have revenge on these police.
FROST. Oh, do consider how beset with snares
   You are – how Government lurks like a tiger,
   Waiting and watching for the least excuse
   To pounce upon you with exulting fury!
   We are no match for it in force and fraud –
   Only by moral means can we hope conquest.
   Our wav'ring friends will turn to foes with fear.
   Obey the law, or you arm tyrants with't.
SHELL. We'll break the law and make a better one.
FROST. Well, since you will not be advis'd, I'll go;
   But with the hope to counsel you to peace.
   March quietly and show yourselves in front;
   Perchance when your hired foes behold your force
   They'll let your friend out, and you'll go in peace.
SHELL. Let's have him out, and then we'll see
   What next we'll do; away, to Albion's gaol.
                                    (Exeunt, shots are heard.)

   (Re-enter Frost. Alone.)
FROST. The soldiers have come in; they fire on them
   Oh! how these shots ring in my stricken ears.
   I was not born for fearful scenes like this.
   I cannot bear the sight of reeking blood,
   It makes my heart sick; I am fit to faint.
   They should have chosen one more stern than I.
   My trade is peace; I'm horror-struck with war.
   Again these shots! my damp hair rises up;
   A mortal coldness spreads upon my brains;
   I must far off; they'll fail – they have no force,
   More moved are they by fury than by reason.
   They'll fail and find no mercy, nor shall I.
   I've too much thought in me for desperate action.
   I'll fly; I was not made for facing death,
   Nor dealing it – those shots strike on my soul.
   I must get out of hearing of those guns.   *(Exit.)*

SCENE II

Frost's Parlour.

Mrs Frost, Britannia, and Henry.

MRS FROST. Why did you let your father go?
BRITANNIA. I could not hold him, he said there would be bloodshed,
   Unless he used his influence to prevent it.
MRS FROST. His influence! who can stop a flood or fire?
   Not they who aided it to burst all bounds.
   Why, they would sweep him with them, yea, o'erwhelm
   And sacrifice him, if opposed to them.
   You should have held him as I would have done,
   Had I been here. But you have always urged him.
BRITANNIA. He did instruct them; who so fit to guide?
MRS FROST. Oh, how foolish he has been; how mad!
   Nothing but woe and trouble for me now,
   Hour after hour, like wave on wave, to sink me;
   And we so comfortable, so well off
   Before this Chartist mania seiz'd on him.
   Go, Henry, say he must come home – he *must!*
   Or I shall die with terror and distress.
HENRY. I'll pull him by the coat laps, mother.   *(Exit.)*
BRITANNIA. Mother, you know poor Albion was arrested?
   And all this rage was but to rescue him.
MRS FROST. Aye, Albion! Albion! let thy father perish,
   So Albion's safe; he should have held his tongue;
   He was right served; I'd serve all rebels so –
   Stirring a lawless mob so apt to rise.
BRITANNIA. Nay, but mother, he did but speak the truth,
   Moved by a spirit of humanity,
   And they have us'd him with indignity.
   Such cruelty might well excite the wrath
   Of those for whom he suffers; they have risen
   And flown to knock his felon fetters off.
MRS FROST. Aye, they will be imprison'd next, or slain.
BRITANNIA. If Government can wrong the people thus,
   And punish those who plead in their behalf,
   The State, indeed, must need a patriot's care.
     (Enter Parson Coal, and Blue Devil.)

Act IV Scene II

COAL. Is Mr Frost within?
MRS FROST. Oh, no; I wish he were.
COAL. So do I too; do you know where he is?
MRS FROST. No, sir; oh, tell me, is he safe?
COAL. If we could find him, we would keep him safe.
   He led the rebels on, and then escaped.
   I thought he might have come back home to you.
MRS FROST. Oh, why was he so fond to leave it?
COAL. He's gone, I'll warrant, to the hills.
MRS FROST. What has been done? what has he done, good sir?
COAL. What he must answer with his head when found.
   I have a warrant to search and seize his goods.
   Where are his papers?
MRS FROST. Alack! alack!
BRITANNIA. I'll get his papers for you, sir.
   (Enter Henry.)
MRS FROST. Have you seen your father, my boy?
HENRY. No, mother; there's such a crowd!
BLUE. This boy was there; I know him, by his cap.
COAL. Like enough; a forager's, I see.
BLUE. Aye, no doubt, he was a foraging.
COAL. Arrest him, officer! we'll take him, too.
MRS FROST. Oh, don't bereave me of my guiltless child;
   I sent him there to fetch his father back.
   Oh, touch him not, lay not your hands on him;
   Or I shall never pardon me for that.
   I've lost my husband; must I lose my son?
   Oh, 'tis too heavy such a double stroke!
COAL. Ma'am, I must do my duty.
MRS FROST. Oh, sir, he's fatherless; and I'm a widow –
   Your duty is to comfort us in this dark hour.
   Not to increase the desolation here.
   If you take him away in this sad time,
   I ne'er can sit and hear you preach again.
COAL. The church door shall stand open for you, ma'am;
   'Twill not be my fault if you stay away.
   I must do my judicial duty, ma'am.
BRITANNIA. Your magistracy spoils your ministry;
   Or one or both you should give up.
COAL. My duty is severe sometimes to me
   As well as others; I must expect hard words
   And reprehension for the doing it.

The officer can swear he saw him there;
He knows him by this most suspicious cap.
BLUE. Aye, and he led one half the mob.
COAL. You hear, ma'am; I cannot leave him – must not;
He is his father's son and that's enough.[97]
HENRY. Don't cry, mother, or I shall cry and all;
They will not kill me, will they, mother?
MRS FROST. I know not what they will not do.
HENRY. Where will they take me to, and what for, mother?
For wearing this cap? I'll not wear't again.
COAL. Come, we must go.
HENRY. What will they do to me? I'll stay with mother
Till father comes. Will you let me come back?
COAL. Officer, do your duty in the name of the Queen!
MRS FROST. Desist in the name of God!
Is't in the Queen to tear my son from me
Just when I've lost his father?
COAL. Resist not, ma'am, or you too we must take.
BRITANNIA. Mother, for my sake and your own, be patient.
Justice must soon return the prey they take;
Let the lamb go awhile.
COAL. Good day, ladies.
    (*Coal and Bluedevil escape with Henry. Mrs Frost falls into Britannia's arms.*)

SCENE III

A Road Leading to the Hills.

Enter Frost.

FROST. I cannot reach the mountains, – I am spent, –
And something seems to pull my heartstrings back.
Perchance my wife and children have been slain,
Or cannot bear the news of my ill fate.
What have I done, that I need run away?
I fired no shot – would fain none had been fired –

---

[97] *He is his father's son*: Henry Hunt Frost, Frost's second son; Henry's arrest attracted negative attention because of his age of 17. Charges were eventually dropped when the government failed to produce a witness implicating him (though historians believe he did take part in the rising).

I'm innocent, – why should I fly like guilt?
'Tis now too late to stop or to return;
My flight has been discovered – that's enough!
Oh! me, my thoughtless fear will be my fate.
Oh! for some quiet solitary nook,
Where I might hide me from the face of man,
Far from pursuit, unknown, forgetting all,
By all forgotten; – oh! for such a spot
To live and die in – nature's lonely hermit. –
The shots have ceased, and stragglers from the town
Too surely show the soldiers have prevailed.
Here comes a fugitive, I'll ask the news.
   (*Enter a Working-man.*)
Pray what has happened, that you run so fast?
MAN. Oh! sir, poor Shell is shot, and many more;[98]
I saw him die, – his last death-utter'd words
Were, 'Kill the murderers!' I turned and fled.
Away with me unto the mountain-sides;
There we may keep a native warfare up
Until all England rises for the Charter,
And government know not which way to turn.   (*Exit.*)
FROST. Shall I return or hide me in this copse?
I'll hide awhile till all pursuit is passed,
Then to some public-house to reconnoitre.
I cannot bear suspense; I will decide
To yield me up, and take my chance of justice.   (*Exit.*)

SCENE IV

Inside of a Public-house.

Soakflesh, Filip, Neutral, – Frost, in a corner, eating bread and cheese.

NEUTRAL. I'm not a Chartist, I never was one;
But for all that, I'll say what's right and just,
And that is this – the Charter is but fair.
FILIP. Aye, so it is, according to the law,
For law is justice, and the Charter's just.
We lawyers vindicate the law, you know;

---

[98] *poor Shell is shot*: see Footnote 4.

    And let the Charter once be made a law,
    We will defend it for you.
NEUTRAL. Why, if 'tis just, you lawyers should be first,
    According to the law, to get us justice.
FILIP. Nay, the old law does well enough for us;
    Better, perhaps, than your new one would do.
NEUTRAL. But lawyers can't be honest, if the law
    Opposes justice.
FILIP. Just or unjust, the law is still the law,
    And we are bound to vindicate the law.
NEUTRAL. As lawyers, maybe; not as honest men:
    Eh, what say you, landlord?
SOAKFLESH. I know nought of the suffrage, or of suffering, –
    Not I. I never bother myself so.
    I've always had good store of meat and drink,
    And always will, I'll take good care of that.
NEUTRAL. Care for yourself alone?
SOAKFLESH. Aye, let each one do that, and all are cared for;
    That is my Charter, and I've grown fat on't.
NEUTRAL. The fatter you are, the fitter for cooking.
    The Whigs will not long pick the poor man's bones,
    They'll leave the lean, and come to such as you.
    Remember Rome – look at the Emperors;
    Did not Tiberius, when he wanted sport,
    Pass o'er the poor, and butcher lordly calves?[99]
SOAKFLESH. Lord! how thou talks – thou's a fine fellow, truly,
    Drink off thy glass, shalt have another one,
    And then I'll tell thee this – prate as thou likes,
    I pay more wages than I finger profits.
NEUTRAL. Why do you hire men if you lose by them?
SOAKFLESH. Content you there, I must keep trade agoing;
    The times will mend, and I shall make it up.
NEUTRAL. Aye, out of workmen's bones, and blood, and marrow.
SOAKFLESH. Just so, my lad; think'st thou I'd keep them on,
    Except in hope to make my losses up?
NEUTRAL. Well, well, the Charter is a Christian scheme,
    And would do good for all: I'll join for it.
FILIP. And so will I when it becomes a law;
    For law, you know, is justice to us lawyers.

---

[99] *Tiberius ... butcher lordly calves*: second Roman emperor; reference to atrocities untraced.

> The language of the law is beautiful,
> And harmonizes well with truth.

FROST. The spirit, too; pity it is perverted.

FILIP. Aye, thousand pities practice should pervert it.

FROST. You seem a righteous, equitable man:
> I'll tell my case to you; I need your counsel!
> I can rely on one so just as you.

FILIP. Put perfect confidence in me, dear sir.

FROST. Good sir, you can befriend me much; then do,
> And I set my anxious mind at ease.
> Sir, I was present at this sad affair, –
> But to prevent it; yet I am afraid
> My presence will be deemed participation.
> What's your opinion, sir? what says the law?

FILIP. You do confess you were among the rebels?
> You hear him, sirs! – sir, you are my prisoner!

FROST. Yours!

FILIP. Yes, sir; let me see, is not John Frost your name?

FROST. It is.

FILIP. I'm glad to hear it – landlord! glasses round.
> I've got the chief – a hundred pounds reward.[100]
> Do you submit, or must I fetter you?

FROST. I do submit – oh, what a fatal thing –
> How suddenly a man may fall to ruin!
> Even by striving for his fellow man.
> Oh, I am wretched, too much so, to live!
> I would do good, and ill is done to me:
> Oh for a ray from Heaven to cheer my soul!

FILIP. Come, sir, I'll drink your health.

FROST. Can you exult in my most wretched state;
> You, for whose good, with all mankind's, I fought?

FILIP. It's the £100, not you, my dear sir.

FROST. You shall have twice as much to let me go.

FILIP. No, 'tis too late; there's more in't than the money.

FROST. Is't possible that man can be my foe?
> I am the friend of man – of you, yourself;
> And you must die, you know not when, nor how,
> You who joy life, as I did, yesterday.

---

[100] *a hundred pounds reward*: rewards for this amount were offered for the capture of Frost, William Jones and Zephaniah Williams.

How can you wish my death, since yours must come?
Man won't forgive, but surely God will pardon.
FILIP. Come, take a glass, to keep your spirits up;
Fortune of war, you know, luck's all.
FROST. I cannot drink; 'twould choke me now.
I wonder you can drink, or follow folly,
Just on the brink of fate, for aught you know,
As I am now, and death's an awful thing.
FILIP. Landlord! get out your gig and go with us;
You are a constable as well as I,
And will assist in taking him to town.
NEUTRAL. I feel for you, good sir; it was for me:
'Twas such as I got you into this scrape.
Had we stood for ourselves, as you for us,
Ourselves might have been righted, and you saved.
FROST. Aye, had not such as you stood off from us,
All this had been prevented; 'tis too late
For me, but not too late to help yourselves.
I trust remorse and shame will spur you on
More briskly for your rights; though I be lost,
Let not the Charter perish; but consider,
The man who does not strive to gain his birthright,
Deserves to lose it – nay, deserves to die!
For he disgraces life, which, without freedom,
Is but the brutes' existence.
NEUTRAL. I am a Chartist, though I meet your fate.
FROST. May I finish my bread and cheese?
FILIP. Oh yes, and have what else you like.
Make yourself comfortable; be at home.
FROST. At home! where is my home? what is at home?
I've lost my home! I've lost my wife! my children!

(Bursting into tears.)
(Scene closes.)

END OF ACT IV.

ACT V
SCENE I

The Council Chamber.

Lord Littlejohn and Lord Noman.

LITTLEJOHN. Good news, good news! the best I ever heard!
  I never was more pleased in all my life!
  We now may crush the people as we please,
  For none will venture now to take their part.
NOMAN. Good news indeed, if only it be true.
LITTLEJOHN. We've got Jack Frost, Jack Cade redivivus.[101]
  Iden, the gentleman that captured Cade,[102]
  Walworth, the mayor that struck Wat Tyler down,
  Were knighted and rewarded for their deeds;[103]
  And lawyer Filip, who has *filip'd* Frost,[104]
  Shall, in like manner, be honour'd for it.
  'Tis fit such loyalty should be encouraged.
NOMAN. I'll ask him to a dinner with us here,
  And stuff him with the best our pantry holds.
  If he can play the trencher-man as well[105]
  As Chartist-taker, why he shall be knight
  Of our round table – dubb'd the pantry-knight!
LITTLEJOHN. Where's Lambkin?
NOMAN. Oh, helping Vic. to feed her marmozets.[106]
LITTLEJOHN. Thanks to the people that supply the means!

---

[101] *Jack Cade*: leader of a popular revolt in England in 1450; *redivivus*: reborn (Latin).
[102] *Iden*: Alexander Iden, who wounded and captured Cade; later Sheriff of Kent.
[103] *Walworth ... for their deeds*: William Walworth, the Mayor of London, killed Wat Tyler, the leader of the Great Rising of 1381, during a parley with King Richard II at Smithfield in London; he was knighted shortly afterward.
[104] *filip'd Frost*: see Footnote 8.
[105] *trencher-man*: dependant or hanger-on; eater with a hearty appetite.
[106] *marmozets*: marmosets, small monkeys. See Footnote 51.

NOMAN. He is the valet, my wife the chambermaid;
   Let me be cook, you shall be butler, John.
LITTLEJOHN. Why, truly, every man to his vocation.
   But this sharp Frost, that thought to nip our blossoms,
   We'll nip his neck: he shall be hanged, I say.
NOMAN. What, before trial? Let the verdict come;
   You know we have him – no expense is spared;
   No doubt the law will soon revenge your hate.
      (*Enter Lambkin.*)
LAMBKIN. They've found Frost guilty!
LITTLEJOHN. Thanks to our friends, the Special Judge and Jury.[107]
LAMBKIN. But recommend the dog to mercy.
LITTLEJOHN. Mercy! mercy to him were none to us.
   Mercy! aye, such mercy he shall have
   As you, Lord Lambkin, would have found from him.
LAMBKIN. Faith! I don't think I stood in so much danger
   From this Welch wolf as you, my little lord.
LITTLEJOHN. Well, well, no Frost; and then sunshine is ours.
   Lord Noman! strict and certain orders send
   To have a gallows made, and made right strong;
   For should it break, the crowd might rescue him.
   Let it be strong enough to hang a horse,
   And fee the hangman double for the job.
NOMAN. But in our haste to get the charge drawn up,
   We did o'erlook a necessary form.
   Objection straight was made on Frost's behalf,
   And, sure enough, the trial had been stopped,
   But that Frost's council did themselves agree
   It should go on; this awkward point reserved
   For the decision of the judges after.[108]
   Should their opinion make the objection good,
   Then Frost not prejudiced by adverse verdict.

---

[107] *the Special Judge and Jury*: the Newport prisoners were tried by a Special Commission, rather than at the quarterly assize. Justice John Williams presided and was assisted by Sir James Parke and the Lord Chief Justice Sir Nicholas Tindal. The participation of Williams, who was notorious for sentencing the Dorchester labourers to penal transportation (see Footnote 45), reinforced the popular perception that the accused had not received a fair trial.

[108] *in our haste ... necessary form ... the judges after*: upon indicting Frost and presenting the jury list, the prosecution delayed providing the defence its witness list for five days, a failure that threatened the validity of the trial. As Watkins describes, the defence allowed the trial to proceed, reserving its right to air the objection after the trial.

LAMBKIN. Just so, my lord, and now the judges sit
  In consultation on this ticklish point.
    (*Enter a Messenger.*)
MESSENGER. Nine of the judges do decide for Frost.
LITTLEJOHN. Nine, but not all.
MESSENGER. No, only nine, out of fifteen, my lord.   (*Exit.*)
LITTLEJOHN. They are not all unanimous, my lords,
  And so this lame objection is no bar.
NOMAN. Are we to act on the majority,
  Or the minority, my loving lord?
LITTLEJOHN. Six loyal voices are enough for us;
  The nine disloyal ones deserve no notice.[109]
  Besides the odium we have cast on Frost
  Will serve us for a weapon and a shield.
LAMBKIN. I say, let him be banished.[110]
LITTLEJOHN. Banished! his friends may bring him back again;
  Why not make sure of him at once?
LAMBKIN. 'Cause his attempt to weaken us will strengthen,
  And give us pleas to put down all his friends.
  We'll issue proclamations, swords and pistols,
  To arm the middlemen against the mob.
  The iron Duke gave us a lift last night;[111]
  He said this row beat all he ever saw
  In all his wars; good thanks to him for that!
  But let us not pursue revenge too far,
  Lest we should chance to lose our way.
NOMAN. Aye, aye, let not our zeal outrun discretion;
  The first *things* to consider are ourselves.
LITTLEJOHN. Well, I consent, but you will see his life
  Will keep alive the flame of disaffection.
NOMAN. Nay, we'll provide 'gainst that by sending him
  To penal Isles, where life is worse than death,
  And he may kill himself and we not blamed.

---

[109] *Nine of the judges ... deserve no notice*: In the Court of Exchequer, nine judges, a majority, voted to sustain the defence's objection concerning the list, but the court also ruled that the defence raised the objection at the improper time and thus upheld the verdict and sentence.

[110] *let him be banished*: Frost's, Zephaniah Williams's, and William Jones's death sentences were commuted to transportation for life to Van Diemen's Land (modern-day Tasmania).

[111] *The iron Duke*: Arthur Wellesley (1769–1852), Duke of Wellington; famous for defeating Napoleon at Waterloo; later, conservative politician and Prime Minister (1828–30).

LITTLEJOHN. Well, I agree, but lest the people rise,
    Remove him under cover in the dark,
    Allow him no leave-taking of his friends,
    That not a hint transpire of his departure.[112]
    Let it take place at midnight to the hulks,
    A steamer ready and a transport ship.
    He hath transported us, we'll transport him –
    Transport for transport, is measure for measure.

SCENE II

A Dungeon.

Frost, reading.

FROST. 'Blessed are the merciful for they shall obtain mercy.'[113]
    From whom shall they obtain it? – not from man –
    Man curses man – cruel e'en in his mercy!
    Me, merciful, they recommend to mercy.
    And what do I obtain? – nor that, nor justice!
    I sought for mercy for the suff'ring poor,
    And am condemn'd for't – aye, for that,
    I'm sentence'd to be hang'd, and drawn and quarter'd,[114]
    My sever'd limbs dispos'd of by the Queen.
    What will she do with them when sent to her?
    Will she, like Ate, make a feast of them?[115]
    'Tis treason now to pity poor men's woes –
    Loyal to laugh at them – the base are thank'd.
    God! thou art merciful – have mercy on me –
    On those who have more need of it than I;
    On those who've none for me, nor for the poor.
    Oh God! if 'tis expedient one man perish
    For thy poor people's sake, – I'll be that man.

---

[112] *no leave-taking ... his departure*: Frost and his fellow prisoners were moved from Monmouth Gaol in the middle of the night on 2 February 1840, circumstances that provoked considerable controversy. They were taken to Portsmouth and embarked for Van Diemen's Land about two weeks later.

[113] *Blessed ... obtain mercy*: see Matthew 5:7.

[114] *hang'd, and drawn and quarter'd*: the traditional punishment for treason – being drawn by a horse to the place of execution, hanging until death, and having the corpse quartered.

[115] *Ate*: Greek goddess of mischief, associated with mad impulses and disaster.

If I have erred 'twas with no bad intent,
But strictest judgment will be dealt on me.
Oh, may my punishment atone my faults –
Oh, hear my prayers, oh, God! and pardon me.
   (Enter Jailer.)
JAILER. Her Majesty most graciously has mercy –
She will not hang you; but transport you, sir.
FROST. I'd rather die – I'd rather far be hang'd!
JAILER. At your pleasure, sir –
But you'll be transported, sir – not hang'd.
I thought you would have lik'd to hear it, sir.   *(Exeunt.)*
FROST. Transported! – 'tis to drag on death alive.
Mercy! 'tis worse cruelty – none but fiends
Would call it mercy – oh, 'tis most sardonic!
Transport, indeed! – transport in penal flames!
They'll next call Hell, an Heaven – and its devils
They'll christen angels, – so, indeed, they are,
Aye, fiends are cherubs when compar'd with these.
England a worser Hell – what shall I do?
Vice reigns on earth, and virtue is her victim. –
They seiz'd me – immur'd me – the very priests
Who pray that God will pity all poor prisoners,
Made me a captive; was't to pray for me?
Betray'd by mine own counsel on my trial;[116]
Condemn'd to human shambles to be slaughter'd,
More like a beast for market than a man;
And now Victoria's mercy for me, is——
What? banishment to earth's remotest bounds,
Far from the hearing of redress or pity;
There to be chain'd with felons 'neath the sun,
A keeper o'er me with a whip of wire,
And when I groan with unhabitual toil,
Or faint with thirst and hunger, or disease,
To have the whip scourge off my blister'd skin,
And be worse tortured for my cries and shrieks.
Nay, when worn nature sinks in torpid sleep,
And dreams of what I was, stir thoughts of home,

---

[116] *Betray'd by mine own counsel*: apparently Watkins's invention as historians cite no evidence of such a betrayal nor does this theme appear prominently in other Chartist discourse. Frost and his co-defendants received excellent representation from their counsellors Sir Frederick Pollock (a former Attorney General) and Fitzroy Kelly.

To be awak'd and goaded to my doom;
I, whose whole course of life has run contrary,
So that my fate will make itself more felt.
I, to end life's last days thus namelessly;
It is too dreadful for my mind to think of.
They cannot mean it, sure; a moment so,
With such companions and such overseers,
In such an irresponsive wilderness,
Where man is authoriz'd to torture man,
And savage beasts seem tame compar'd with him:
A moment of such life, were like whole years,
Aye of such misery as I have deplor'd.
And must I go, with memory, and spend
The last sad remnant of my being thus?
I shall go mad; or, worse, become a fiend!
And this they call their mercy – royal mercy!
Be merciful, indeed; and give me death!
Oh, let me die while yet I am a man!
Give me some chance of leaving earth for Heaven!
   (Re-enter Jailer.)
JAILER. Your wife seeks an admittance to you, sir.
FROST. My wife! my children! Have I wife and child?
I've kept them from me; durst not think of them;
My mind was conscious it would fail me there,
And shifted from the thought – thrust it away –
But now my heart flies open at their names,
They rush within – they overpower me all –
Oh, now it is I feel! – all else was nothing –
She comes herself – my wife! my wife! oh! oh!
   (Enter Mrs Frost.)
MRS FROST. My husband!
FROST. Oh, let me weep! I'll drown thee with my tears!
I have not wept till now – my poor, dear wife!
Oh, how I feel for thee – my children, too.
This blow were nothing, fell it not on you –
It is too much for me – I am a father! –
Oh, they do torture me in my affections,
And pain of body would relieve my mind.
Oh, tell me all – what of Britannia? Henry?
MRS FROST. Britannia has not wept; but oh, her looks!
They are so mournful, so serene and fix'd, –
She speaks not, eats not – but her eyes are bright

With an etherial lustre, like two stars,
And seem to gaze upon another world.
I fear she'll die, and give no sign of death.
FROST. What of poor Ned? must he be quarter'd, too?
MRS FROST. They have releas'd him; but he plays no more:[117]
He wishes they had prison'd him with you.
FROST. And then thyself – hast thou not come to chide?
MRS FROST. Oh, no, I come to sympathize with thee –
'Twas never hate, but fear that made me scold.
FROST. Oh, hadst thou seen the Christian parson Coal?
How mild he look'd! – with what complacency
He sat in judgment on me! on his brow
I read no hope, as on the gate of Hell.[118]
What of the country? is there much excitement?
What do the people say?
MRS FROST. They have themselves to care for, more than thee, –
They are amaz'd, and keep at home in quiet.
FROST. Man knows not how to deal with demons.
MRS FROST. If thou hadst kept at home that fatal day.
FROST. Or when I found I'd no control o'er them,
Had I return'd, and not flown out of town –
But reason fled before I fled myself.
Who can keep cool amid such harrowing scenes?
MRS FROST. And must thou be the scape-goat for them all?
FROST. Aye, I must go – far, far away from thee, –
Far from the country I have loved too well –[119]
Too far to hear of it, or make it hear.
Where, should I call on thee with dying voice,
No answer could I get except the roar
Of a whole ocean that will roll between.
MRS FROST. I'll go with thee.
FROST. No, no, thou shalt not go, nor follow me –
'Twould double ev'ry pang to see thee suffer.
The best alleviation of my lot
Will be to think ye are exempt from it.
MRS FROST. Ah me! suspense must rankle in my heart,
And make me ever feel what you endure.

---

[117] *They have releas'd him*: see Footnote 97.
[118] *no hope ... gate of Hell*: Allusion to Dante's *Inferno*, in which the gate of hell is inscribed with the motto, 'Abandon every hope, who enter here' (Allen Mandelbaum's translation).
[119] *the country I have loved too well*: echoes Othello in Shakespeare's tragedy: 'one that loved not wisely, but too well' (5.2.404).

FROST. Nay, think not of it – account me as no more –
 Train up our boy to love his country, too.
 Cheer poor Britannia with some hope of joy –
 And tell my friends they must not think of me;
 But of themselves: tell them to get the Charter!
 That will revenge and recompense me all.
MRS FROST. When Henry asks of me, in winter nights,
 Where is poor father now? what is he doing?
 What answer can I give but sighs and tears?
FROST. The people should prevent my drear exile –
 At least they should resolve to bring me back.
MRS FROST. They wish me to petition Majesty!
 I'd sooner take a sword and lead them on:
 No, not e'en for thy precious life I'd kneel
 Unto the Queen that robs me of my husband
 Just at the moment she is taking one.
FROST. That is my wife! welcome martyrdom,
 Since I must leave my land for loving it;
 Leave it a prey to its well-paid protectors.
 I must be punish'd for my patriotism,
 Because I am too honest to be loyal.
MRS FROST. Oh, how can I remain behind from thee,
 And know and feel what thou wilt feel and know?
 I must fly to thee, though it be to death.
FROST. And aggravate my suff'rings with thine own.
 No! for our children's sakes and thine, stay here.
MRS FROST. But should'st thou sicken, as 'tis like thou wilt,
 What hand shall 'minister thy wants to thee?
 What ear shall listen to thy feeble plaints?
 What tongue shall soothe thee with heart-sympathy?
 Whose but thy wife's – thy Mary's – mine?
FROST. God's hand will make my bed for me in sickness,
 And close my dying eyes if need should be,
 Or smooth my pillow with returning help.
 God, to whose throne my prayers shall be address'd,
 For comfort to my children and my country,
 Will fortify and not forsake us both.
MRS FROST. We stand in need of God's good providence;
 For I have parted with all things for thee:
 In thy defence most bootlessly 'twas spent.
 We're now as poor as those whom thou didst pity.
 Will they have pity on us?

FROST. They will if they are men, not worse than whigs,
   Those worse than fiends; they will, or else deserve
   The doom that falls unmerited on me,
   A doom incurred through them, and for them, too.
   The bitterest portion of my grievous lot
   Will be neglect from those for whom I suffer.
   But yet I wish thou hadst reserved them, Mary.
MRS FROST. Thy life was more than all.
JAILER. The time is over, ma'am – we can't allow
   No more this time; so come, ma'am, if you please.
MRS FROST. Who gave thee power to part us?
JAILER. Lord Noman, ma'am.
MRS FROST. Whom God hath join'd, let *no man* put asunder.
JAILER. He is head-jailer, ma'am – I'm but his servant –
   It is my duty to obey his orders.
FROST. Curse on the system that requires such duty!
MRS FROST. And must we part – and part in such a place?
   The time has been when you have but left home
   To go a journey, for a day, or two,
   I murmur'd, and repin'd; and now, oh me!
   What journey you must take, and to what place,
   And on what errand!
FROST. One last embrace! – do not come here again –
   Seek not to see me more – oh, if thou knew'st
   If thou couldst feel what now I feel, and more,
   What I must feel when left alone by thee,
   How I am haunted by thy weeping form –
   Thou wouldst not break afresh my bleeding heart,
   By more such pains of parting.
MRS FROST. Nay, do not weep!
FROST. I must, or my full heart will burst.
MRS FROST. Then weep thy fill – I'll join my tears with thine,
   As we erewhile were wont to share our joys.
FROST. Oh, when we part, to what a wild I go!
MRS FROST. And I to what a desolate, drear home!
FROST. Would I might die, to part no more from thee!
   Give my Britannia all I have to give –
   This kiss – and one for Henry, too.
JAILER. Come, madam, I must part you.
MRS FROST. I cannot leave thee in this sore distress.
FROST. Why, then I'll smile on thee – God bless my wife!

MRS FROST. Vulture! (*to the gaoler*) thou tear'st my heart out by its strings.
(*She is forced out.*)

FROST. Villain! Thou'rt murd'ring her and murd'ring me!
   This is to make me feel all woes at once –
   Sure, all that follows will be nothing, now –
   Have mercy, God! – 'tis more than I can bear.
   Oh, God! bethink thee, I'm a husband! father!
     (*Re-enter Jailer.*)

JAILER. Come, sir; I'll knock your fetters off.

FROST. What! am I free? am I repriev'd? releas'd?
   Oh, let me fly to wipe their tearful eyes –
   Oh, thanks to Heaven! thanks to the Queen! to thee!

JAILER. Nay, sir, not so fast. You must to Botany –[120]
   The convict-ship is waiting for you, sir.

FROST. 'Tis far to sail – far as a ship can sail –
   I'm sick at sea; but sick of land, of life.
   Transport me to my grave – oh, let me rest!
   When I quit England, let me quit the world.
   Our country with our liberty is lost,
   And last of Englishmen is poor JOHN FROST! (*Exeunt.*)

THE END.

---

[120] *to Botany*: to penal servitude in the Australian colonies; after Botany Bay in Sydney, the site of the first such penal colony.

3

The Trial of Robert Emmet (1841)

Editor's introduction

The Chartists staged re-enactments of Robert Emmet's 1803 treason trial far more than any other work, creating a veritable cult of celebrity around the executed United Irishman. The young revolutionary's defiance in the face of oppression struck a chord with members of a movement that repeatedly saw its ranks depleted by arrests, imprisonment, and penal transportation, and Emmet's anti-imperialism resonated with the Chartists' own. Productions provoked strong reactions and audiences demanded repeat performances, leading Chartist groups to mount the trial at least thirty-six times and possibly fifty or more. In particular, the representation of Emmet's address to the court in the face of imminent death, in which he reaffirmed his commitment to an independent Ireland and condemned the tribunal before which he stood, inspired passionate responses. During Emmet's speech at an Ashton performance, 'tears were seen trickling down many cheeks'.[1] In Keighley in West Yorkshire, one Thomas Knowles delivered the same part with 'soul-stirring effect', causing 'nearly the whole audience [to melt] into tears, as if they had actually seen the original Emmett, with all the dignity of youth and love of country, placed before their eyes'.[2] At a meeting in Birmingham, the chair's recitation of Emmet's 'thrilling [speech] … created the greatest sensation among the people present'.[3] These events illustrate both the potential of dramatic art within a political context and the way the Chartists mobilised history as an emotionally resonant resource for their ongoing campaign.

The trial's popularity was such that three different troupes mounted touring productions in the early 1840s, likely the only examples of travelling theatre within the movement. Following performances by the Ashton Juvenile Chartist Association in the Manchester region in 1840–41, two companies toured Scotland in 1843. The Universal Suffrage Association of Greenock performed

---

[1] 'Ashton', *Northern Star* (31 October 1840), p. 1.
[2] 'Keighley. – Chartist Festival', *Northern Star* (2 January 1841), p. 1.
[3] 'Birmingham – The Welsh Victims', *Northern Star* (28 November 1840), p. 1.

the trial in Glasgow, Paisley, Johnston, the Vale of Leven, and possibly elsewhere.[4] The Glasgow Chartist Association planned an even more ambitious circuit that comprised twenty-one towns and cities.[5] How many of the projected performances occurred, however, is unknown. After the Greenock group complained about its competitor's performances depressing turnout for its own, the *Star* ceased covering the events, expressing 'regret ... that private and local differences should exist among Chartists – still more that they should be made public. Each party has now had its "say" on the Emmet-trial matter, and we must have no more of it.'[6]

Spilling beyond the stage, Emmet's trial touched other aspects of Chartist life. Speakers lectured on the 1803 rising or read or performed his speech from the dock.[7] As a *Star* obituary remembered, S. Dixon of Hollinwood 'took great delight in delivering' Emmet's address 'to a large number of crowded meetings, in different parts of the country'.[8] Those who encountered Emmet's oratory in print could also be moved by its power. Robert Gammage recalled how he so admired 'the daring courage of the young Irish rebel that [he] was never weary of reading his speech. [He] read and re-read until every word was fixed in [his] then tenacious memory.'[9] Emmet's trial also formed part of Chartist visual culture. A portrait of Emmet addressing the court, one in a series of pictures of radical heroes the *Star* distributed, ornamented many meeting rooms and homes.[10] William Farish, a handloom weaver from Carlisle, recollected that 'among the many portraits that were given with the *Northern Star*, none was more popular than that of Robert Emmet ... I had one of the portraits myself, which, after being framed by my own hand, served for years to adorn the wall of my bedroom.'[11]

Still more intimately, some Chartist parents christened their 'young patriots' after the martyred hero. A Mountsorrell couple was one of many who named their offspring 'in honour of that illustrious patriot who fell a victim to factious cruelty in 1803'.[12] Nor was the practice confined to boys: Cornelia

---

[4] 'To the Chartists of Scotland', *Northern Star* (13 May 1843), p. 4.
[5] 'Glasgow', *Northern Star* (22 April 1843), p. 1.
[6] 'To Readers and Correspondents', *Northern Star* (13 May 1843), p. 5.
[7] 'Star Coffee House', *Northern Star* (24 September 1842), p. 8; 'Golden Lion, Dean Street, Soho', *Northern Star* (5 August 1843), p. 1; 'Lecture', *Northern Star* (18 November 1843), p. 7.
[8] 'Death', *Northern Star* (23 February 1850), p. 8.
[9] Robert Gammage, *Reminiscences of a Chartist* (Manchester: Manchester Free Press, 1983), p. 39.
[10] Malcolm Chase, 'Building identity, building circulation: engraved portraiture and the *Northern Star*', in Joan Allen and Owen Ashton (eds), *Papers for the People: A Study of the Chartist Press* (Bodmin: Merlin Press, 2005), p. 31.
[11] William Farish, *The Autobiography of William Farish: The Struggles of a Handloom Weaver* (London: Caliban Books, 1996), p. 50.
[12] 'More Young Patriots', *Northern Star* (15 January 1842), p. 5.

Emmett Chippendale and Janet Elizabeth Emmett Howie both bore the United Irishman's name.[13] Finally, the Chartists of Marylebone commemorated Emmet by calling themselves the 'Robert Emmett brigade' while their 1848 alliance with Irish Confederates embodied their namesake's politics.[14] All told, the reverence shown Emmet provided 'a thorough contradiction to the silly assumption that *English* working men have no sympathy for the wrongs endured by *Irishmen*'.[15]

Because no performance text of *The Trial of Robert Emmet* is extant – nor indeed was ever published – one cannot know for certain what Chartist productions looked like. Nevertheless, two prose accounts of the trial circulated widely in radical milieux and likely formed the basis of many performances. First, the anonymous 1836 chapbook *The Life, Trial, and Conversations of Robert Emmet*, which enjoyed numerous re-printings in England, Ireland, and the United States, sold in Chartist circles.[16] John Doherty, an Irish emigrant, Manchester union activist, and eventual Chartist produced a version that would have been available in Ashton and other Lancashire towns where the trial was popular.[17] In 1841, the important radical publisher John Cleave produced his own Emmet biography, which copied verbatim whole sections of *Life, Trial, and Conversations*. Condensing and editing the latter text, which Cleave had previously sold, the *Memoir of Robert Emmett and the Irish Insurrection of 1803*, appeared serially in the *English Chartist Circular* and as a 1s. pamphlet.[18] The *English Chartist Circular* consistently addressed Irish issues and voiced support for the repeal of the Act of Union, concerns growing out of Cleave's own Irish ancestry but consistent with Chartism's wider programme. Cleave's memoir reached a Scottish audience as well; the Glasgow-based *Chartist Circular* reprinted it in spring 1842, twelve months before the Greenock and Glasgow Chartists toured Scotland with productions of the trial.[19] As references to no other Emmet biographies appear in Chartist sources, it is probable that many local groups utilised the speeches and

---

[13] 'More Young Patriots', *Northern Star* (11 September 1841), p. 5; 'More Young Patriots', *Northern Star* (10 June 1843), p. 1.
[14] 'Bradford', *Northern Star* (4 December 1841), p. 1; 'Central Criminal Court, Sept. 27', *Morning Advertiser* (28 September 1848), p. 4.
[15] 'Emmett and the Men of 1798', *Poor Man's Guardian and Repealer's Friend*, 4 (n.d.), p. 25.
[16] Marianne Elliott, *Robert Emmet: The Making of a Legend* (London: Profile Books, 2003), p. 129.
[17] *The Life, Trial and Conversations of Robert Emmet, Esq., Leader of the Irish Insurrection of 1803: Also, the celebrated speech made by him on that occasion* (Manchester: John Doherty, 1836).
[18] *Memoir of Robert Emmett and the Irish Insurrection of 1803; with the Trial of Emmett for High Treason, His Memorable Speech, &c.* (London: Cleave, [1841]); 'Memoires of Celebrated Patriots. No. 2 – Robert Emmett', *English Chartist Circular*, 1:11–1:21 (n.d.). Cleave advertised *The Life, Trial and Conversations* in the *Northern Star* in 1840–41.
[19] 'Memoir of Robert Emmett', *Chartist Circular* (5 March–14 May 1842).

testimony these editions provided for their dramatic endeavours.[20] Composed overwhelmingly of direct and indirect discourse, their accounts of Emmet's trial were readily adaptable to performance. This volume, therefore, reproduces Cleave's version of the trial in its entirety and includes in Appendix 3 all substantial passages of *Life, Trials, and Conversations* omitted by Cleave.

Both memoirs begin by sketching Emmet's Dublin childhood and studies at Trinity, where he pursued a career in law before withdrawing in March 1798 in the face of a purge of student members of the United Irishmen. Following a massive rebellion against British rule that spring and summer, Emmet departed for France to serve as an emissary to Napoleon's government. He returned clandestinely in autumn 1802 and set to organising the rising that took place on 23 July 1803. The conspirators' plan was to seize government buildings in Dublin, which Emmet and other leaders intended as a signal for a national rebellion. The insurrection, however, went awry even before its commencement.[21] On 16 July, an explosion at one of the rebels' depots and the prospect of a government crackdown forced Emmet to act before preparations were complete. Compounding difficulties, the United Irishmen had hoped to operate in concert with France (Britain and France had renewed hostilities in May 1803), but no French expeditionary force materialised. These circumstances led to a fatal lack of firearms. Learning this, veteran contingents who had travelled to Dublin from outlying districts decided to withdraw. Faced with a huge shortage of men and guns, Emmet led a small corps against the Dublin Castle – likely as a feint in the hope that other cadres could escape – before himself fleeing to the Dublin mountains.[22] Following a return to the capital, Emmet was captured on 25 August and stood trial for treason about one month later.

Emmet's bravery and eloquence at trial transformed the rising's failure into an act of Romantic sacrifice. His address from the dock became one of the most famous speeches 'in modern Irish history' and placed the fallen revolutionary, in W.B. Yeats's estimate, 'foremost among [Ireland's] saints of nationality'.[23] Emmet's speech itself articulates history as a contested domain, raising in its opening moments the question of how the rising will be commemorated. Emmet asserts he would endure punishment in silence were he only to suffer death but that he is compelled to speak because 'the sentence of the law which

---

[20] Cleave's misspelling of Emmet's name provides a helpful marker of the reach of his memoir. A majority of reports on trial performances sent to the *Star* utilise Cleave's misspelling, suggesting the writers' familiarity with his text.

[21] For accounts of the rising, see Ruán O'Donnell, *Robert Emmet and the Rising of 1803* (Dublin: Irish Academic Press, 2003); Patrick Geoghegan, *Robert Emmet, A Life* (Dublin: Gill & Macmillan, 2002).

[22] *Memoir of Robert Emmet*, p. 22; O'Donnell, *Robert Emmet*, p. 86.

[23] Ibid., p. 10; W. B. Yeats, 'Emmet the Apostle of Irish Liberty', in Colton Johnson (ed.), *The Collected Works of W. B. Yeats* (New York: Scribner, 2000), vol. 10, p. 103.

delivers [his] body to the executioner, will, through the ministry of that law, labour in its own vindication, to consign [his] character to obloquy. For there must be guilt somewhere: whether in the sentence of the Court or in the catastrophe, posterity must determine.'[24] Emmet's address thus bequeaths to the future the work of political judgment. Emmet's contemporaries responded by memorialising him in prose and verse. Robert Southey, Percy Bysshe Shelley, and above all Thomas Moore celebrated his youthful idealism and heroic patriotism. At the same time, Emmet's very words became a matter of dispute as radical accounts of the trial competed with versions based on likely falsified government reports.[25] Chartist performances, therefore, entered a long-standing field of strife when they recalled Emmet to life.

Among the first in a tradition of theatrical adaptations of Emmet's rising and subsequent trial and death, *The Trial of Robert Emmet* was followed by George Dibdin Pitt's *Terry Tyrone* (1845), James Pilgrim's *Robert Emmet, The Martyr of Irish Liberty* (1853), Dion Boucicault's *Robert Emmet* (1884), Lennox Robinson's *The Dreamers* (1915), and Denis Johnston's *The Old Lady Says No!* (1929). All told, some fifty plays have dramatised the events of 1803.[26] A crucial difference separating the Chartists' trial from other dramatic works, however, is the former's omission of Emmet's doomed love affair with Sarah Curran, for whom he is supposed to have returned to Dublin. Popularised in Thomas Moore's *Irish Melodies* (1808), the story of this relationship became a vital part of the Emmet legend and a staple for nineteenth- and twentieth-century playwrights. For the Chartists, by contrast, Emmet's revolutionary politics remained front and centre. His narrative presented an opportunity to make common cause with the Irish seeking an end to British rule and to lay claim to a Jacobin tradition that linked British radicalism with internationalist currents. It provided a means of considering revolutionary violence as a political strategy after the failure of the Newport rising.[27] And perhaps most of all, it offered a movement wrestling with its own series of devastating losses a vision of redemption even in defeat.

---

[24] *Memoir of Robert Emmet*, p. 37 (p. 175).
[25] Geoghegan, *Robert Emmet*, p. 244.
[26] Maureen S. G. Hawkins, 'Heroic Kings and Romantic Rebels: The Dramatic Treatment of Brian Boru and Robert Emmet as Irish National Heroes' (PhD dissertation, University of Toronto, 1992), p. 180.
[27] Mike Sanders, *The Poetry of Chartism* (Cambridge: Cambridge University Press, 2009), p. 136.

Figure 3.1 Frontispiece and title page of John Cleave's *Memoir of Robert Emmet and the Irish Insurrection of 1803; with the Trial of Emmett, for High Treason, his Memorable Speech, &c.*

MEMOIR OF ROBERT EMMET AND THE IRISH INSURRECTION OF 1803;

WITH THE TRIAL OF EMMET, FOR HIGH TREASON, HIS MEMORABLE SPEECH, &c.[1]

London:
Cleave, Shoe-Lane, Fleet-Street.

Information for these footnotes derives in part from *The Oxford Dictionary of National Biography*; Patrick Geoghegan, *Robert Emmet, A Life* (Dublin: Gill & Macmillan, 2002); and Ruán O'Donnell, *Robert Emmet and the Rising of 1803* (Irish Academic Press: Dublin, 2003).

[1] *Emmet*: Cleave spells Emmet's name with a second 't', a somewhat common misspelling this edition emends.

CHAPTER VII.

What though your cause be baffled – freemen cast
In dungeons – dragged to death, or forced to flee;
Hope is not withered in affliction's blast –
The Patriot's blood's the seed of Freedom's tree.
                    CAMPBELL.[2]

[The chapter opens with a brief account of Emmet's arrest.]

With a blood-thirsty precipitancy, the government appointed a Special Commission to *try* Emmet and nineteen other prisoners in Dublin. This Commission was opened on the 21st of August, just six days after the arrest of Emmet, and was presided over by Lord Norbury, of execrable memory, and Barons George, and Daly.[3]

Of the nineteen unfortunate individuals referred to, we may observe, *en-passant*, that one was acquitted, and a second reprieved; the rest were condemned and butchered 'according to law.'[4]

On Monday, the 19th of September, 1803, commenced

THE TRIAL
OF
ROBERT EMMET,
UPON AN
Indictment for High Treason.

To the indictment, charging him with compassing the deposition and death of the king, and conspiring to levy war against the king, within the said king's realm, Emmet pleaded in a firm, manly tone 'Not Guilty.'

The indictment was then opened by the Attorney General, Standish O'Grady,

---

[2] *What though ... Freedom's Tree*: excerpted from Thomas Campbell's 'To the Memory of the Spanish Patriots Latest killed in Resisting the Regency and the Duke of Angouleme'; first published in the *New Monthly Magazine* in 1823.

[3] *Lord Norbury*: John Toler, first earl of Norbury (1745–1831); chief justice from December 1800; as Attorney General in 1798, prosecuted several United Irishmen. [*Baron*] *George*: Denis George, Second Baron of the Exchequer. [*Baron*] *Daly*: George Daly.

[4] *en-passant*: in passing (French).

whose address to the *impartially* selected jury, was precisely such an one as 'Plain John Campbell', would under similar circumstances have, and to our sorrow has, made in England.⁵ We shall therefore be excused its non-repetition in this place, and proceed at once to the evidence adduced by the Crown.⁶ The first witness,

Joseph Rawlins, Esq., deposed to a knowledge of the prisoner, and recollected having been in his company some time in the month of December last, when he understood from him that he had been to see his brother at Brussels.⁷ On his cross-examination the witness said, that in conversations with him on the subject of continental politics, the prisoner avowed that the inhabitants of the Austrian Netherlands execrated Bonaparte's government;⁸ and from the whole of the prisoner's conversation, the witness had reason to believe, that he highly condemned Bonaparte's conduct and government.

Mr George Tyrrel, an attorney, and Michael Trayne, proved the execution of the lease of a house in Butterfield Lane, Rathfarnham, to the prisoner, who assumed the name of Ellis.⁹ Mr Tyrrel was one of the subscribing witnesses to the lease, and a person named William Dowdall was the other, who, with the prisoner, lived in the house in the most sequestered manner, and apparently anxious of concealment.

John Fleming, a native of the county Kildare, deposed, that on the 23ʳᵈ of July, and for the year previous thereto, he had been hostler at the White Bull Inn, Thomas Street, kept by a person named Dillon.¹⁰ The house was convenient

---

⁵ *Standish O'Grady*: (1766–1840) made Attorney General after Lord Kilwarden was killed by rebels on 23 July 1803.
  such an one as 'Plain John Campbell' ... has made in England: as Attorney General, Sir John Campbell (1779–1861) prosecuted the Chartist leaders of the Newport Rising for treason.
⁶ See Appendix 3 for O'Grady's address from the source from which Cleave copied most of his text, *The Life, Trial and Conversations of Robert Emmet, Esq., Leader of the Irish Insurrection of 1803: Also, the celebrated speech made by him on that occasion* (Manchester: John Doherty, 1836). *The Life, Trial and Conversations* was also read in Chartist circles and likely served as the basis for some performances. Other than omitted passages (which are all included in the appendix), the two accounts of the trial are nearly identical.
⁷ *Joseph Rawlins*: the Emmets' family attorney.
  brother at Brussels: Thomas Addis Emmet (1764–1827), Robert Emmet's older brother and important leader of the United Irishmen. Following the death of the Emmets' oldest brother Christopher Temple, Thomas gave up his career in medicine to pursue Christopher's occupation of law. Arrested in March 1798, he was released in June 1802 and exiled to the Netherlands.
⁸ *Austrian Netherlands*: a province of the Holy Roman Empire, located in present-day Belgium and Luxembourg; annexed by the French revolutionary government in 1795.
⁹ Cleave condenses testimonies of two witnesses into one account where *The Life, Trial and Conversations* gives both.
  Rathfarnham: village approximately four miles south of Dublin.
¹⁰ *John Fleming*: having fought with the rebels 23 July, agreed to give testimony against fellow conspirators.
  county Kildare: county west of Dublin.
  hostler: a groom who cares for stabled horses, usually at an inn.

to Mass Lane, where the rebel depot was, and to which the witness had free and constant access; having been in the confidence of the conspirators, and employed to bring them ammunition and other things.[11] He saw the persons there making pike-handles, and heading them with the iron part; he also saw the blunderbusses, firelocks, and pistols in the depot, and saw ball cartridges making there. Here the witness identified the prisoner at the bar, whom he saw in the depot for the first time on the Tuesday morning after the explosion in Patrick Street (that explosion took place on Saturday the 16th July).[12] The witness had opened the gate of the inn yard, which opened into Mass Lane, to let out Quigley, when he saw the prisoner, accompanied by a person of the name of Palmer;[13] the latter got some sacks from the witness to convey ammunition to the stores; and the prisoner went into the depot, where he continued almost constantly until the evening of the 23rd July, directing the preparations for the insurrection, and having the chief authority. He heard the prisoner read a little sketch, as the witness called it, purporting, that every officer, non-commissioned officer, and private, should have equally everything they got, and have the same laws as in France. Being asked what it was they were to share, the prisoner replied, 'what they got when they were to take Ireland or Dublin'. He saw green uniform jackets making in the depot by different tailors; one of whom was named Colgan. He saw one uniform in particular: a green coat laced on the sleeves and skirts, &c., and with gold epaulettes, like a gentleman's dress. He saw the prisoner take it out of a desk one day, and show it to all present (here the witness identified the desk, which was in court;) he also saw the prisoner at different times, take out papers, and put papers into the desk; there was none other in the store: Quigley also used sometimes to go to the desk. On the evening of the 23rd July, witness saw the prisoner dressed in the uniform above described, with white waistcoat and pantaloons, new boots, and cocked hat, and white feather. He had also a sash on him, and was armed with a sword and case of pistols. The prisoner called for a big coat (but did not get it) to disguise his uniform, as he said, until he went to the party that was to attack the castle.[14] Quigley, and a person named Stafford, had uniforms, like that of Emmet, but that they had only one epaulette: Quigley wore a white feather, and Stafford a green one.[15] Stafford was a

---

[11] *Mass Lane*: more commonly called Marshal Lane, the name used in *The Life, Trial and Conversations*.

[12] *explosion in Patrick Street*: explosion at a rebel depot during the manufacture of armaments – particularly fuses for rockets – which led to one conspirator's death.

[13] *Quigley*: Michael Quigley (1768–1849), leader of 1798 rebellion in county Kildare and a key lieutenant in 1803; a bricklayer by occupation; survived arrest by turning king's evidence.

[14] *the castle*: administrative centre of British government in Ireland.

[15] *Stafford*: Nicholas (c.1767–1816), a leader of the 1803 rising; had participated in the 1798 rebellion in his home county Kildare; afterward relocated to Dublin where he pursued his trade of baker.

baker in Thomas Street. About 9 o'clock the prisoner drew his sword, and called out, 'Come on, boys'; he sallied out of the depot, accompanied by Quigley and Stafford, and about 50 men, as well as the witness could judge, armed with pikes blunderbusses, pistols, &c. They entered Dirty Lane, and went from thence into Thomas Street. The prisoner was in the centre of the party. They began to fire in Dirty Lane, and also when they got into Thomas Street. The witness was with the party. The prisoner went, in the stores, by the name of Ellis. He was considered by all of them as the General and Head of the business; the witness heard him called by the title of General. In and out of the depot it was said they were preparing to assist the French when they should land. Quigley went in the depot, by the name of Graham.

Terence Colgan (the tailor named in the foregoing evidence), being sworn, deposed, that on the Sunday previous to the insurrection, he came to town from Lucan, where he lived; and having met with a friend, they went to Dillon's, the White Bull Inn, in Thomas Street, and drank, until the witness, overcome with liquor, fell asleep, when he was conveyed in this state of insensibility, into the depot in Mass Lane; and when he awoke the next morning, he was set to work, making green jackets and white pantaloons. He saw the prisoner there, by whose directions every thing was done; and who, he understood, was the chief. He, witness, also corroborated the general preparations of arms, ammunition, &c., for the insurrection.[16]

Patrick Fraser deposed, that as he was passing through Mass Lane, between the hours of 9 and 10 o'clock on the evening of Friday the 22nd of July, he stopped before the malt-stores, or depot, on hearing a noise therein which surprised him, as he considered it a waste house.[17] Immediately the door opened, and a man came forth who caught him, and asked him what he was doing there? The witness was then brought into the depot, and again asked what brought him there, or had he ever been there before? He said he had not. They asked him did he know Graham? He replied that he did not. One of the persons then said the witness was a spy, and called out to 'Drop him immediately;' – by which the witness understood that they meant to shoot him. They brought him up stairs and after some consultation they agreed to wait for some person to come in, who would decide what should be done with him. That person having arrived, he asked the witness if he knew Graham? – He replied, that he did not; a light was brought in at the same time, and the witness having looked about, was asked if he knew any one there? – he answered that he knew Quigley. He was asked where? – He replied, that he knew him five or six years ago at Maynooth, as a bricklayer, or

---

[16] Cleave omits a small amount of testimony of tailor Terence Colgan present in *Life, Trials, and Conversations*. See Appendix 3.

[17] *Patrick Fraser*: name changed (incorrectly) from Patrick Farrell in *Life, Trials, and Conversations*.

mason.[18] The witness then identified the prisoner as the person who came in and decided that he should not be killed, but that he should be taken care of, and not let out. The witness was detained there that night, and the whole of the next day (Saturday the 23rd), and was made to assist the different kinds of work; during that time he saw the prisoner, who appeared to have the chief direction. Here the witness described the weapons and missiles of various kinds; also the uniforms, and particularly that on the evening of the 23rd, he saw three men dressed in green uniforms, richly laced; one of whom was the prisoner, who wore two gold epaulettes; but the other two only one each.

On his cross-examination, in which the interrogatories were suggested by the prisoner, the only thing remarkable in the evidence of the witness was, that he heard a printed paper read; part of which was, that nineteen counties were ready to rise at the same time to second the attempt in Dublin. The witness also heard them say 'that they had no idea as to French relief, but would make it good themselves'. – To a question by the Court, the witness said, that he gave information of the circumstances deposed in his evidence, the next morning, to Mr Ormsby, in Thomas Street, to whom he was steward.[19]

Sergeant Thomas Rice and others proved the proclamation of the Provisional Government found in the depot; identified the desk which the prisoner used there; and a letter signed 'Thomas Addis Emmet'; and directed to 'Mrs Emmet, Milltown, near Dublin', beginning 'My dearest Robert'.[20]

Edward Wilson, Esq., recollected the explosion of gunpowder which took place in Patrick-street, previous to the 23rd of July; it took place on the 16th. He went there and found an apparatus for making gunpowder; was certain that it was gunpowder exploded. Proved the existence of a rebellious insurrection; as did also Lieutenant Brady. The latter added that on an examination of the pikes, which he found in Thomas-street, four were stained with blood on the iron part, and on one or two of them the blood extended half-way up the handle.

John Doyle, a farmer, being sworn, deposed to the following effect: – That on the morning of the 26th of July last, about two o'clock, a party of people came to his house at Ballymace, in the parish of Tallaght, seven miles from Dublin. He had been after drinking, and was heavy asleep; they came to his bedside, and stirred and called him, but he did not awake at once; when he did and looked up, he lay closer than before: they desired him to take some spirits, which he refused. They then moved him to the middle of the bed, and two of them lay down, one on each side of him. One of them said, 'you have a French general and a French

---

[18] *Maynooth*: town in county Kildare.
[19] Cleave omits some testimony of Patrick Fraser/Farrell that is present in *Life, Trials, and Conversations*. See Appendix 3.
[20] Cleave omits several minor witnesses present in *Life, Trials, and Conversations*. See Appendix 3.

colonel beside you, what you never had before'. For some hours the witness lay between asleep and awake. When he found his companions asleep he stole out of the bed, and found in the room some blunderbusses, a gun, and some pistols. The number of blunderbusses he believed were equal to the number of persons, who, on being collected at breakfast, amounted to fourteen. Here he identified the prisoner as one of those who were in the bed with him.

The witness then further stated that the prisoner, on going away in the evening, put on a coat with a great deal of lace and tassels (as he expressed it.) There was another person in a similar dress: they wore on their departure great coats over these. The party left his house between eight and nine o'clock in the evening, and proceeded up the hill. The next morning the witness found under the table, on which they breakfasted, one of the small printed proclamations, which he gave to John Robinson, the barony constable.[21]

Rose Bagnal, residing at Ballynascorney, about a mile further up the hill from Doyle's, proved that a party of men, fifteen in number, and whom she described similar to that of the preceding witness, came to her house on the night of the Tuesday immediately after the insurrection. Three of them wore green clothes, ornamented with something yellow; she was so frightened she could not distinguish exactly. One of them was called a general. She was not enabled to identify any of them. They left her house about nine o'clock the following night.

John Robinson, constable of the barony of Upper Cross, corroborated the testimony of the witness Doyle, relative to the small proclamation which he identified.

Joseph Palmer deposed that he was clerk to Mr Colville, and lodged at his mother's house, at Harold's Cross.[22] He recollected the apprehension of the prisoner, at his mother's house, by Major Sirr; and that he had lodged there the preceding spring, at which time, and when he was arrested, he went by the name of Hewitt. The prisoner came to lodge there, the second time, about three weeks before the last time; and was habited in a brown coat, white waistcoat, white pantaloons, hessian boots, and a black stock. The pantaloons were of cloth. Those who visited the prisoner inquired for him by the name of Hewitt. At the time he was arrested there was a label on the door of the house, expressive of its inhabitants. It was written by the witness, but the prisoner was omitted, at his request, because he said he was afraid government would take him up. – The prisoner in different conversations with the witness, explained why he feared being taken up. He acknowledged that he had been in Thomas Street on the night of the 23rd of July, and described the dress he wore on that occasion, part of which were the waistcoat, pantaloons, and boots already mentioned, and particularly his coat, which he described as a very handsome uniform.

---

[21] *barony constable*: police officer of a barony, a subdivision of a county.
[22] *Harold's Cross*: village on the outskirts of Dublin.

The prisoner had a conversation with witness about a magazine, and expressed much regret at the loss of the powder in the depot. The proclamations were likewise mentioned by the prisoner, and he planned a mode of escape, in the event of any attempt to arrest him, by going through the parlour window into the back house, and from thence into the fields. Here the witness was shown a paper, found upon a chair in the room in which the prisoner lodged, and asked if he knew whose handwriting it was – He replied, that he did not know, but was certain that it had not been written by any of his family, and that there was no other lodger in the house besides the prisoner.

The examination of this witness being closed, extracts from several papers found in the possession of Emmet were then read. We quote the following passage from one of his manifestos, as evidencing his generous feeling towards all classes and denominations: – viz.

> Orangemen, add not to the catalogue of your follies and crimes, already have you been duped to the ruin of the country in the legislative union with its tyrants; attempt not an opposition – return from the paths of delusion – return to the arms of your countrymen, who will receive and hail your repentance.[23] Countrymen, of all descriptions! let us act with union and concert. All sects, Catholic, Protestant, and Presbyterian, are equal and indiscriminately embraced in the benevolence of our object, &c.

Major Henry Charles Sirr, sworn and examined.[24] Deposed to the arrest of the prisoner, as follows: – I went, in the evening of the 25th of August, to the house of one Palmer. I had heard there was a stranger in the back parlour. I rode, accompanied by a man on foot; I desired the man to knock at the door. He did, and it was opened by a girl. I alighted, and ran directly into the back parlour. I saw the prisoner sitting at dinner: the woman of the house was there, and the girl who opened the door was the daughter of the woman of the house. I desired them to withdraw. I asked the prisoner his name; he told me his name was Cunningham. I gave him in charge to the man who accompanied me, and went into the next room to ask the woman and daughter about him; they told me his name was Hewitt. I went back, and asked how long he had been there? He said he came that morning. He had attempted to escape before I returned,

---

[23] *Orangemen*: members of the Orange Order, a political society founded in 1795 to maintain the Protestant ascendancy in face of efforts seeking Catholic Emancipation.
legislative union: union joining Britain and Ireland that came into effect 1 January 1801 and was passed as a response to the Irish Rebellion of 1798; dissolved the Irish Parliament while granting Ireland representation in the British upper and lower Houses (though only Protestant property-holders possessed the franchise). Emmet's condemnation of the union resonates with the Chartist call to repeal the Act of Union in their 1842 national petition.

[24] *Major Henry Charles Sirr*: (1764?–1841) town-major, or chief of police, in Dublin from 1798; conducted frequent raids and organised an extensive network of spies and informers to weaken the United Irishmen.

for he was bloody, and the man said he knocked him down with a pistol. I then went to Mrs Palmer, who said he had lodged there for a month. I then judged he was a person of some importance. When I first went in, there was a paper on the chair, which I put into my pocket. I then went to the canal bridge for a guard, having desired him to be in readiness as I passed by. I planted a sentry over him, and desired the non-commissioned officer to surround the house with sentries, while I searched it. I then examined Mrs Palmer, and took down her account of the prisoner, during which time I heard a noise, as if an escape was attempted. I instantly ran to the back part of the house, as the most likely part for him to get out at; I saw him going off, and ordered a sentinel to fire, and then pursued myself, regardless of the order. The sentry snapped, but the musket did not go off. I overtook the prisoner, and he said, 'I surrender!' I searched him, and found some papers upon him.

On the witness expressing concern at the necessity of the prisoner's being treated so roughly, he, the prisoner, observed, 'that all was fair in war'. The prisoner, when brought to the Castle, acknowledged that his name was Emmet.

The case for the Crown having closed, Emmet calmly declined to enter into any defence.

Mr Conyngham Plunket then rose to address the jury, previous to the judge's charge. To this, the prisoner's legal adviser very naturally objected, as the counsel for the crown could not be said to have a right to reply to evidence, when *no defence had been made*.

The *upright* and *impartial* Lord Norbury, however, decided otherwise; and thereupon, 'the father of all the Hannibals', as Cobbett called him, proceeded to deliver a speech of considerable length, and marked by the most disgusting tone of legal and political asperity.[25]

Plunket having thus earned the 'wages of infamy' – infamy, increased by the fact, that he had, but a short time previous, been the *friend* – the associate of Emmet; one, that to adopt the language of the latter, had, 'in their early intimacy actually *inculcated* into his mind those principles for which he was now about to offer up his life'.[26] This disgraceful exhibition over, Lord Norbury recapitulated the evidence to the jury.

---

[25] *proceeded to deliver a speech*: this speech is also omitted in *Life, Trials, and Conversations*. As no published accounts of performances of the trial reference it (unlike O'Grady's opening address), it likely was not part of Chartist productions.

[26] *'father of all the Hannibals' ... 'offer up his life'*: William Conyngham Plunket's participation in the prosecution of Emmet made him especially notorious to supporters of Irish independence because of his earlier support for United Irishman principles and his friendship with Thomas Addis Emmet at Trinity. Opposing the Act of Union, Plunket had said he would 'like the father of Hannibal, take my children to the altar and swear them to eternal hostility against the invaders of their country's freedom'. The radical journalist William Cobbett vociferously attacked Plunket for his betrayal, for which Plunket sued Cobbett for libel and recovered £500 damages.

The jury, without leaving the box, and as a matter of course, pronounced a verdict of – GUILTY!

CHAPTER VIII.

Glory to them that die in this great cause!
  Kings, Bigots, can inflict no brand of shame,
Or shape of death, to shroud them from applause: –
  No! – manglers of the martyr's earthly frame!
Your hangmen fingers cannot touch his fame.
  Still in your prostrate land there shall be some
Proud hearts, the shrines of Freedom's vestal flame.
  Long trains of ill may pass unheeded, dumb,
But vengeance is behind, and justice is to come.[27]
                                    CAMPBELL.

The immediate judgment of the court having been prayed upon the accused, and the customary proclamation for silence made, the Clerk of the Crown asked him, 'what he had to say why judgment of death and execution should not be awarded against him, according to law?'

ROBERT EMMET'S REPLY.

'MY LORDS,

'What have I to say that sentence of death should not be passed on me according to law? I have nothing to say that can alter your predetermination, nor that will become me to say, with any view to the mitigation of that sentence which you are here to pronounce, and I must abide by. But I have that to say, which interests me more than life, and which you have laboured (as was necessarily your office in the present circumstances of this oppressed country) to destroy – I have much to say, why my reputation should be rescued from the load of false accusation and calumny which has been heaped upon it. I do not imagine that, seated where you are, your minds can be so free from impurity, as to receive the least impression from what I am going to utter. I have no hopes that I can anchor my character in the breast of a Court constituted and trammeled as this is. I only wish, and that is the utmost I expect, that your Lordships may suffer it to float down your memories untainted by the foul breath of prejudice, until it finds some more hospitable harbour to shelter it from the storm by which it is at present buffeted.

'Were I only to suffer death, after being adjudged guilty by your tribunal, I should bow in silence, and meet the fate that awaits me without a murmur: but

---

[27] *Glory to them … justice is to come*: see Footnote 2.

the sentence of the law which delivers my body to the executioner, will, through the ministry of that law, labour in its own vindication, to consign my character to obloquy; for there must be guilt somewhere, whether in the sentence of the Court or in the catastrophe, posterity must determine. A man in my situation, my Lords, has not only to encounter the difficulties of fortune, and the forces of power over minds which it has corrupted or subjugated, but the difficulties of established prejudice: the man dies, but his memory lives; that mine may not perish – that it may live in the memory of my countrymen – I seize upon this opportunity to vindicate myself from some of the charge alleged against me. When my spirit shall be wafted to a more friendly port, – when my shade shall have joined the bands of those martyred heroes who have shed their blood on the scaffold and in the field, in defence of their country and virtue, this is my hope – I wish that my memory and name may animate those who survive me, while I look down with complacency on the destruction of that perfidious government which upholds its domination by blasphemy of the Most High; which displays its power over man as over the beasts of the forest; which sets man upon his brother, and lifts his hand, in the name of God, against the throat of his fellow who believes or doubts a little more than the government standard – a government steeled to barbarity by the cries of the orphans and the tears of the widows which it has made.

[*Here Lord Norbury interrupted Mr Emmet – saying, that the mean and wicked enthusiasts who felt as he did, were not equal to the accomplishment of their wild designs.*]

'I appeal to the immaculate God – I swear by the throne of Heaven, before which I must shortly appear – by the blood of the murdered patriots who have gone before me, that my conduct has been, through all this peril and through all my purposes, governed only by the conviction which I have uttered, and by no other view than that of their cure, and the emancipation of my country from the superinhuman oppression under which she has so long and too patiently travailed ; and I confidently and assuredly hope that, wild and chimerical as it may appear, there is still union and strength in Ireland to accomplish this noblest enterprise.

'Of this I speak with the confidence of immense knowledge, and with the consolation that appertains to that confidence. Think not, my Lords, I say this for the petty gratification of giving you a transitory uneasiness; a man who never yet raised his voice to assert a lie, will not hazard his character with posterity, by asserting a falsehood on a subject so important to his country, and on an occasion like this. Yes, my Lords, a man who does not wish to have his epitaph written until his country is liberated, will not leave a weapon in the power of envy, nor a pretence to impeach the probity which he means to preserve even in the grave to which tyranny consigns him.

[*Here he was again interrupted by the Court.*]

'Again I say, what I have spoken was not intended for your Lordships, whose situation I commiserate rather than envy – my expressions were for my countrymen; if there is an Irishman present, let my last words cheer him in the hour of affliction.

[*Here he was again interrupted; Lord Norbury said he did not sit there to hear treason.*]

'I have always understood it to be the duty of a judge, when a prisoner has been convicted, to pronounce the sentence of the law; I have also understood the judges sometimes think it their duty to hear with patience, and to speak with humanity, to exhort the victim of the laws, and to offer with tender benignity their opinion of the motives by which he was actuated in the crime, of which he was adjudged guilty. That a judge has thought it his duty so to have done, I have no doubt; but where is the boasted freedom of your institutions – where is the vaunted impartiality, clemency, and mildness of your courts of justice, if an unfortunate prisoner, whom your policy, and not your justice, is about to deliver into the hands of the executioner, is not suffered to explain his motives sincerely and truly, and to vindicate the principles by which he was actuated.

'My Lords, it may be a part of the system of angry justice to bow a man's mind by humiliation to the proposed ignominy of the scaffold; but worse to me than the proposed shame, or the scaffold's terrors, would be the shame of such foul and unfounded imputations as have been laid against me in this Court. You, my Lord, are a Judge; I am the supposed culprit; I am a man; you are a man also; by a revolution of power we might change places, though we never could characters. If I stand at the bar of this Court, and dare not vindicate my character, what a farce is your justice! If I stand at this bar, and dare not vindicate my character, how dare you calumniate it? Does the sentence of death, which your unhallowed policy inflicts on my body, also condemn my tongue to silence, and my reputation to reproach? Your executioner may abridge the period of my existence, but while I exist, I shall not forbear to vindicate my character and motives from your aspersions; and as a man to whom fame is far dearer than life, I will make the last use of that life in doing justice to that reputation which is to live after me, and which is the only legacy I can leave to those I honour and love, and for whom I am proud to perish.

'As men, my Lords, we must appear on the great day at one common tribunal, and it will then remain for the Searcher of all hearts to show a collective universe, who was engaged in the most virtuous actions or actuated by the purest motive – by the country's oppressors, or –

[*Here he was again interrupted, and told to listen to the sentence of the law.*]

'My Lords, will a dying man be denied the legal privilege of exculpating himself, in the eyes of the community, of an undeserved reproach, thrown upon him during his trial, by charging him with ambition, and attempting to cast away, for a paltry consideration, the liberties of his country? Why did your Lordships insult me – or rather, why insult justice, in demanding of me why sentence of death should not be pronounced? I know, my Lord, that form prescribes that you should ask the question; the form also prescribes the right of answering. This, no doubt, may be dispensed with, and so might the whole ceremony of the trial, since sentence was already pronounced at the Castle before your jury was empanelled. Your Lordships are but the priests of the oracle, and I submit: but I insist on the whole of the forms.

[*Here the Court desired him to proceed.*]

'I am charged with being an emissary of France.[28] An emissary of France! and for what end? It is alleged that I wished to sell the independence of my country! and for what end? Was this the object of my ambition? and is this the mode by which a tribunal of justice reconciles contradictions? No, I am no emissary, and my ambition was to hold a place among the deliverers of my country – not in power, nor in profit, but in the glory of the achievement. Sell my country's independence to France! and for what? Was it for a change of masters? No, but for ambition! O! my country, was it personal ambition that could influence me? Had it been the soul of my actions, could I not, by my education and fortune – by the rank and consideration of my family, have placed myself among the proudest of the oppressors? My country was my idol; to it I sacrificed every selfish, every endearing sentiment, and for it I now offer up my life. Oh God! No, my Lord; I acted as an Irishman, determined on delivering his countrymen from the yoke of a domestic faction, which is its joint partner and perpetrator in the patricide, for the ignominy of existing with an exterior of splendour and a consciousness of innate depravity; it was the wish of my heart to extricate my country from this doubly-rivetted despotism. I wished to place her independence beyond the reach of any power on earth – I wished to exalt her to that proud station in the world.

'Connection with France was, indeed, intended – but only as far as mutual interest would sanction or require. Were they to assume any authority inconsistent with the purest independence, it would be the signal for its destruction.[29] We sought aid, and we sought it as we had assurance we should obtain it – as auxiliaries in war, and allies in peace.

---

[28] *emissary of France*: Emmet indeed travelled to France in 1800 and worked to secure French aid for the 1803 rising. Government reports of the trial have Emmet's final speech vociferously denounce French tyranny whereas nationalist and radical versions (including Cleave's) present Emmet's remarks on France as much more tempered. United Irishmen not unreasonably assumed the government account had been falsified.

[29] *the signal for its destruction*: Cleave makes a significant change from *Life, Trials, and Conversations*, which reads 'the signal for their [i.e. the French's] destruction'. In Cleave's version, Emmet says if the French assumed 'authority inconsistent with the purest independence', it would lead to a dissolution of the alliance between Ireland and France, not necessarily to military conflict.

'Were the French to come as invaders or enemies, uninvited by the wishes of the people, I should oppose them to the utmost of my strength. Yes, my countrymen, I should advise you to meet them on the beach with a sword in one hand and a torch in the other; I would meet them with all the destructive fury of war, and I would animate my countrymen to immolate them in their boats before they had contaminated the soil of my country. If they succeeded in landing, and if forced to retire before superior discipline, I would dispute every inch of ground, burn every blade of grass, and the last entrenchment of liberty should be my grave. What I could not do myself, if I should fall, I should leave as a last charge to my countrymen to accomplish, because I should feel conscious that life, any more than death, is unprofitable when a foreign nation holds my country in subjection.

'But it was not as an enemy the succours of France were to land. I looked indeed for the assistance of France, but I wished to prove to France and to the world, that Irishmen deserved to be assisted; that they were indignant at slavery, and ready to assert the independence and liberty of their country.

'I wished to procure for my country the guarantee which Washington procured for America. To procure an aid which, by its example, would be as important as its valour – disciplined, gallant, pregnant with science and experience; who would perceive the good, and polish the rough points of our character; they would come to us as strangers and leave us as friends, after sharing our perils and elevating our destiny. These were my objects – not to receive new taskmasters, but to expel old tyrants; these were my views, and these only became Irishmen. It was for these ends I sought aid from France, because France, even as an enemy, could not be more implacable than the enemy already in the bosom of my country.

[*Here he was interrupted by the Court.*]

'I have been charged with that importance in the efforts to emancipate my countrymen as to be considered the keystone of the combination of Irishmen, or as your Lordship expressed it, 'the life and blood of the conspiracy'; you do me honour over much: you have given to the subaltern, all the credit of a superior. There are men engaged in this conspiracy who are not only superior to me, but even to your own computation of yourself, my Lord; before the splendour of whose genius and virtues I should bow with respectful deference, and who would think themselves disgraced to be called your friend; and who would not disgrace themselves, by shaking your blood-stained hand.

[*Here he was again interrupted.*]

'What, my Lord! shall you tell me on the passage to that scaffold, which that tyranny, of which you are only the intermediary executioner, has erected for my murder, that I am accountable for all the blood that has and will be shed in this struggle of the oppressed against the oppressor – shall you tell me this, and shall I be so very a slave as not to repel it!

'I do not fear to approach the Omnipotent Judge to answer for the conduct of my whole life, and am I to be appalled and falsified by a mere remnant of mortality![30] By you, too, who, if it were possible to collect all the innocent blood that you have shed in your unhallowed ministry, in one great reservoir, your Lordship might swim in it.

[*Here the Judge interfered.*]

'Let no man dare, when I am dead, to charge me with dishonour; let no man attaint my memory, by believing that I could have engaged in any cause but of my country's liberty and independence, or that I became the pliant minion of power in the oppression or the miseries of my countrymen. The proclamation of the Provisional Government speaks for our views; no inference can be tortured from it to countenance barbarity or debasement at home; or subjection, humiliation, or treachery, from abroad; I would not have submitted to a foreign oppressor, for the same reason that I would resist the present domestic oppressor. In the dignity of freedom I would have fought on the threshold of my country, and its enemy should only enter by passing over my lifeless corpse. And am I, who lived but for my country, and who have subjected myself to the dangers of the jealous and watchful oppressor, and the bondage of the grave, only to give my countrymen their rights, and my country her independence – am I to be loaded with calumny, and not suffered to resent or repel it! No, God forbid![31]

'If the spirits of the illustrious dead participate in the concerns and cares of those who are dear to them in this transitory life – O, ever dear, and venerable shade of my departed Father, look down with scrutiny upon the conduct of your suffering Son; and see if I have, even for a moment, deviated from those principles of morality and patriotism which it was your care to instil into my youthful mind, and for which I am now about to offer up my life.[32]

'My Lords, you are impatient for the sacrifice – the blood which you seek is not congealed by the artificial terrors that surround your victim; it circulates warmly and unruffled through the channels which God created for nobler purposes, but which you are bent to destroy, for purposes so grievous that they cry to Heaven. Be ye patient! I have but a few words more to say. I am going to my cold and silent grave: my lamp of life is nearly extinguished: my race is run: the grave opens to receive me, and I sink into its bosom! I have but one request to ask at my departure from this world; it is the charity of its silence! Let no man write my epitaph; for as no man who knows my motives dare now vindicate

---

[30] *to be appalled*: to be dismayed, shocked or terrified.
[31] Cleave Omits Norbury's final interruption of Emmet's speech, which provides context as to why Emmet begins speaking about his father. See Appendix 3.
[32] *departed Father*: the elder Robert Emmet (1729–1802); served as the Irish state physician from 1770.
suffering Son: Emmet calls to mind Jesus's appeal to God the Father in the garden of Gethsemane; see Matthew 26:39–42.

them, let not prejudice or ignorance asperse them. Let them and me repose in obscurity and peace, and my tomb remain uninscribed, until other times, and other men, can do justice to my character. When my country takes her place among the nations of the earth – then, and not till then – let my epitaph be written. I HAVE DONE!'

4

St John's Eve (1848) – Ernest Jones

Editor's introduction

In certain respects, Ernest Jones's gothic melodrama *St John's Eve* is atypical of Chartist drama. It is not explicitly political and neither concerns a historical event nor depicts a popular uprising. Furthermore, its use of stage technology and special effects evidence Jones's intention of having the play performed at commercial venues rather than by amateurs (in the event, however, it was never staged). At the same time, the play, published in 1848 in the 6*d*. Chartist journal the *Labourer*, speaks to the campaign's engagement with a diverse body of drama. Activists mounted plays from a wide range of genres, including many without obvious political import. Indeed, on at least two occasions Chartist benefits featured gothic works – *The Haunted Grange* and Matthew Lewis's *The Castle Spectre*.[1] Chartist literature too encompassed a more eclectic array of writing than the topical poetry and fiction upon which critics have generally focused – sentimental verse and nautical adventure tales existed side by side with Chartist songs and social problem fiction. Yet any literature appearing in a Chartist context could not help but take on new significance. The preface to the *Labourer* suggests that 'poetry and romance' should play a part in the movement's liberatory struggle:

> Our object has been more instruction than amusement – we, however, had one great goal before our eyes – the redemption of the Working classes from their thralldom – and to this object we have made the purpose of each article subservient. Yet, convinced that all which elevates the feelings or heightens the aspirations, can but strengthen the political power of a people, we have placed poetry and romance side by side with politics and history.[2]

How then would the inclusion of *St John's Eve* in a journal with this announced purpose have inflected the play's meaning? Edited jointly by Jones and Feargus

---

[1] 'Standard', *Northern Star* (1 June 1850), p. 3; 'The Longton Amateur Theatricals', *Northern Star* (1 February 1851), p. 5.
[2] 'Preface', *Labourer* (1847), vol. 1, p. 1.

O'Connor, the *Labourer* featured poetry and fiction alongside historical essays, dramatic criticism, and frequent editorials promoting the Chartist land plan. The latter initiative was a widely popular effort to establish model agricultural communities of resettled urban workers. Tens of thousands of weekly subscribers provided funds sufficient to purchase five estates, which stood as 'islands of practical Chartism' while projecting how society might be transformed by democratic rule.[3] In this context, *St John's Eve*'s pastoralism carries political weight. The action opens with the heroine Gemma longing to join a group of 'merry village-dancers' but knowing her despotic father resents her even looking 'on others' bliss and liberty', a stricture that parallels the demand she forswear her attachment to the penniless Rudolf in order to wed a rich stranger.[4] Aligned with the pastoral, romantic love seems to embody the freedom and joy of the villagers' festivity. In this light, the play's conclusion mobilises the utopian possibilities implicit in its comedic happy ending. For Louis James, 'the climactic resolutions' of melodrama express 'desire, not for the conservative status quo, but for a redemptive restoration of justice and harmony'.[5]

At the same time, the play's depiction of gender relationships is more fraught than much writing in the *Labourer*, especially essays and fiction supporting the land plan. Such work imagines the Chartist scheme restoring a traditional sexual division of labour as an antidote to the disruption that industrialisation has caused working-class family life.[6] Jones, on the other hand, emphasises the mercenary and suffocating aspects of Gemma's life with her father while casting doubt on what marriage to Rudolf will mean for the heroine. Even as the play encourages the reader's wish that Gemma escape her father's rule, the hero traffics in sorcery, expresses murderous desires, and nearly abandons his beloved (because he doubts her fidelity). Rudolf's compromised nature, his affinities with the villain, and the way the rivals act in concert to endanger the heroine thus problematise marriage as a proffered resolution. Union with the jealous and amoral hero threatens to recapitulate Gemma's life with her tyrannical parent or fulfil her fears of what existence with the villainous cavalier would represent. If these undercurrents disturb the play's pastoralism, they link the drama to Jones's fiction. Both his short stories and his explicitly feminist novel-

---

[3] Dorothy Thompson, *The Chartists* (New York: Pantheon, 1984), p. 306; Malcolm Chase, *Chartism: A New History* (Manchester: Manchester University Press, 2007), pp. 253, 256. On the Chartist land plan, see Chris Vanden Bossche, *Reform Acts* (Baltimore: Johns Hopkins University Press, 2014), pp. 75–84; Chase, *Chartism*, pp. 247–53 and passim; Thompson, *Chartists*, pp. 299–306.

[4] Ernest Jones, 'St. John's Eve: A Romantic Drama, in Three Acts', *The Labourer* (1848), vol. 3, pp. 203–4 (p. 189).

[5] Louis James, *The Victorian Novel* (Oxford: Blackwell Publishing, 2006), p. 91.

[6] See, for instance, the short story, 'The Charter and the Land', *Labourer* (1847), vol. 1, pp. 44–48.

las *Woman's Wrongs* criticise the patriarchal family while ironising plots of male rescue.[7]

The class politics of *St John's Eve* resemble that of many contemporary melodramas, which frequently cast the poor as virtuous and the rich as predatory. These stereotypes accorded well with the *Labourer*'s outlook, but they took on particular significance given Jones's own background. Indeed, the play's portrait of Gemma's wealthy but repressive home bears affinities to Jones's depiction of his childhood in 'The Better Hope', an autobiographical poem that Jones published in the *Northern Star* in September 1846: 'My father's house, in the lordly square, / Was cold in its solemn state, / And the sculptures rare – on the walls so bare, / Looked down with a quiet hate. / … And the dwellers were filled in that solemn place, / With the trance of a sullen pride; / For the scutcheoned grace – of a titled race, / Is the armour the heart to hide!'[8] Although Miles Taylor has shown how Jones's self-presentation distorted his background by exaggerating his wealth and connections, Jones's life circumstances were profoundly different from those of the great mass of Chartists. Consequently, his road-to-Damascus conversion to radical politics in winter 1845–46 generated much attention in the movement.[9]

Born in Berlin in January 1819 to a retired British officer and the daughter of a Kentish landlord, Jones grew up on a small estate in Holstein.[10] Educated in childhood by his father, he learned several languages, published a volume of juvenile verse, and studied at the 'aristocratic college of St. Michael'.[11] In 1838, Jones's family relocated to London. In the capital, the young man moved in literary and theatrical circles rather than among the social elite. Nevertheless, he attended the Queen's levee three times after being presented by a friend of his father's, the Duke of Beaufort.[12] His marriage to Jane Atherley in the summer of 1841 also elevated him socially by connecting him to a landed Kentish family.[13]

---

[7] Ernest Jones, 'The Pirates' Prize', *Labourer* (1848), vol. 3, pp. 143–49, 168–80; Ernest Jones, 'The Confessions of a King', *Labourer* (1847): vol. 1, pp. 83–87, 131–33, 211–18, 253–59; vol. 2, pp. 39–43, 67–77; Ernest Jones, *Woman's Wrongs*, in Ian Haywood (ed.), *Chartist Fiction*, vol. 2 (Burlington, VT: Ashgate, 2001). On plots of male rescue in Jones's fiction, see Gregory Vargo, *An Underground History of Early Victorian Fiction* (Cambridge: Cambridge University Press, 2018), pp. 156–59.

[8] Ernest Jones, 'The Better Hope', *Northern Star* (5 September 1846), p. 3.

[9] Miles Taylor, *Ernest Jones, Chartism, and the Romance of Politics* (Oxford: Oxford University Press, 2004).

[10] John Saville, 'Introduction', in John Saville (ed.), *Ernest Jones: Chartist. Selections from the Writings and Speeches of Ernest Jones* (London: Lawrence & Wishart, 1952), p. 13.

[11] *Ibid.*; Simon Rennie, *The Poetry of Ernest Jones: Myth, Song, and the 'Mighty Mind'* (New York: Legenda, 2016), p. 6.

[12] Manchester County Record Office, MS. f28189 J5/30, Ernest Jones Diary, 12 May 1840.

[13] Taylor, *Ernest Jones*, pp. 54–55.

On 8 March 1841, Jones entered the Middle Temple to prepare for a career in law, but his life already revolved around the theatre. Between 1840 and 1844, he saw at least fifty plays and operas (and maybe many more), mostly at the patent houses of the Haymarket, Covent Garden, and Drury Lane.[14] Moreover, in the winter of 1841–42, Jones became friends with some of the most important actors and playwrights of his time, whom he met through the salon of the novelist Lady Catherine Stepney.[15] He was particularly close to the tragedian Charles Kean, with whom he frequently dined and attended plays. Via Kean, Jones was able to sit in on rehearsals and watch performances backstage at the Haymarket. He also visited and occasionally entertained the actor-manager Charles Matthew (of Covent Garden), Matthew's wife and business partner Madame Vestris, and the playwright Dion Boucicault while knowing more loosely the actor William Oxberry, the famous tragedian William Macready, and the actor, playwright, and theatre-manager Charles Kemble.

These connections were professional as well as personal. Having published the novel *The Wood Spirit* in 1841 and fiction and poetry in magazines such as the *Court Journal*, Jones's ambitions turned to drama. He wrote at least eleven plays, including three tragedies, *The Student of Padua*, *The Folkungar* and *Lavagna*; a farce, *Love and the Monkey*; two operas (one adapted from his novel and another titled *The Syren*); and others that his diary fails to classify: *The Gray Man*, *King Death*, *The Libertin*, and *The Fairy of Montberceau*. Jones completed these (as well as *St John's Eve*) by early 1844, two years before he became a Chartist. It is impossible to know whether and how much Jones adapted *St John's Eve* before it appeared in the *Labourer*, though Simon Rennie's study of Jones's poetry shows how he made strategic revisions to his earlier verse for publication in an activist context.[16] No play other than *St John's Eve* survives, and none were ever staged, despite the writer's best efforts.[17] Jones offered *St John's Eve* to Drury Lane, the Adelphi, Prince's, and Covent Garden before 'Boyd, Moore, & Brooks' of the Lyceum accepted it over 'a most successful dinner' in February 1844.[18] The theatre, however, failed before production could begin, the circumstance to which Jones probably alludes in a March diary entry: 'If ever mortals suffered mental agonies I have today!!!!!!!!'.[19] Previously (in 1842), his opera

---

[14] Jones's diary records roughly fifty visits to theatres over these years (nearly fifty percent of which to the Haymarket). Jones also attended many performances and rehearsals backstage, and other theatre visits may have gone unrecorded due to gaps in the diary.

[15] Taylor, *Ernest Jones*, p. 56; Ernest Jones Diary passim.

[16] Rennie, *Mighty Mind*, passim.

[17] Ernest Jones, *The Student of Padua* (London: William Henry Cox, 1836). Ernest Jones Diary, 3 November 1842 and passim.

[18] Ibid., 17 September 1844. Thomas Serle, the manager of Drury Lane rejected the play, finding it ill-suited to the theatre given that the house was not a 'melodramatic company'. Quoted in Taylor, *Ernest Jones*, 58.

[19] Ernest Jones Diary, 1 March 1844; 'London Literary Chit-Chat', *Leeds Times* (30 March 1844), p. 6; 'Behind the Scenes', *Illustrated London News* (30 March 1844), p. 10.

The Wood Spirit had met a similar fate. Covent Garden and the ill-starred Lyceum agreed in turn to mount it, but each went bankrupt before it saw the stage.[20]

More serious difficulties lay ahead for Jones and his family. Speculating on a property he intended to rent out to tenants, Jones entered a contract for a Kentish estate for £57,000 in autumn 1844.[21] His failure to secure loans to complete the contract, however, led to a loss of £3,000 followed rapidly by bankruptcy, the loss of family possessions, and a drastic change in lifestyle. 'We have saved', Jones wrote in his diary, 'our clothing and a few pet books ... A great deal of china, glass, plate, and books have been claimed ... The other part of the things was sold by auction on the 22nd and realized about £300.'[22] After relocating to a cottage in Hampstead, Jones eventually found work as secretary to a railway company for four guineas per week.[23] His connection to the world of theatre largely ceased from this period.

It was in the wake of these tumultuous events that Jones threw in his lot with the Chartists. In his account of the circumstances, he happened upon a copy of the *Northern Star* in winter 1845 'and finding the political principles advocated harmonized with my own, I sought the executive and joined the Chartist movement'.[24] Jones's ascent through the ranks was rapid. By July 1846, he had been 'elected Permanent Chairman' of the 'Democratic Committee for Poland's Regeneration' and began lecturing in London on such diverse subjects as 'Poland and England', Byron's tragedy *Werner*, and 'Spring time thoughts'.[25] The following year he became sub-editor of the *Northern Star*, earning a yearly salary of £250, and spoke regularly at Chartist associations throughout Britain.[26] In 1848, he addressed the Kennington Common demonstration as a leading speaker and travelled to Paris as part of a three-person delegation to the French revolutionary government.

Despite Jones's activist role, his poetry was perhaps his greatest contribution to Chartism. Like many writers of humbler background, Jones was inspired by his participation in the cultural side of the movement. When the Chartist publisher Thomas MacGowan brought out his first book of verse, *Chartist Poems*, Jones remarked in his diary, 'I am pouring the tide of my songs over England, forming the tone of the mighty mind of the people.'[27] Besides this volume, Jones published more poems in the *Northern Star* than any other individual, some forty

---

[20] Ernest Jones Diary, 3 November 1842; 17 September 1844.
[21] *Ibid.*, 20 September 1844; Taylor, *Ernest Jones*, pp. 62–65.
[22] Ernest Jones Diary, 23 February 1845.
[23] *Ibid.*, 20 September 1845.
[24] Quoted in Saville, 'Introduction', p. 17.
[25] Ernest Jones Diary, 16 July 1846; 8 November 1846; 18 April 1847; 25 April 1847.
[26] Saville, 'Introduction', p. 24.
[27] Ernest Jones Diary, 8 October 1846.

between 1846 and 1848.[28] This corpus, in the words of Simon Rennie, 'inspired a generation of working-class radicals'.[29] Shaped by the German Romantics, whom Jones frequently translated for Chartist papers, Jones's verse contrasted the ills of industrial modernity with an idealised rural past.[30] *St John's Eve*, which unlike Jones's poetry and fiction has received almost no critical attention, also shows German Romantic influence, even as the hero's suspect qualities unsettle some of the oppositions present in Jones's verse.

Jones's involvement in politics came at a high cost. When the final act of *St John's Eve* appeared in the *Labourer*, Jones was beginning a term of two-years solitary confinement in Tothill Fields prison in London for a speech made at Bishop Bonner's Field in the capital in June 1848. Jones had urged his audience to 'organise ... and you will yet see the green flag floating over Downing-Street. Let that be accomplished, and John Mitchell will be brought back to his own country, and Sir [George] Grey, and Lord [John] Russell will be sent to exchange places with him.'[31] Arrested for sedition, Jones remained defiant, pledging that 'the last words on my lips now as the first when I issue from my cell, shall be: THE CHARTER AND NO SURRENDER'.[32] True to his promise, Jones emerged from prison to become the most important Chartist leader and publisher of the 1850s even as the movement contracted and splintered. He also continued to write poetry and fiction, publishing such seminal works as *Woman's Wrongs* and the anti-colonialist epic 'The New World, a Democratic Poem' (reissued in the wake of the Indian Rebellion of 1857 as *The Revolt of Hindostan; or, the New World*). Although Jones never returned to drama, his fiction borrowed freely from the plots, characters, and sensibility of the early Victorian stage.[33]

After enduring a decade of financial hardships, Jones quit radical journalism for a belated legal career, in which he took a number of political cases, representing unions and radical defendants, including the Irish Fenians.[34] Active around the agitation for the Second Reform Act of 1867, he remained popular as a speaker and politician until his death in winter 1869. The 50,000–100,000 mourners who attended his funeral came to pay tribute not only to an activist and politician but to Chartism's most important poet and writer.

---

[28] Rennie, *Mighty Mind*, p. 6; Anne Janowitz, *Lyric and Labour in the Romantic Tradition* (Cambridge: Cambridge University Press, 1998), p. 179.
[29] Rennie, *Mighty Mind*, p. 41.
[30] Ibid., pp. 38–40; Taylor, *Ernest Jones*, pp. 19–31.
[31] 'Arrest of Chartist Leaders', *Northern Star* (10 June 1848), p. 5.
[32] Ernest Jones, 'To the Chartists', *Northern Star* (1 July 1848), p. 1.
[33] Vargo, *Underground History*, pp. 148–71.
[34] Saville, 'Introduction', p. 77.

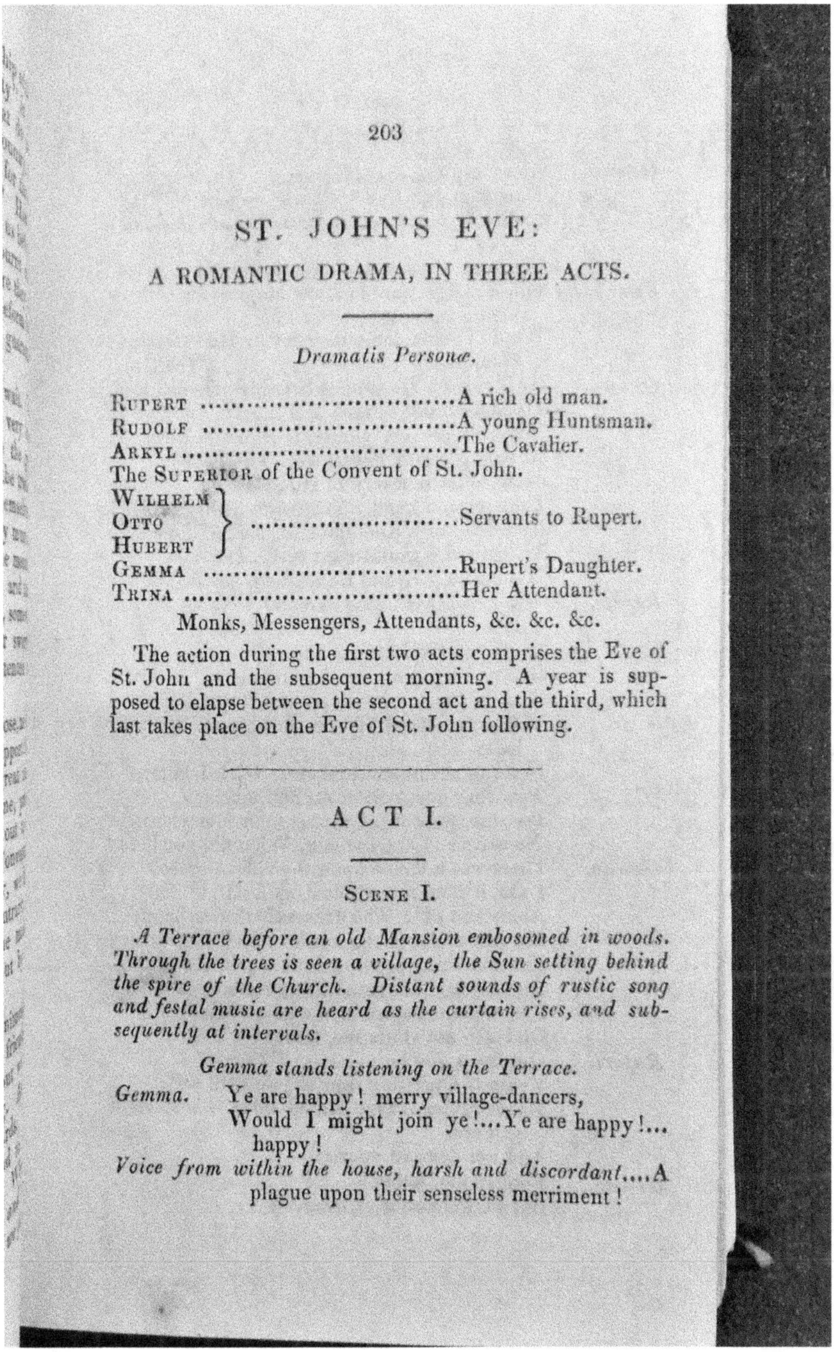

203

ST. JOHN'S EVE:

A ROMANTIC DRAMA, IN THREE ACTS.

Dramatis Personæ.

RUPERT .... A rich old man.
RUDOLF .... A young Huntsman.
ARKYL .... The Cavalier.
The SUPERIOR of the Convent of St. John.
WILHELM ⎫
OTTO   ⎬ .... Servants to Rupert.
HUBERT   ⎭
GEMMA .... Rupert's Daughter.
TRINA .... Her Attendant.

Monks, Messengers, Attendants, &c. &c. &c.

The action during the first two acts comprises the Eve of St. John and the subsequent morning. A year is supposed to elapse between the second act and the third, which last takes place on the Eve of St. John following.

ACT I.

SCENE I.

A Terrace before an old Mansion embosomed in woods. Through the trees is seen a village, the Sun setting behind the spire of the Church. Distant sounds of rustic song and festal music are heard as the curtain rises, and subsequently at intervals.

    Gemma stands listening on the Terrace.
Gemma.   Ye are happy! merry village-dancers,
            Would I might join ye!...Ye are happy!...
            happy!
*Voice from within the house, harsh and discordant....*A
            plague upon their senseless merriment!

Figure 4.1 The opening of *St John's Eve* as it appeared in the *Labourer*, 1848 (vol. 3), p. 203

ST JOHN'S EVE: A ROMANTIC DRAMA, IN THREE ACTS.

Dramatis Personae:
Rupert — A rich old man.
Rudolf — A young Huntsman.
Arkyl — The Cavalier.
The Superior of the Convent of St John.
Wilhelm / Otto / Hubert — Servants to Rupert.
Gemma — Rupert's Daughter.
Trina — Her Attendant.
Monks, Messengers, Attendants, &c. &c. &c.

The action during the first two acts comprises the Eve of St John and the subsequent morning.[1] A year is supposed to elapse between the second act and the third, which last takes place on the Eve of St John following.

---

[1] *Eve of St John*: 23 June; day before the Catholic feast day of Saint John the Baptist.

ACT I
SCENE I

A Terrace before an old Mansion embosomed in woods. Through the trees is seen a village, the Sun setting behind the spire of the Church. Distant sounds of rustic song and festal music are heard as the curtain rises, and subsequently at intervals.

(Gemma stands listening on the Terrace.)

GEMMA. Ye are happy! merry village-dancers,
   Would I might join ye! ... Ye are happy! ... happy!
     (Voice from within the house, harsh and discordant) ... A plague upon their senseless merriment!
GEMMA. Alas! my father chides again. Ah, me ...
   Dear Rudolf! Rudolf! must we part?
     (Music and bursts of laughter behind the scene.)
                      Again! ...
   The voice of mirth sounds strangely to mine ear.
     (Voice from within) ... The Caitiffs know no pleasure without noise.[2]
   Would I could damp their joy; ... Ho! Gemma! Gemma! *(Calling.)*
GEMMA. He'll chide! He cannot bear his prisoned bird
   To look on others' bliss and liberty.
   'Tis hard, so very young, to sigh and weep
   At seeing others' happiness ... Yon sounds
   Seem bitter mockery of my solitude
   That voice, a knell ... Yet 'tis my father's voice!
   Rudolph! my Rudolph! for the last time here
   I promised I would meet thee ... and, alas!
   'Tis but to give and take a long farewell.
RUPERT. *(Entering from the house in anger.)* What do you here?
   Mark you the loitering throng

---

[2] *Caitiffs*: contemptuous, miserable wretches.

Gazing in gaping wonder from afar,
Because 'tis strange to see old Rupert's child?
While you stand here, and with your drooping looks
Seem to accuse me to them. Oh! I know,
That they speak ill of *me* and pity *you*,
Because, forsooth, I thwart your idle whims.
No matter! Let them talk. What did you here?

GEMMA. There was a dance upon the village green,
I saw it from my window, as I sat
Alone and sad. The dancers looked so happy ...
My heart beat to the music ... Oh! forgive me!
For something prompted me to join the throng,
And I could not resist ... but came to gaze
Like a pained spirit at the gate of Heaven.
Oh! Do not chide me, father!

RUPERT. Out upon you![3]
Yourself forgetting thus to join with serfs.
My daughter ... You should think whose child you are,
And not demean yourself.

GEMMA. Forgive me, father!
But we were once as *those*.

RUPERT. What now? ... We? ... we?
That I have raised myself from humbler state,
Through dint of talent and of energy,
Can be no reason I should sink again.
Peace! well befits it for a promised bride
To dance with serfs upon a village green!

GEMMA. Speak not of that strange man. I love him not.

RUPERT. You love him not. Ha! ha! and do you think
That is an argument to urge to me?
You think to cover every childish whim
With those unmeaning words ... *I love him not!*
You have not seen him since your early childhood;
When ye were affianced. Many years
He has been absent in the Indies far,[4]
And won high honours and a princely wealth.

---

[3] *Oh! Do not ... Out upon you!*: Jones commonly uses iambic pentameter lines split between two lines of dialogue, but does not follow the standard lineation of such lines (where the second line would begin directly below where the first line ends).

[4] *Indies*: unspecified whether India or the West Indies; the former is perhaps more likely considering the emphasis on the locale's exoticness and wealth, Orientalist stereotypes commonly applied to India.

GEMMA. The *rank* and *wealth* of man are in his *soul*.
RUPERT. What still that vagrant Rudolf in thy head?
GEMMA. No! In my *heart*.
RUPERT. Then I'll erase him thence!
   To kill thy darling and rebellious love,
   Learn: thine affianced comes across the sea
   To claim thee as his bride. My letters say,
   The ship that bears him hitherward, has sailed,
   And in a month we may expect him here.
   Therefore I warn thee.
GEMMA. He too once was poor
   And you opposed *him* not.
RUPERT. So *we* were then;
   We're wealthy now.
GEMMA. And Rudolf may become so.
RUPERT. Become! No! *He* is not the man for that.
   He's far too *proud*, girl! ever to grow *rich*.
   Who would grow rich, must *stoop* to pick the gold,
   The proud man *scorns* to *lift* from the *low mire*.
   But now no more of this, and have a care
   Thy looks be brighter ... I hate moody brows.
     (*Exit to the house.*)
GEMMA. His heart may change. Oh! heaven change his heart.
   He is gone. The rapid sun sinks low and wanes,
   The village dance is o'er, and Rudolf comes not.
   Poor Rudolf! Playmates in our childish days,
   Must we be strangers now? I promised here
   To meet him, where so oft in happier hour
   We met. He comes not, and my heart is breaking.
     (*She seats herself on a stone bench, and sings the following song to her lute.*)

   POOR BIRD[5]

     At break of day – its matin lay[6]
     A bird all blithely sang and gay;
     Ere noon its note had died away!
         Poor bird! Poor bird!

---

[5] This song has been set to music by Benedict. [Footnote in original].
  Benedict: Sir Julius Benedict (1804–85), German-born composer and conductor.

[6] *matin lay*: a morning song.

It has no nest – to take its rest,
It roves all homeless and unblest
Far from the spot it loves the best.
  Poor bird! Poor bird!

Its wings wave slow ... and weary grow,
It wounded heart beats faint and low,
Is there no resting place for woe?
  Poor bird! Poor bird!

It pleads in vain ... In plaintive strain;
Will none have pity on its pain
And guide it to a home again?
  Poor bird! Poor bird!

 (*Rudolf has entered during the last stanza. He is attired in the dress of a huntsman, with a plume and hanger.*)[7]

RUDOLF. Sweet Gemma! This is kind to let me see you.
 You weep ... sad augur! Have we then no hope?
GEMMA. In heaven! That may change my father's heart,
 And in thy Gemma, who will never yield
 Unto another's love.
RUDOLF. Sweet girl! I came
 While yet I may, for soon the time approaches
 When I must hasten hence to distant lands,
 To seek a fortune, that may make thee mine.
 But much I fear it is a hopeless quest.
 Oh! That the noblest still must be defiled!
 That gold should measure honour, love, and faith!
 Out on the world! We are at war together!
GEMMA. Thou art most strange. Forsooth, a look so stern
 I never saw thee wear.
RUDOLF. Times alter men.
 Oft have I seen the meek, defenceless lamb
 Turn fierce as tiger in extremity.
 Believe me, Gemma! there are times, in which
 Men change to fiends. Methinks they are at hand.
GEMMA. Oh, Rudolf! Rudolf! Art thou come to this?
RUDOLF. Nay! Fear not, sweetest! For whate'er betide,
 To thee I'll aye be gentle, though the world
 Turn what is blood in me to fire.

---

[7] *plume*: a feather; *hanger*: a short sword.

GEMMA. Beware!
>For thoughts like these lead never unto good.
>Soft mercy dwells above, that, if we trust,
>From darkest fortunes lifts to brightest ends:
>But if self-willed, we grasp our fate's strange woof,[8]
>We rush but unto ruin and destruction!
>—— Thou hearest not ... Art buried in deep thought ...
>—— Thy brow is dark and frowning!

RUDOLF. (*Starting as from a dream.*) Should we part
>Then I may ne'er see thee again ... perchance
>I never may return ... and absent ... thou ...
>Mayest fall a sacrifice to tyrant power!
>I hence ... what may not happen? ... Oh! thy father
>Spurned me. He reviled me. Slandered foully!
>Girl! Were he not thy father!! ... Ha! that word
>Sends the hot blood all cold back to my heart.
>Thy father ... Peace! peace! ... Yes ... He is thy father.
>>(*Pause.*)
>And he alone is hindrance to our union.
>Gemma! Thy father's very, very old.

GEMMA. (*Anxiously.*) He is ... and what of that?

RUDOLF. Why ... nothing ... but ... (*embarrassed.*)

GEMMA. But what?

RUDOLF. He is infirm.

GEMMA. What thought is that?
>Rudolf! I scarce can think ...

RUDOLF. He numbers eighty winters, does he not?

GEMMA. He does, may heaven increase them!

RUDOLF. At such age
>Life is uncertain, and a sudden blast
>Will oft extinguish its fast failing lamp.

GEMMA. (*With growing anxiety.*) Rudolf! I know thee not.
>What mean thy words?

RUDOLF. Ay! He may die ere long, and then ... and then ...

GEMMA. (*Starting up.*) Rudolf, farewell! if e'er again such words
>Shall pass thy lips, we part to meet no more!
>To build one's fortunes on another's death,
>Is murder, though it lack the hand and steel!

---

[8] *fate's strange woof*: reference to mythological motif that describes the Fates as three female figures, who spin and cut the threads of human destiny. *woof*: in weaving, threads crossing the warp at right angles.

And 'tis my father! Rudolf! ... 'Tis my father!
   (*Exit Gemma.*)
RUDOLF. (*Calling after her.*) Forgive me, Gemma! dearest Gemma! Stay.
I meant it not ... 'Twas but an idle thought.
Oh! she is gone, and I am all alone
With but a busy devil prompting here.
   (*Touching his heart.*)
I do not *wish* him dead! No! Heaven's my judge!
This moment would I throw my life away,
To save his, were it perilled.
(*Hesitatingly.*) No! no! no!
Sure am I that I do not wish him dead ...
I merely thought, IF it pleased heaven above
To TAKE his life ... we might be happy then!
   (*Pause.*)
Ah! I feel uneasy! wretched! wretched!
I fear me that I know not mine own heart.
   (*He crosses the stage in visible agitation.*)
Gemma is gone in anger ... and the world
Grows dark and darker round me ... Life's stars wane!
Men scowl and frown upon me ... and for *why?*
Oh, yes! I have the greatest fault ... I'm poor!
Is there no justice yonder in high heaven?
   (*With clenched hands lifted upwards.*)

>   (*It has been growing darker and darker gradually, so that it is almost night. At the last words of Rudolf a tall figure, veiled in a dark flowing robe, with overshadowing cap and sable plume, steps forth from among the trees, and advances behind the speaker. An expression of triumph gleams upon his countenance, which is pale as that of one long buried.*)

STRANGER. (*Aside.*) Ah! I have watched thee long and tracked thee far,
   And seldom until now, by word or sign,
   Hast thou yet given me the power of nearing thee!
   Henceforth thou shalt be mine. The time is come.
      (*Rudolf, who has stood buried in deep thought, turns suddenly, and starts on beholding the Stranger.*)
RUDOLF. Ha! Who art thou?
STRANGER. Dost recognise me not? (*His manner is at once contemptuous and familiar.*)
   A brother student of your younger days ...
   An old ... a very good old friend of yours.
   Dost not remember me?

RUDOLF. I never saw thee!
STRANGER. Oh! You but forget. I'll prove it to you.
   Do you remember when into the church
   You stole, and broke the sculptured cherubim?
   I WAS WITH YOU THEN!
RUDOLF. Yes! Heaven forgive me!
   But you I can remember not
STRANGER. Perchance, –
   Friendship has a slippery memory.
   I was with you ne'ertheless. Again,
   You bore a young maid from her father's house!
   I WAS WITH YOU THEN!
RUDOLF. But, moved at heart,
   Pure I restored her to her father's arms.
STRANGER. Ha! Ha! you did! I was NOT with you then!
   But I was with you, when one night you won
   His pittance from a gambler. I WAS THERE!
   You drove him to despair and self-sought death!
   I stood behind your chair that live-long night.
   I prompted you the cards – *I* shook the dice! –
   You ruined him!
RUDOLF. Good Heaven! what bitter pangs
   It cost me: But the ill-won spoil I gave
   Unto a widowed mother.
STRANGER. For the which
   Some robbers came and murdered her. Ha! ha!
RUDOLF. 'Tis strange that I should not remember you.
STRANGER. Oh! there are many strange things in the world.
RUDOLF. And where hast been these years?
STRANGER. Far – very far.
   I have returned in secret, and I feel
   Death's hand upon me; – you do need a friend.
RUDOLF. I do – and have none.
STRANGER. I will be one, then.
   But tell thou none I have returned again,
   For *none* have seen me – I have *spoke with none!*
   For I have enemies in yonder convent,
   And they might seek me out *with mass and bell*,
   And drive me hence!
RUDOLF. Thy speech, thy manner's strange! –
   The bell and mass *are only for the dead!*

STRANGER. Oh, heed not that. Mark! you alone of all
   Have seen me. Keep your secret *with* the grave.
RUDOLF. *With* the grave?
STRANGER. Or *like* the grave. But tell me of your life –
   How fares your suit with Gemma?
RUDOLF. Haplessly.
STRANGER. I know it, and your rival hastens here,
   While you go hence to mend your fortunes. Ha!
   Your rival thanks you for thus flying him.
RUDOLF. 'Sdeath! How! – But Heaven! How did'st thou learn that,[9]
   Saying but now *thou had'st seen none, save me?*
STRANGER. Oh! secrets soon reach even strangers' ears,
   And Common news are scarce thought worth the telling.
   Rudolf! methinks your suit stands *not* so bad:
   Her father's old, and *ere the year may die!*
RUDOLF. Ha! think you that as well?
STRANGER. *Dost wish him dead?*
RUDOLF. How darest thou? – it were a thought profane.
STRANGER. But were he dead your fortunes were more bright, –
   You would be happy.
RUDOLF. *But I wish it not.*
STRANGER. Say, would you at the least not wish to know
   Whether this year bringeth his death or not?
   For it might spare much sorrow, – nay, might save
   Your life from misery! with you away,
   Gemma may pine and die – may yield to force, –
   She may be wronged – who knows? – while, were you here
   All this might be avoided, and perchance
   The old man dies within the year! Too late
   You would return, the evil had been done!
   Now, could you know whether old Rupert died,
   This endless, helpless sorrow might be spared.
RUDOLF. Oh! could I know! – But 'tis unhallowed quest.
STRANGER. Nay, the mere knowledge does not cause his death.
   And might thus save long years of agony;
   I could inform you how to gain it.
RUDOLF. (*Eagerly.*) How?
   Where? – Tell me! tell me!
STRANGER. Nay! – it were unsafe; –
   You are not bold enough to dare it.

---

[9] *'Sdeath*: His death (i.e. Christ's); a mild oath.

RUDOLF. Try!
STRANGER. Then listen: This is *St John's holy eve*.
  Repair at midnight to the village church,
  But enter not; – rest thee upon a tomb,
  With grave-earth on thy breast, and as the clock
  Strikes twelve, thou'lt mark a gleam illume the aisles,
  And phantom funeral-service peal within.
  Then through the gate, that to the hamlet leads,
  Will enter one by one the shrouded ghosts
  Of those, who in the year shall slumber there!
RUDOLF. Ha! but 'tis sinful!
STRANGER. How men's coward hearts
  Apply dread words to things, they know not why.
  Knowledge is not sinful.
RUDOLF. It was erst so.[10]
  And then 'twill drive me mad. Oh! should I see –
STRANGER. Perchance *thyself!* Does that arouse thy fears?
  But rest assured men see not their own ghosts.
RUDOLF. Dost think, that I fear death? ... No! But the dead.
STRANGER. Then rest contented, coward, with thy fears!
  Seek not to fathom glories that may come!
  Shrink from the chance of misery, drag on
  The lagging year in agony and care ...
  I leave thee!
RUDOLF. Stay! I'll brave it, by my life!
STRANGER. (*Aside.*) Say by thy soul! 'Tis nearer to the mark.[11]
RUDOLF. Wilt thou be there?
STRANGER. *I'll not be far away!*
  From this hour on thou shalt not be alone.
    (*Exit Stranger.*)
RUDOLF. Yes! I will go! ... I can bear *this* no longer.
  This dread uncertainty will drive me mad.
  I feel it! ... But I must see Gemma first.
  She went in anger, and I cannot brave
  The fearful hour with Gemma's anger on me.
  I've cast! I will be there ... I must ... I will.

---

[10] *Knowledge ... erst so*: see Genesis 2:17: 'But of the tree of the knowledge of good and evil, thou shalt not eat of it: for in the day that thou eatest thereof thou shalt surely die' (*King James Version*).
[11] *Say by thy soul*: evokes Goethe's *Faust*, in which Faust sells his soul to the devil Mephistopheles.

Down! restless heart! Thou shalt not hinder me.
(*Exit Rudolph.*)

SCENE II

Chamber in Rupert's House. Rupert and Otto.

RUPERT. Come hither, Otto! I would speak with you. You know I always have been kind to you.

OTTO. (*Aside.*) Yes. When you'd a point to gain.

RUPERT. And now I fain would render you some service.

OTTO. (*Aside.*) Ay! There it comes. (*Aloud.*) What do you want me to do for you, Sir?

RUPERT. Oh! Nothing, friend!

OTTO. (*Aside.*) Oh! It's to come out by degrees. It's no joke, then.

RUPERT. There has been a festival this evening in the village. You were there? Merry? Eh?

OTTO. Yes! … (*Aside.*) … I wonder what he's driving at?

RUPERT. Now, did they talk of me?

OTTO. Oh yes! Of nothing else!… (*Aside.*) … Here's a capital opportunity of telling him some pleasant truths.

RUPERT. Caitiffs! What said they?

OTTO. Oh! I dare not tell you.

RUPERT. Nay, but I command.

OTTO. (*With eagerness and warmth.*) Well, then, but recollect! *I* say it not, *they* said it … Well, one said, 'Otto! your master's an old scoundrel!' … Another, 'The upstart villain!' … Another, 'The miser, who has coined orphans' and widows' tears, and keeps them locked up in chests to be the curse of whoever inherits them.'

RUPERT. Hounds! Every ducat shall be buried with me.[12]

OTTO. 'Old anatomy! who crawls about the incarnation of a foggy November's day!' … 'Tyrannous old croaking monster!' …

RUPERT. How? Slave!

OTTO. Oh! *I* say it not. It is but what *they* say. 'Libel on white hairs, who can do nothing, but mar the happiness of others' …

RUPERT. Sirrah! Have done, I say! I'll hear no more.[13]

---

[12] *ducat*: coin, from the name of a Venetian gold coin used widely in Europe and beyond until the nineteenth century.

[13] *Sirrah*: expression of contempt for a man or boy.

OTTO. 'Who seems to delight in his child, as fiends would create an angel to have the pleasure of torturing it.' ...

RUPERT. Hold! villain! Hold!

OTTO. (*Aside.*) Oh! that was delicious! I have not had an opportunity of telling him my mind for a long time.

RUPERT. The foul-mouthed hounds! Now, Otto. There they lie ... I love my child ... For her I've won, for her I've kept my wealth ... For I too could have spent it in fair joys! But I will not see all this labour lost ... To fall into the first young gallant's hands ... with whom my child may chance to fall in love! ... No! no! She must have one who will prize both ... my *daughter* and my *gold*, my *gold* and *daughter*! ... Aye. Rudolf shall not have them, if I slay him. Here! Otto! listen! from what I have heard I much suspect that they will meet tonight ... Now, then, *watch Rudolph well where'er he goes*, and tell me whether he comes near my daughter! ... I will reward you, Otto! I will reward you! ... To-morrow I will give you ... ugh! ... ugh! ... ugh!
  (*Exit Rupert.*)

TRINA. (*Enters from opposite side.*) Hist! Is nobody here? No. That's right!¹⁴

OTTO. That's right ... Why, what do you call ME?

TRINA. Why ... Otto ...

OTTO. Oh, no; of course, I'm nobody ... look at me! ... I'm nobody! ... Feel me! I'm nobody! Why, I declare, you're right ... I'm quite *platonic*! ... as father Andrew said, when he was caught with ...

TRINA. Now, don't be a fool, Otto! for I want you to do something for me.

OTTO. Oh! Then that won't do at all!

TRINA. Yes! And my young mistress too!

OTTO. Oh, dear! The deuce she does!

TRINA. Yes! You see, because she has parted with Rudolf in anger. Do you understand?

OTTO. Oh yes! Now I understand you perfectly.

TRINA. Well, I said I knew I could trust you.

OTTO. To be sure you can.

TRINA. Then she told me to beg you to carry this letter from her to Rudolph ...

OTTO. Well, is that all?

TRINA. Yes! You'll do it for *me*, won't you?

OTTO. Oh, ah! ... Hum! ... Why, yes. If I'm rewarded.

TRINA. For love of me!

OTTO. Then your love must reward me ... This comes capitally, I *am* to hunt after Rudolf ... and now I've got something to say to him when I've found him.

---

¹⁴ *Hist!*: expression demanding silence or for a person to listen.

TRINA. Now, why don't you hurry? Haste, good Otto! – go! ... Why don't you go!

OTTO. Because I can't. (*With a tender leer.*)

TRINA. Why can't you?

OTTO. The *maggot* is held by the pole, you know ... Now, then, give me one kiss before I go.[15]

TRINA. No! not for another month.

OTTO. Oh! won't you?

TRINA. No! not for a year.

OTTO. Oh! won't you?

TRINA. No; not as long as I live.

OTTO. Well, never mind; good by ... (*Trina pouts.*) ... Well, what's the matter?

TRINA. You needn't be off in such a great hurry, I should think.

OTTO. Oh! but I am; you told me, you know.

TRINA. Stay; I'm very ill.

OTTO. I'll send the doctor.

TRINA. I'm dying!

OTTO. I'll run for him.

TRINA. I'm dead.

OTTO. Well, then, I'll prescribe for you. I carry my medicine about with me ... *First dose*: An insinuating look; if that has no effect, repeat the dose, and add a gentle pressure of the hand ... (*Takes her hand.*) ... Do you feel any better.

TRINA. Get away; I am very ill, indeed.

OTTO. That failing, stronger remedies become necessary. *Dose third*: Application of arm round the waist, a squeeze, and some soft nonsense. Do you feel any better now, my dear?

TRINA. Oh! I'm fainting; leave me; I shall fall.

OTTO. Oh! Then the case is becoming desperate. A kiss is absolutely necessary ... (*Kissing her.*) ... That's it. Do you feel easier now? ... Well, good by; I'll send the doctor.

TRINA. Otto, suppose we were to look for the doctor together?

OTTO. Come then, quickly; for now it's kill or cure.

(*Exeunt.*)

---

[15] *maggot ... the pole*: likely reference to fishing.

SCENE III

Bright moonlight. The village Churchyard. The Church in the background. Church porch on L. Gate to Churchyard on R. Tombs thickly scattered about. The Stranger standing beside a low, flat tomb in the centre of the stage.

STRANGER. This is the spot whence springs thy ruin, Rudolf!
   This is the stone on which he'll cast him down.
   It suits me well, for here a murderer lies,
   Whose crime, unproved, still yields a holy grave;
   Thence in the Churchyard desecrate I'm free.

   Now I'll send slumber o'er thee, Rudolf, call
   Such phantoms o'er thy sleep, will drive thee mad;
   Kill thy fond Gemma's heart with false alarms,
   And make ye both turn rebels unto heaven.

   For I too loved his Gemma – might have won her –
   He thwarted me – despair drove me to sin.
   I stand all dedicate to heavenly wrath,
   But to eternal Justice cry: forbear!
   They're guilty, for they made me what I am.
   And thence it is permitted me to tempt them.
   Now, Powers of Evil, listen to my voice.

   By slanderer's smile at calumny's success.
   Rise to the work of Evil! Rise! Arise!

     (*The moon is overcast. Darkness.*)

   Heaven veils its light: then hell begins to see.
   By the fine sophistry that lures to sin.

     (*Thunder under the earth, deep and faint.*)

   They answer from beneath me, but as yet
   Loud thunders rolling upward from deep hell
   Stay half-way on their course. Oh! Rise, Arise.
   By the dark thought upon a murderer's heart
   Before he strikes his victim, Rise, Arise.

     (*Groans and shrieks under the earth, loud thunder.*)

   Ye shriek; then I disturb your sleep of anguish,
   And ye will come anon. Now, by the terror
   That walks beside the culprit to the scaffold.

> (*Laughter, loud and ascending, from under the earth, echoed from the tombs and rocks.*)

Ye laugh. Oh, then ye feel that ye may come.
Come! By the black, but deeply-burning fire,
That drops its pulses through incestuous veins.

> (*The graves open, and the chorus of laughter sounds as on the stage. A light is seen gleaming against the grave-stones, thrown upward through their openings. Lightning wheels around the church.*)

By the last death-pang of an atheist.

> (*Sheets of fire flash upward through the open graves – the storm bursts – the form of the murderer rises slowly out of the grave by which the Stranger stands, and a fiend peers out of every tomb.*)

THE PHANTOM. Thou mayest be spared, but 'tis on one condition.
(*The form begins to sink.*)
STRANGER. (*With imploring eagerness.*) Name it. Stay. Oh, answer me. Stay; speak.
On what condition, and what time for trial?
(*The phantom gradually disappears below.*)
THE VOICE FROM THE GRAVE. List. They or you, before the clock strikes twelve
At St John's Eve next year, are ours for ever.

> (*He disappears amid thunder and tempest; the graves close, the fiends vanish, and all is as before, calm and bright moonlight, save that for a time the thunder, shrieks and laughter are heard gradually dying away underground, as though descending back to hell, while the Stranger stands with outstretched arms over the tomb.*)

> (*Pause. Rudolf enters the churchyard through the gate next the village; the Stranger is discovered leaning against a tombstone in the background, and the church clock begins to strike twelve very slowly.*)

RUDOLF. It is the field of death, where Time sows seed
For dread eternity. It is the Church,
And yet I cannot pray. I'm faint: I'll rest here.
(*He seats himself on the tomb in the centre.*)
It is the time; then come. Chill, death-damp earth,
And cool my burning heart.
(*He takes some grave-earth, places it on his breast, and lies down.*)
Ah, thus 'tis well,
For some strange slumber's on me: I must rest.

(*He falls asleep. The clock ceases to strike, and immediately a sudden gleam illumines the interior of the church, the organ sounds, and funeral service is heard performing within, though no one is visible. Presently, one by one, in their white shrouds, each holding a burning taper, a phantom funeral train enters the churchyard by the gate from the village, and passes in a slow procession into the church, the funeral service pealing all the time, and the Stranger waving them on with his arm, as he stands towering in the background. Many of Rudolf's friends and relatives are among them, as appears from the exclamations he makes in his sleep.*)

Last of the train Gemma appears. As she ascends the steps of the porch she turns round, pauses, looks with a melancholy expression of countenance on Rudolf, who still lies asleep, thrice waves her hand to him in farewell, and as he starts up, passes within the porch. At the same instant she, the lights, the phantoms disappear, and all is as before, silence and moonlight.)

RUDOLF. Gemma, where am I? I will come, my love.
    (*Pause.*)
Where is she? Silence, solitude, and night.
Oh, my foreboding heart. Then all is lost.
Why came I here. Oh, tempter thrice accurst.

    (*The Stranger advances with a smile of triumph.*)

Art thou a fiend, to triumph in my pain.
STRANGER. If so, reproach me not. The fiend ne'er comes
Until man's heart has whispered prayers for him.
Trust me, no fiend can injure man so much
As by fulfilment of his own desires.
    (*Rudolf sinks overpowered at the Stranger's feet, who laughs in triumph over him, and the curtain falls.*)

END OF ACT I.

ACT II
SCENE I

Garden saloon in Rupert's house. Rupert; a Messenger, strangely attired.

RUPERT. How came you then? (*With letters in his hand.*)
MESSENGER. Across the sea.
RUPERT. Strange, that your vessel was not signaled.
MESSENGER. A thick mist concealed us.
RUPERT. Is your vessel now in port?
MESSENGER. It sailed again, for it is a ship that bears strange freightage, and there are many on board who have mysterious missions. It landed us with early dawn, and then stood out to sea again.
RUPERT. Where is your master now?
MESSENGER. He's nearing fast, but I sped first to herald his approach.
RUPERT. 'Tis sixty miles to that old seaport town. You left it but at dawn, and here already?
MESSENGER. We travel fast, we travel very fast.
RUPERT. 'Tis almost superhuman speed, and why near those deserted ruins land?
MESSENGER. 'Twas once a famous city.
RUPERT. By the sea engulfed. A mouldering tower the beacon, without flag or light. They say unholy spirits haunt the spot.
MESSENGER. They did so once, for man made it his dwelling place.
RUPERT. Oh! a sneerer too. What said your master, then? Repeat.
MESSENGER. Commend me to friend Rupert, say today I come to see and claim my promised bride, pledged to me ere I left my native land.
RUPERT. We'll bid him welcome and redeem our pledge. He has been absent long, and, if report speaks true, has amassed a princely wealth.
MESSENGER. Enough to buy a princedom, which wealth he now lays humbly at your daughter's feet.
RUPERT. (*Eager and delighted.*) My lord is kind; my lord is very kind. Is he far? He will not tarry long. Haste, haste! (*Calling.*) Wilhelm! Hubert! Otto! (*Servants enter.*) Send out scouts to see if he be coming. Would he were here.

Methinks he tarries long. Give him welcome. Bid him speed – my pledge shall be redeemed ... My daughter – pledge – gold – promise – by my soul. (*The messenger smiles.*) Ha! You laugh?

MESSENGER. Did I? No! You fancied. (*The Messenger disappears unperceived.*)

FIRST SERVANT. (*To second.*) He sneers, and seems to chuckle at some secret thought.

RUPERT. (*Aside.*) Perchance I seem too eager. One must always be on one's guard with these great people. They laugh at us poor citizens. I must behave with greater dignity. (*Aloud and pompously.*) What ho! Sir Messenger! What ho! I say. Give your master fair welcome. Tell him, if my daughter wills, he may come and lay his homage at her feet. (*Forgetting himself.*) He won't be long, will he? I mean, Sir Messenger – (*Turning round.*) Ha! – Is he gone? – Which way did he go? – I thought he stood beside me.

FIRST SERVANT. So did I.

SECOND SERVANT. And I.

RUPERT. Look if he's in the passage still. He must be.

FIRST SERVANT. (*From the passage.*) No.

RUPERT. How fast he went; he's on the terrace then.

FIRST SERVANT. (*From still more distant.*) No.

OTTO. Strange! Lord have mercy on us.

RUPERT. How quickly these great folks always do things. Quite surprising.

OTTO. Sir!

RUPERT. What?

OTTO. I beg your pardon, sir – but I don't think – (*Hesitates.*)

RUPERT. What, sir?

OTTO. That it's all right with that gentleman, who left us just now, or with his master either.

RUPERT. Insolent blockhead. Why not?

OTTO. Why, Sir! his comings and goings are not to my liking. He goes away, somehow, like the smoke out of the chimney, no one knows where it goes to, and he comes like –

RUPERT. Sir! What do you mean?

OTTO. And that landing. Sir! At those ill-favoured ruins! I'm afraid it's not all right with them!

RUPERT. Idiot! I tell you it *is* all right, and do not let me hear you buzzing your idle fooleries about the house. It is all right, I tell you; is he not as rich as a gold mine? Has he not got plenty of money; and what can be wrong with a man who has got plenty of money?

OTTO. But, Sir!

RUPERT. Silence, Sirrah! – You make me forget all I have to do. See that the green chamber be put in order, and the covers taken off the chairs –

and – d'ye hear? – see that – oh! – I forget! – ah yes – d'ye hear – where is my daughter – my daughter – His coming so suddenly makes me forget everything. She does not yet know of my lord's arrival; in fact, I could not expect it for a month at least – go and seek her – where is she – let me see her – She must prepare to receive him. Here – Wilhelm, Hubert, come – where is my daughter? Gemma, Gemma. (*Exit.*)

OTTO. I don't like the looks of it, anyhow. I don't think the old gentleman, himself, a bit better than he should be. If he wasn't in league with the devil he'd be more afraid of him.

TRINA. (*Without.*) Otto, Otto.

OTTO. Ay, Otto, Otto – I don't know what they'd do in the world without me – that I'm sure I don't. It's 'dear Otto, come here.' It's 'dear Otto, go there' – from the master and the mistress, and the maid: Lord bless you, they ought to have three Ottos, at least.

TRINA. (*Entering.*) Otto, Otto; tell me; is it true?

OTTO. What, my love?

TRINA. And have you told him what you saw Rudolf do last night?

OTTO. To be sure I have; why, wasn't I sent to find out?

TRINA. Oh, you dolt! How could you?

OTTO. There it is again; other people get themselves into a scrape, and I'm sure to suffer for it. Well, I don't care. I'm straightforward and plain.

TRINA. Yes, I see – but don't you know you've placed poor Rudolf quite in the old man's power?

OTTO. Oh, have I – sooner he than I, then.

TRINA. Why, don't you see, he could have him taken up for sorcery.[16]

OTTO. Well, I always thought no good could come of it; and this same outlandish devil we have got coming now.

TRINA. Lord bless you! Why, it's only the foreign gentleman.

OTTO. A foreign gentleman – Ugh! It's my opinion many a devil comes into the country in the disguise of a foreign gentleman.

TRINA. Well, as long as I don't see horns and tail –

OTTO. That's because you won't see. You see them every day, only they curl their tails upward and you take them for moustachios; and as to their horns – why, bless you, what do you think they wear that lot of hair on their heads for, if it wasn't to hide them? For my part, when I see a fellow enter a house with long rowley-powleys dancing about his shoulders, I always look out for

---

[16] *taken up for sorcery*: prosecutions for sorcery ended with the Witchcraft Act of 1735. The theme of magic and this suggestion of a temporally distant setting are examples of the play's use of gothic conventions.

horns, somewhere or other.[17] Well – never mind, I'm determined to make something out of it.

TRINA. Didn't he promise to reward you today?

OTTO. Yes, he said he'd give me: ugh! ugh! ugh! – a coughing fit always seizes him when he's promising. – But this wedding shall bring me something.

TRINA. Oh, Otto! I wonder when I shall be married.

OTTO. Patience, patience, my dear.

TRINA. Yes, it's very well for you to cry patience, who hasn't got any beauty to lose, but look at me, I'm absolutely wasting away, I'm sure.

OTTO. Well, all comes at last.

TRINA. At last! Yes, when it's too late to do any good. You cold, unfeeling wretch; you shall hear the effects of waiting, I wish I could make you feel them; now listen:

(*Sings*) A maiden lived in a cottage lone
    And Love he lived there too.
One morning Hymen passed that way:[18]
    She stepped unto the threshold stone,
And how she begged of him to stay!
    But Hymen answered: 'No! no! no!

I have no time, for I must go
    To marry an old dowager[19]
Unto a toothless beau!
    And you are young – and you can wait;'
And Hymen wandered past the gate,
    And murmured: 'No! no! no!'

Once more he passed that cottage lone,
    His torch was dark and low;
All anxiously he pressed the latch
    And asked for leave in blandest tone,
His torch to kindle with a 'match.'
    But then she answered: 'No! no! no!'

I cannot now – for I did go
    With Love who travels rapidly,
When Hymen's coach is slow':
    For maids, when Hymen tries them sore,

---

[17] *rowley-powleys*: coiled hair.
[18] *Hymen*: Greek God of marriage.
[19] *dowager*: widow who possesses property or title from her late husband.

> Will fly with Love, and close the door,
> And murmur: 'No! no! no!'

OTTO. Hark!

TRINA. What do you hear?

OTTO. A distant trumpet.

TRINA. Folly! It was the sea wind among the witch elms.

OTTO. No! – Again! Heard you not a sound like the distant trampling of horses?

TRINA. The thunder among the hills. See! a black cloud has risen from them.

OTTO. It seems to my fancy, as though it announced the approach of mischief to some one here. But see! I must have heard rightly, for old Rupert is hastening across the garden-terrace yonder! I must away and join him – he is calling. Here! here! Sir, here! Small hope for Rudolf now his rival comes. (*Exit Otto.*)

TRINA. Heigho, Otto! I wish you had a rival too. But what a storm is driving across the hills. I like not guests who come in such foul weather. (*Rudolf meets her.*)

RUDOLF. Stay, for the love of heaven! Stay! Where is she? – Gemma! I must see her! see her!

TRINA. Oh! what brings him at such a moment. Away, this is no time.

RUDOLF. Time! time and I will soon have turned to strangers. I must – I will see Gemma! Let me see her, or I will raise a tempest through the house shall mock the one approaching – Hence, I'm maddened. Ah! she comes. She lives! She lives! She lives! 'Twas her heart told her I was here and sought her. (*Gemma enters.*)

GEMMA. Oh! Rudolf! Rudolf! Dost thou linger yet, the free bird hovering round the captive one. 'Tis rash to come thus openly and brave my father's anger, Rudolf.

RUDOLF. Should I fear? What have I now to fear? A whirlwind, Gemma drove me to thee! A wreck unto a wreck.

GEMMA. Why art thou so dejected? Pale despair is written on thy face! Be sure that heaven will not let two young hearts, like ours, be rent. Thou wilt return with wealth from foreign lands.

RUDOLF. I go not, Gemma.

GEMMA. How? You will not go?

RUDOLF. And wherefore should I? Hope is dead and buried, yes, it was buried yesternight.

GEMMA. A phoenix! from its undying ashes it will rise! Could I but give you something of my thoughts! They are so full of dreams of a bright future. But one cloud o'er me hangs: the tide of years seems weighing heavy on my father's head.

RUDOLF. That care I can remove. He'll not die yet. He will not die this year.
GEMMA. Thank you for this. The words are kind – their truth no man can know.
RUDOLF. I know it. Therefore smile thy short, sad hour. Poor Gemma! Death has daintier work in hand.
GEMMA. (*Amazed.*) What sudden sorrow shakes thee? What strange fear? Why thus abandon thy long-cherished plan, today should see enacted? Why not hence, seeking love's flowers upon fortune's path?
RUDOLF. Why hence – why here – why anywhere? For now no hope is here, nor hence, nor anywhere! We part and yet I go not.
GEMMA. What means this?
RUDOLF. That life's a curse, and fortitude a jest.
GEMMA. There lurks some hidden meaning under this. Oh, tell me, Rudolph, tell me.
RUDOLF. Ask me not.
GEMMA. By our dear love, I do adjure you, tell.
RUDOLF. I cannot.
GEMMA. Ha! – Did you not say? – oh, speak. My father's life was safe? – Whence know you that? Oh, boding heart – where were you yesternight? Speak – answer me – where were you yesternight? Speak. I bethink me of an ancient tale of death-foreboding sights on St John's Eve.[20]
RUDOLF. Hold! – silence! – Seek no more.
GEMMA. You were to church last midnight, but no priest was in the aisle. Shake not your head thus. On your death-white cheek 'tis written. Oh, what saw you there? Oh say! or I go mad.
RUDOLF. (*Bitterly.*) Your father was not there.
GEMMA. Then why this grief?
RUDOLF. Now spare me! heaven spare me!
GEMMA. Rudolf, turn not away. Look at me well. Now answer me, who was there? (*A long pause.*) I was there! I see it! (*She stands riveted to the spot.*)
RUDOLF. Heaven! If thou hast mercy, strike me dead. Gemma! beloved! She hears not – heeds me not. Gemma! one smile, one sign. Oh! she is dead, and this a marble statue for her grave. Speak to me, Gemma.
GEMMA. Rudolf, 'tis in vain. For at that moment – in that pause I felt death's spirit pass into my heart. 'Tis o'er! you have seen truly, Rudolf.
RUDOLF. Say not so. Phantoms are sent of hell, and dreams are false.
GEMMA. (*Heeding him not.*) Rudolf, 'tis cruel doom to die so young. My heart was full of hope, and love, and dreams. Oh! golden dreams of visionary bliss!

---

[20] *death-foreboding sights on St John's Eve*: likely Jones's invention; Shakespeare's *Midsummer Night's Dream* may have served as a source for Jones's setting, a night near the solstice associated with the supernatural. The plot of crossed lovers also links the plays.

And to be laid beneath the chill, damp earth; while yet so full of these, – 'tis bitter, bitter! We might have been – oh! very, very happy.

RUDOLF. We might have been. All – all the joys of earth are compassed in these words: 'We might have been!'

GEMMA. You will not leave me, Rudolf?

RUDOLF. Leave you, Gemma, never. Not even in the grave, for death may take, but has no power to refuse. Fear not that I will leave you.

GEMMA. I fear you!

RUDOLF. Then fear not, I am calm. Calm, said I? Calm? The calm that follows on the thunderburst.

GEMMA. (*In broken tones.*) My Rudolf, will you love me, when I'm dead?

RUDOLF. If the dead love! – But no, no, no! my Gemma! you must not – shall not die! By penance long, by self-inflicted rack, by agonies, I'll win your life from heaven! I'll die for you.

GEMMA. 'Tis sweet to be loved thus; but oh! I feel a cold foreboding freezes young hope dead.

RUDOLF. No, Gemma, cheer thee. Smile, mine own beloved. Give me one little smile before I go. We will be happy yet; thy hated suitor, perchance, may ne'er arrive; so many things may save us yet to happiness. Bethink thee, he has to cross far seas, they're like a grave, the storms are fierce, his barque may founder, he may perish.

GEMMA. Rudolf! this is sinful, Rudolf! Oh God! But yesternight – and now again.

RUDOLF. Forgive me – oh! forgive me, for I'm maddened – I mean it not. Oh! May he live – possess the world – the heavens – all – but not my Gemma.

GEMMA. Hush, hush! For pity's sake! Thy every thought is sin!

RUDOLF. I feel thou art too good for me; my soul would perish, were it not for thee. Thou art the angel calls me back from hell. May heaven bless thee, Gemma, noble girl! Too good, too pure, too beautiful for earth (*folding her in his arms.*)

GEMMA. Hush! may we meet in heaven.

RUDOLF. To my heart! On earth thou shalt be mine. Despite the world I fold thee in mine arms and brave them all. Nought – nought shall part us. (*Rupert has entered unperceived.*)

RUPERT. Part!

GEMMA. The voice of fate. (*She sinks in Rudolf's arms.*)

RUPERT. (*To Rudolf.*) How dare you, sir, intrude into this house? Have I not forbid? (*To Gemma.*) How dare you, insolent child, forget yourself, and sink so low as to admit that villain here?[21] (*To Rudolf.*) Hence, sir, or I will have

---

[21] *villain*: low-born rustic; scoundrel.

you scourged away. Hence, minion! bandy not those looks with me, or I will strike you to the ground.
RUDOLF. Ha, Sir! No, no! You are her father, you may speak.
RUPERT. How, now?
RUDOLF. (*Going.*) I go – but of mine own accord.
GEMMA. Rudolf! Rudolf! He abandons me.
RUDOLF. No, no, beloved! beloved! See, see, she dies!
RUPERT. Better die, than thus disgrace herself. Rise, idle minion. (*To Rudolf.*) Villain! hence this instant.
RUDOLF. I go not, till I see her safe.
RUPERT. How, slave!
GEMMA. Go, dearest Rudolf. Go, incense him not.
RUDOLF. Oh! do not break my heart and bid me go.
RUPERT. Wilhelm! Otto! – Ho! without there, ho. (*Servants enter.*) Now, slave.
RUDOLF. Touch me not, I warn ye.
GEMMA. (*Throwing herself between them.*) Father!
RUPERT. Now, girl! thy paramour is in my power, for know that he was traced last night consorting with hell itself. Renounce him or he'll perish. Hence from my path, girl, or I trample on thee. (*Sounds of trumpets. Rupert starts.*) Hush, hark! What was that sound? He comes, he comes. Ha! he must not see this – Rise, dry thy tears. Thy hair is dishevelled – 'Tis thy bridegroom comes.
GEMMA AND RUDOLF. Oh! heaven. All is lost – so soon, so soon. (*Trumpets approaching.*)
RUPERT. Ha! List! What shall I do? Away, away, get to thy chamber – Don thy festal robe. It is too late – He's on the terrace! – Quick! – He's here.
(*A splendid train defile along the terrace past the windows to the sound of music, in gorgeous array, and enter the saloon bearing costly gifts.*[22] *Lastly enters a cavalier of majestic presence and almost fabulous splendour of attire.*)
RUPERT. My Lord. (*Bowing.*)
CAVALIER. Well met, at last, well met. How beats my heart towards my promised bride.
(*Rudolf starts, steps aside, and remains watching the Cavalier with marks of the utmost astonishment.*)
RUPERT. (*Aside to Gemma.*) Smile, daughter, smile. At peril of thy life.
CAVALIER. (*To Gemma.*) Silent – yet eloquently beautiful. Lo! at thy feet I cast these treasures rich –
RUDOLF. It is! – yet cannot be – (*Aside, still eyeing the Cavalier with astonishment.*)
CAVALIER. The spoils of ocean – incense – jewels rare, this morning landed –

---

[22] *defile*: march in a row.

RUDOLF. (*Rushing forward.*) This morning? But I saw thee yesternight.
CAVALIER. (*With haughtiness.*) Unto whom speaks the serf?
RUDOLF. To thee, to thee!
RUPERT. (*To Rudolf in an under-tone.*) I warn you, sir! be silent. (*To servants.*) Bear him hence.
RUDOLF. (*To the servants.*) Back, hounds; at peril of your lives, hold back. (*To Cavalier.*) Stand me that question – answer me I say. Wast thou not with me yesternight?
RUPERT. He's mad.
CAVALIER. (*In calm scorn.*) Sooth, friend! you wander strangely. I with you! Fair company to pass a summer's eve.
RUDOLF. Not in the churchyard?
CAVALIER. (*Sternly.*) In the churchyard, serf? What did you in the churchyard yesternight?
RUDOLF. (*Staggering back.*) Oh Heaven!
GEMMA. Hush, hush! This implicates your life. 'Twas sorcery, that's visited with death.
RUPERT. Here, seize him; self-arraigned of sorcery. Besides I've proof, I have a witness too, our Otto saw him to the churchyard wander. Now then, your life is forfeit to my will.
RUDOLF. (*Half unsheathing his hanger.*) Then be your blood on you own heads. Forbear.
GEMMA. Oh! spare him, spare him, father.
RUPERT. (*Aside to Gemma.*) Then speak smooth unto my lord, or else he dies.
GEMMA. (*Aside to Rupert.*) I will. (*Aloud to Cavalier.*) You're welcome. Oh! you're welcome, Cavalier. (*Aside to Rupert.*) Father, you see I smile – I smile – and kindly. (*Aloud to Cavalier.*) Dear Cavalier, you're welcome. – Oh! Thrice welcome.
RUDOLF. (*Starting.*) What do I hear?
CAVALIER. Then deign accept these gifts. A pilgrim's offering to his sweet saint.
GEMMA. (*Hurriedly.*) Yes – yes – I smile – you promised – Father – mark – dear Cavalier, I thank you.
RUDOLF. Can it be? Oh, heart of woman, faithless, frail and light.
CAVALIER. Fair lady; here in homage at your feet the pleasures of the Indies.
RUDOLF. (*Casting himself at Gemma's feet.*) At your feet breaking heart, that breaks for love of you.
RUPERT. (*Aside to Gemma.*) Remember.
RUDOLF. Choose!
GEMMA. (*In broken accents.*) Oh, dear sir Cavalier! – Your honoured suit –
RUDOLF. (*Starting up.*) Oh! Gemma! Gemma! Death.
GEMMA. See! Father – Spare him – spare him – spare him – It is done!

(She sinks insensible into her father's arms, Rudolf stands in an agony of despair, the Cavalier towers in triumph, and the curtain falls.)

END OF SECOND ACT.

ACT III
SCENE I

Chamber in Rupert's House. Otto, Wilhelm and Hubert busied in decorating the Apartment.

OTTO. Bustle – bustle – friends! This is St John's Eve again. You know what the day portends.
WILHELM. Yes, for this day, a year ago, poor Gemma first began to droop and fade.
HUBERT. Yes – this day, a year ago, the Cavalier first made his appearance.
OTTO. Ay – and this evening she is to be married to the Cavalier. Poor girl – she's dying.
HUBERT. Her father's as hard-hearted as ever. He thinks it but assumed.
WILHELM. What says the doctor?
OTTO. What doctors always say – he looks wise, shakes his head and says – '*Hum!*'
HUBERT. She has said that this evening will be her death.
WILHELM. Some one had told her he had seen her shadow last St John's Eve, and it made such an impression on her, that she has gradually declined ever since.
HUBERT. Poor girl! The leech did say, if she survived this evening she would soon recover, her illness being of the mind.[23] But he gives no hopes.
WILHELM. No chance! – no chance! Her death is foredoomed, this evening! Who ever has escaped, whose spirit has been seen on St John's Eve?
HUBERT. I say, Otto! why is the rite to take place at the old deserted Abbey among the hills, instead of the church, as usual?
OTTO. What know I? It was the special will of the Cavalier. But bustle! See you not the sun is westering? and the rite is to take place as soon as it is dark! Speed! speed! you to the green chamber, – you to the Garden saloon – Quick! We have not got a moment to spare – not one of us – there – go! go! – work! – toil! – bustle! – that's right! go! go! (*Exit Wilhelm and Hubert.*)

---

[23] *leech*: doctor.

And I'll sit quietly and think for you all! (*Seating himself. After a pause taking forth a bag of gold.*) Now then, we'll look at what we've got. A purse of gold – this the Cavalier gave me. I don't much like his gifts – but – open! (*opens the purse.*) Pah! I know not what the fancy is, but this purse smells like an opened grave. Ha! Ha! Folly! gold is gold! – (*Taking out a handful, and dropping it back with a cry of pain.*) Ah! It burns! it burns! Should he – as Trina sometimes says, be a fiend, and this gold – pah! perhaps I but fancied – and it can do no harm just to handle it a little. (*Takes more.*) Ah! it's cooler now! I find, 'tis but at first it burns, the hand soon grows accustomed to it. (*Takes more.*) Why, I protest, it's quite cold and comfortable now. – Lord! What a lot! (*calling.*) Trina! Trina! (*Trina enters.*) Now, Trina! brighten up that pretty face of yours. You are mine and I am yours, I am yours and you are mine! Clap your hands for joy, girl! you've got a rich man! You've got *me*!

TRINA. What new foolery have you afloat?

OTTO. Foolery if you please! *This* is no foolery! (*shewing the purse.*)

TRINA. Where did you get that?

OTTO. Never you mind. You see I have got it.

TRINA. Where did you get that? Let me know, or I tell directly.

OTTO. Hush! Hush! No! No! For that would spoil all.

TRINA. Spoil what? I am not trifling! – There is more behind this! – Tell directly – or! –

OTTO. Well! – Well! – but be discreet! – The Cavalier.

TRINA. As I thought! What for?

OTTO. But you must be very discreet! Why, you must know, my master bade me fetch the Superior and the Holy brotherhood of St John to the Abbey this evening, to solemnise the rite between the Cavalier and Gemma.

TRINA. Well! – well! –

OTTO. Well, the Cavalier gave me this gold, *if I would not fetch them, but keep them away*! He said he had a Priest, *one of his own*, would serve as well.

TRINA. Just Heaven! 'Tis as clear as day! He is in league with the Evil one. He has some design upon us, that the powers of the Church would thwart.

OTTO. What is it, Trina? you frighten me.

TRINA. Yes, yes! Or else why choose the ruined Abbey instead of the Church? Why keep them hence? – Away, away! unhappy wretch. Touch me not, you're lost, you've sold yourself!

OTTO. How? – sold! –

TRINA. To the fiend! – Away! – I smell sulphur about you! go, go! That gold was coined – (*pointing downwards.*)

OTTO. (*In fear.*) What – in the place – where – people are warm! –

TRINA. Yes, yes! You're a lost man! He's got you! – safe and sound! good bye, poor Otto!

OTTO. Oh stay! – Stay! – Trina! – I *do* feel very uncomfortable! – don't I look – Oh! this gold! – What shall I do? –

TRINA. There is but one thing! Return him his accursed gift, – hurry at once to the Superior! – bring the holy brotherhood to the Abbey this evening – and –

OTTO. But I dare not! He will – I swore! – he –

TRINA. You love me! – Well then, if you do not obey me, I will never be yours – if you go and they come in time, I pledge you my hand tonight.

OTTO. Oh! here I am placed between the devil and a woman, a woman and the devil! – Lord have mercy on me!

TRINA. Well, sir! you hear me!

OTTO. Lord bless you – who would'nt!

TRINA. Well!

OTTO. Oh! I go! – of course! (*aside.*) Out of the frying-pan into the fire. Good bye, my sweet — (*shudders.*) Oh! (*Going, and then turning back.*) I say – Trina! – do you think – I know – that gold – it's a pity the devil should have it, after all, when you know it could be in so much better hands, eh? (*aside.*) I don't like to take it myself, but I don't see the harm of her taking care of it for me. – (*Aloud.*) So I think you might as well –

TRINA. No, no! I would not touch it for worlds!

OTTO. Well, as you like, but, you see (*putting as he speaks, piece after piece of gold into her hand.*) that's a new red gown, and that's a pink trimming to it, and that's a yellow bonnet with cherry-coloured ribbons, la! how it will become your pretty face, and that's a shawl, like the steward's wife's, all pea-green and chocolate, and that's a scarf sky-blue, and then won't you look like a sunset in June!

TRINA. (*Who had been holding out her hand, every moment more pleased.*) Well, after all, I don't see the great harm there can be in taking a little foolish money, so, come along, and I'll get the Priest to give me a blessing for it.

(*Exit.*)

(*Enter Rupert.*)

RUPERT. (*In thought.*) They say she's dying! – What? My poor, poor child!
Perchance I am too harsh! Could it be true,
What Otto fears? Pah, pah! The Cavalier's
A noble knight – and I but weak and foolish?

(*The Cavalier enters, unperceived by Rupert.*)

CAVALIER. (*Aside.*) King Satan's ancient lure has failed me now.
Gold, power, wealth, rank, what? Have ye lost your charms,
That whilome worked so well on woman's heart?[24]

---

[24] *whilome*: formerly; some time in the past.

Act III Scene I

Then – then I must assay the Passions! yea[25]
Resentment, Fear and Pride shall do my work.
RUPERT. (*Perceiving the Cavalier.*) My noble Lord!
CAVALIER. Good morrow, Father Rupert!
How fares my lovely bride?
RUPERT. But ill, my lord! The leech says she is dying.
CAVALIER. Ha! ha! ha!
RUPERT. (*Incensed.*) You laugh above the death-bed of my child?
CAVALIER. No, no! at you. You promised me her hand!
RUPERT. I promised what was human, more I cannot,
She dies! I cannot sacrifice her thus!
CAVALIER. (*Carelessly.*) What? you retract?
RUPERT. I cannot murder her.
CAVALIER. (*Quietly and tauntingly.*)
Ha, ha! you play the doting father well.
'Tis kind, 'tis very kind of you indeed,
To sacrifice your greatness, hopes and will,
To the caprices of a wayward child.
I go, Sir! I admire you – but – I go!
RUPERT. Stay! stay!
CAVALIER. No, no! Our compact is at end.
But I must still admire, in leaving you,
How fierce young blood now grows unto white hairs.
You boasted you could tame her to your will,
And now that St John's Eve is come again,
I find her still rebellious as before.
No doubt 'tis very amiable in you.
RUPERT. But would you have me murder her?
CAVALIER. Oh no!
By no means. Play the poor, kind, weak old man.
RUPERT. But she is dying.
CAVALIER. Oh! that grieves me much. (*With bitter quiet irony.*)
Pity, though, that I should not believe it.
Ungentle doubt in me! But 'tis my way.
Yet pity, too, if we had spoiled her game!
For certainty, a game, that's played so well.
Deserves success.
     (*Affecting to speak in thought.*)
Yes! How she oft will laugh
Above her father's grave. Ay! Laugh to think

---

[25] *assay:* try or attempt.

How well she cheated *you* and broke *my* heart!
While in the arms of her dear paramour.
Good Father! Most good father! Fare you well!
A pretty game! Well played! You're very kind!
   (*Going.*)

RUPERT. Stay, stay! You open a new light to me!
I see it all! I plainly see it all!
 – Stay, Cavalier! I pray you! Thick and fast
A thousand things now flit before my mind,
That give me confirmation of your thoughts!
No! I will not be outraged and deceived!
Weak, doting fool I was! I see it all!
She shall be yours! I swear it!

CAVALIER. By no means!
'Twere pity to disturb your kind resolve.
Perhaps 'twere better otherwise. Oh! Think!
How happy you might in some cottage be,
Beside your peasant son, your peasant child,
While gilded chariots whirl in distance past!
Think of your Gemma on her Rudolf's arm
Gone forth to tend the kine! How sweet a sight![26]

RUPERT. Ha! Loathsome image.

CAVALIER. No! 'Tis very fair! (*Mocking.*)
Poets, you know, still praise it, – then it must
Be something very fine! – Now fare you well!
   (*Going.*)

RUPERT. No! I implore you stay! Stay! Cavalier!
She shall be yours, I swear! Now hear me pray
Hear me beseech you not to go! I've set
My heart upon this union, more than ever!
'Twill kill me, if you go.

CAVALIER. Oh! Then I'll stay.
But are you sure she will consent at last.

RUPERT. Consent! She shall obey me!

CAVALIER. I have doubts.

RUPERT. Ay! If I drag her by the very hair
Unto the altar, still she shall be yours.

CAVALIER. That sounds like resolution. Yes, I'll stay.
But methinks I can make light your labour.
She certainly is charmed by this same Rudolf.

---

[26] *kine*: plural of cow (archaic).

He's put some spell upon her, I can break.
Does not your daughter wear an agate ring,
That was her mother's?
RUPERT. Yes.
CAVALIER. Then give it me.
'Twill be of use to turn her heart.
RUPERT. But how
Procure it? For she never parts with it.
CAVALIER. Take it from her.
RUPERT. She will not permit it!
But I could steal it from her when asleep!
CAVALIER. (*Mocking.*) That sounds like resolution too, indeed.
RUPERT. Well, you shall have it. Come! No longer now
Will I be played with thus! Come! Will you follow?
CAVALIER. Ay! For lo! This once, who follows, leads.
(*Exit.*)

SCENE II

A Chamber in Rudolf's Cottage. Through the windows are seen the house and grounds of Rupert. Rudolf is reclining on a couch.

RUDOLF. (*Starting up.*) – Sweet Gemma! Do they say she dies! She dies!
Oh! I must see her! Cruel, cruel I!
To have neglected her! – She meant it not!
She never, never loved the Cavalier!
Why did blind pride e'er drive me from beside her?
In vain I sought forgetfulness in absence!
Love draws me back from my far wanderings.
And have I but returned to hear she dies?
The words she spoke, I misconstrued. – They were
Mere courtesy! – 'Dear Cavalier!' – Nought else!
'Dear Cavalier.' – Yet 'dear!' – That's nothing – nothing!
She'd say it to her dog – to soulless things!
Oh! I have killed her in my idle pride,
My false resentment, and she loved me still!
Poor Gemma! – Dearest Gemma! – Peace, my heart!
Break not, till thou hast seen her, been forgiven.
'Dear Cavalier!' – Thrice cursed Cavalier!
Thou art the cause, the ruin and the foe!

Ha! I will seek thee out athwart a world[27]
And take a fearful retribution on thee!
'Dear Cavalier!' – Thrice cursed Cavalier.
   (*The Cavalier has entered.*)

CAVALIER. (*Calmly.*) Good morrow! Thank you.

RUDOLF. (*Drawing the instant he sees him.*) Can it be? – Ripe to my vengeance! Ripe!
Have at thee! – Canst thou come to me? To me!
And dost thou dare to taunt me to my face?

CAVALIER. I come as your good friend!

RUDOLF. What! Mocking too?
Draw! Strike! At once!

CAVALIER. I? – Not with you!

RUDOLF. Thou shalt! Or I strike thee!

CAVALIER. You dare not!

RUDOLF. Why!

CAVALIER. Because I am unarmed.

RUDOLF. A coward's idle plea!

CAVALIER. Were I a coward, I had not come here.

RUDOLF. It shall not serve thee! Here are weapons! Here!
Take! What? They suit you not? Then here are more.

CAVALIER. They're not the weapons, with the which I strike!

RUDOLF. Oh! Triple coward! Then I'll strike thee thus!

CAVALIER. (*Standing motionless.*) Man! Have a guard! 'Tis murder! Now I strike!

RUDOLF. (*Sheathing his sword.*) Villain! I scorn thee! Leave me!

CAVALIER. No! Not yet.
I come on the behalf of Gemma.

RUDOLF. Thou?

CAVALIER. You love her – do you not!

RUDOLF. Oh! Can you ask? (*Passionately.*)

CAVALIER. Then you can render her a service.

RUDOLF. How?

CAVALIER. 'Tis by renouncing her. She loves you not,
  But sense of duty binds her to you,
  And raises painful conflict in her breast,
  That undermines the fabric of her life,
  And to rebellion ever prompting her
  Thus brings her grey-haired father to the grave.

RUDOLF. She loves me not!

---

[27] *athwart*: across.

CAVALIER. I've said!
RUDOLF. She loved – she loves! (*With proud confidence.*)
CAVALIER. Her heart is mine.
RUDOLF. Liar! Recreant! That is false![28]
CAVALIER. I can prove my words.
RUDOLF. I dare thee prove them!
CAVALIER. Behold! Know you this ring?[29] (*Lifting his hand.*)
RUDOLF. (*Starting back.*) Her mother's ring!
   She ne'er would part with it! Not e'en to me!
CAVALIER. She gave it me!
RUDOLF. I've asked her for that ring!
CAVALIER. Are you convinced?
RUDOLF. No! There is art in this!
   She – give it *you*!
CAVALIER. Upon that very morn
   When in your very presence she did smile
   Upon my suit, received my proffered gifts
   And all unasked this pledge gave in return.
   You heard – and now you see?
RUDOLF. Yes, Yes! I heard!
   Her own lips told me! Fool! That I could doubt!
CAVALIER. Are you convinced!
RUDOLF. I AM! (*Utterly dejected.*)
CAVALIER. Then write to her,
   And tell her you renounce her, bid her wed
   The man, she loves, *your rival*! Tell her, too,
   You long have ceased to love her – 'tis a kindness
   That rendered, spares her many pangs of conscience!
RUDOLF. Bid me renounce my heaven, and I'll do it!
   But Gemma! Oh! I loved her truly – fondly!
   Ungrateful and unkind!
CAVALIER. Ah! But for you
   She might have been all blythe and happy still!
   You have been the blight of her young life!
   You knew her rich, and that the world had placed
   A bar 'twixt you and her; still, still you urged
   Your suit, and won her heart, entailing thus

---

[28] *Recreant*: traitor, villain.
[29] *Know you this ring*: Jones apparently draws on a central plot of Shakespeare's *Othello*, in which Iago uses Cassio's possession of the hero's handkerchief – a gift from his mother – to convince Othello of Desdemona's unfaithfulness.

    Keen misery upon her. From that hour
    Her love and duty waged destroying war,
    And as they fought long battles with her life,
    Her blooming cheek grew paler day by day,
    Her form more shadow-like, her voice more low,
    She pined, – she drooped, – she faded!
RUDOLF. Oh! Forbear.
CAVALIER. Call you this Love? 'Tis Cruelty! The while
    Had you forborne and chained down love and pain,
    And passed her by, and said: I will not bring
    Blight and death on one so young and gentle,
    She, who now dies within yon trellised porch,
    Had now been dancing on the village green!
    Call you this Love? 'Tis Murder!
RUDOLF. No, no, no! (*With passionate energy.*)
CAVALIER. Such is the love of man, and even now
    You still refuse to write the few, brief words
    That may allay the tempest of her soul.
RUDOLF. (*Writing hurriedly.*) There! – There! – She shall not perish! – Break, my heart!
    Live Gemma! And be happy! – There! I go
    To see her yet tonight – and then to die! (*Exit.*)
CAVALIER. I thank you. You have played your part to end.
    Tonight she must be mine and I am saved!
    And should I fail, still, I will baffle Hell:
    Even though St John's Eve's last hour have struck!
    The rite will be at midnight in the Church –
    They dare not cross the threshold sanctified
    And I within will tarry, and be saved!
    But she *will* yield! Now – now then to my work!
    The heart of woman is but a weak fortress. (*Exit.*)

SCENE III

    The interior of a deserted and decayed Gothic Cathedral. Night. Attendants and Servants of Rupert entering.

ATTENDANTS. Ho! Hollo! Hollo! Here! Is no one here?
    Where is the old man, who guards this ruined Church?

MONK. (*Entering with a lamp from a side aisle.*) Who summons me on this
    tempestuous night?
  Say! Are there any, who assistance need,
  Assailed by storm or midnight murderers?
1ST ATTENDANT. No! We come, father! to crave the loan of your church for
  a short hour or so.
MONK. Come ye for shelter or for penance here?
2ND ATTENDANT. No! On a merrier errand far, for at this shrine tonight a
  Cavalier and Lady fair are to unite in wedlock's holy bands.
MONK. These ruins are unfit for such a rite.
  Why choose they not the convent church at hand?
1ST ATTENDANT. What know I? A fancy! But in sooth! We've had to brave
  the storm for it.
2ND ATTENDANT. Beshrew me! 'Tis a fearful night, the clouds drive wildly
  from the mountains.
1ST ATTENDANT. And how fares Gemma?
2ND ATTENDANT. Like a martyr! Calm despair sits so palely on her cheek, ye
  know not if 'tis death's or sorrow's hue.
1ST ATTENDANT. Beshrew thee, Monk![30] Stir! Stir! Set wide the gate, and
  trim that niggard lamp, that seems a very miser of its light.[31]
    (*Music without approaching.*)
2ND ATTENDANT. Hark! Hark! D'ye hear the strain? They come! They come!
    (*Enter the bridal train, with numerous attendants bearing torches, the Cavalier
    walks on the one side of Gemma, while Rupert supports her on the other, and
    Trina follows.*)
MONK. Say! Who is he, who walks beside the maid?
    (*Starting with horror on perceiving the Cavalier.*)
ATTENDANT. Why do you look thus? The Cavalier! An old friend of my
  master.
MONK. Whence came he?
ATTENDANT. From afar. I know not.
MONK. His name?
ATTENDANT. The Cavalier. I know not.
MONK. You know not! Ha! I shudder. (*Crossing himself.*)
ATTENDANT. Why? What ails you?
MONK. Nothing! Nothing! (*hurriedly.*)
RUPERT. (*To Gemma.*) Now, child! resist no more! The hour is past,
  In which a father's kindness weakly swayed. –
  Here, Cavalier! My daughter and your bride.

---

[30] *Beshrew*: mild oath; to invoke evil upon.
[31] *niggard*: mean, miserly.

GEMMA. (*Faltering.*) My father! Bear with me a little yet!
   I shall not pain thee long!
RUPERT. Ha! What means this?
   So pale! – So cold! – My child! Break not my heart!
GEMMA. 'Tis my heart breaks, my father! Oh! my father!
CAVALIER. (*Aside to Rupert.*) The phantasy of girlhood! Art! Mere art!
RUPERT. Child! I command thee! Ha! Too long I've prayed!
   At peril of my curse!
GEMMA. Stay! Father! Stay!
RUPERT. Wilt thou obey?
GEMMA. I cannot! Oh! I cannot!
RUPERT. Then hear me, Heaven! –
GEMMA. At thy feet my heart! (*Casting herself down.*)
   Now crush it, – spurn it, – but oh! Curse it not.
CAVALIER. (*Aside to Rupert.*) Ha! Wavering now? 'Tis but the last poor shift![32]
   She'll yield anon, be firm!
RUPERT. Then hear and perish!
   Once more I ask thee.
GEMMA. (*Rising with majesty.*) Oh! Then thunder burst!
   From outraged nature I appeal to God!
   My father! You transgress the law of man!
   I'm free! and answer: No!
   (*Kneeling again.*) Now then, thy curse!
   Curse! While I bless thee, father!
RUPERT. Oh! I cannot. (*Overpowered by emotion.*)
GEMMA. What? Is the thunder silent? Rudolf! Rudolf!
CAVALIER. Ha! Then the time is come! You call on one
   Who thinks of you no more, for Rudolf's false!
GEMMA. False is the tongue that says so!
CAVALIER. Yes! For he renounces thee himself!
GEMMA. 'Tis false again!
CAVALIER. His own hand witnesses his perfidy!
   Behold! Where he resigns thee unto me,
   And says, that he has ceased to love thee long!
   Now, girl! What say you? At your feet I lay
   Love, Power and Rank and Wealth! How stands the scale?
   'Tis balanced by a faithless outcast's heart?
GEMMA. 'Tis balanced by my love and not by his!
   He loved me truly once, I love for ever!

---

[32] *shift*: a device to accomplish something.

CAVALIER. Ere that the clock strikes twelve, thou art a corse?[33]
  Become but mine and live! I have the power!
GEMMA. What? Live, and Rudolf faithless!
  Then it is time to die! You rung my knell
TRINA. (*Aside.*) Now, Otto! haste, the fiend is blasting her!
  Hark! Hark! (*Sound of a Mass bell, and sacred chaunt heard approaching.*)
CAVALIER. (*In extreme awe and terror.*) Who summoned those? I bade him
      keep them hence?
  I fear they stood not in my reckoning! (*To Rupert.*)
RUPERT. How now? Why turn you pale? (*To Gemma.*) My child! My child!
  What ails thee? Ha! She falters!
CAVALIER. (*Bending over Gemma.*) Now once more!
  Once more! Time presses! Say thou will be mine!
  Quick! Quick! Or they'll be here! –
  Now speak! (*The chaunt without draws nearer.*)
GEMMA. My father. (*Faintly and wildly.*)
  Your blessing, ere I go – no! – not a curse! –
  Oh! – I am – faint! – (*Chaunt nearer still.*)
CAVALIER. Still 'tis time!
  Say yet thou wilt be mine and thou art saved!
GEMMA. (*Scarcely conscious.*) My Rudolf! – Father! – No, no! Curse me not!
      (*She sinks on the pavement.*)
  Forgive me! –
RUPERT. Ha! She dies! She dies. My child! My daughter.
  Fiend! 'Tis thou hast slain her! –
  Ha! Why turns thine eye so ghastly?
  Ha! Thy form dilates.
CAVALIER. Still 'tis time! – There's but a moment's span.
  I give thee life and love. Reject them not.
  Thy shadow falls upon thy grave already.
RUPERT. Hence! Hence! Let her pained spirit pass in peace!
  Thy hateful voice disturbs her. (*Chaunt close to the Church.*)
  (*Starting.*) What was that?
  Hark! How the tempest bursts! – See, horrid forms
  Peer through the casement!
CAVALIER. Ay! They do! They do!
  Heaven drives me hence, and Hell awaits without!
      (*A Holy Procession, the Superior at their head, with cross and bell, enters the
      Church, and Otto is seen by the side of the Superior, pointing to the Cavalier.*)

---

[33] *corse*: a corpse.

RUPERT. My daughter, Gemma! I have slain my child.
　Is there no voice will call her from the grave?
RUDOLF. (*Rushing in.*) Gemma!
GEMMA. (*Reviving.*) Rudolf called! You love me?
RUDOLF. (*Passionately.*) Love you!
GEMMA. Oh! I am answered. Hark! The hour of death.
CAVALIER. Lost! The time is past!
　　　(*As the clock strikes twelve, fiends arise and seize him and drag him
　　　　downwards.*)
GEMMA. (*Kneeling to the Superior.*) The hour it strikes!
　Father your blessing – for I die this hour. (*Pause.*)
　Ha! It has struck. 'Tis past and yet I live!
RUDOLF AND RUPERT. She lives.
SUPERIOR. (*To Gemma.*). Your faith has saved you – or you perished.
　The fiend a cheating vision held before you
　To tempt you and mislead, and you are saved!
　Thus in the hour of peril, woman proves
　An angel ministrant 'twixt man and heaven!
　Live happy – children! Heaven is satisfied.
　　　(*They kneel before him, Trina gives her hand to Otto, Rupert folds his hands in
　　　　prayer and*
　　　　　　　　THE CURTAIN FALLS.)

Appendix 1

Chartist dramatic performances

This appendix provides a list of documented Chartist performances. Although some planned events may not have actually occurred, more productions likely went unrecorded: the source for the large majority of performances is the *Northern Star*, a newspaper by no means comprehensive given its reliance for gathering news on local groups sending in accounts of their activity. Other reports from the *Star* and elsewhere have not yet been identified. In consequence, it is probable that the total number of Chartist dramatic performances is significantly higher than what is reflected here.

Additionally, newspaper coverage was often incomplete. The chart reflects gaps in the coverage by using the term 'unknown' to indicate if reports fail to list titles staged or the specific date or location of a performance. Finally, the date of performances is sometimes ambiguous (for instance, when an article states 'last Saturday', the performance might have occurred earlier than suggested because of the time it took to file the report or run the article). Dates in brackets indicate cases where the date is not explicitly stated but can be inferred. In ambiguous instances, a question mark is added.

Most Chartist performances lasted only a single night (at least as reported in the *Star*). Any productions that extended to a second evening are indicated. Variant titles for *The Trial of Robert Emmet* are listed as they appear in the source texts.

Table 5.1 Chartist dramatic performances

Source and date (Northern Star indicated as NS)	Date performed	Place	Location	Work(s) performed
Yorkshire Gazette 16.03.1839; Morning Advertiser 25.03.1839	8.03.1839	Whitby	Whitby Theatre	John Watkins's *Wat Tyler*
NS 20.04.1839	Unknown but future	Carlisle (Scotland)	Carlisle Theatre	*William Tell; or, the Swiss Patriot*
NS 16.11.1839	'Hallowe'en' 1839	Kilbarchan (Scotland)	Unknown	Unknown
NS 5.09.1840	26.08.1840	Perth (Scotland)	Outdoor meeting	'Indictment, Trial and Condemnation of Reynard Maule' (mock trial)
NS 12.09.1840; 19.09.1840	2 performances Unknown, likely mid-September	Manchester	Thespian Theatre	Unknown
NS 31.10.1840	Unknown but future	Darlington	Darlington Theatre	*Wat Tyler*
NS 31.10.1840	'Saturday evening last' [24.10.1840]	Ashton	Charlestown Meeting room	*Trial of Robert Emmett*
NS 31.10.1840	7.11.1840	Ashton	Charlestown Meeting room	*Trial of Robert Emmett*
NS 5.12.1840	Unknown but previous	Stalybridge	Unknown	*Trial of Robert Emmett*
Preston Chronicle 12.12.1840	'Saturday Evening last' [5.12.1840]	Oldham	Mr Braddock's large room	*Trial of Robert Emmett*
NS 12.12.1840, 2.01.1841; Northern Liberator 19.12.1840; Dublin Evening Mail 21.12. 1840	12.12.1840	Oldham	Mr Braddock's large room	*Trial of Robert Emmett*

NS 19.12.1840; Freeman's Journal 21.12.1840	19.12.1840	Manchester	Hall of Science	Trial of Emmett
NS 2.01.1841	'Christmas Day' [1840]	Keighley	Working Man's Hall	Trial of Emmett
Manchester Courier 9.01.1841	'Saturday evening' [2.01.1841?]	Middleton	Radical Chapel, Barrowfields	Trial of Emmet
NS 6.02.1841	'Saturday evening' [13.02.1841?]	Ashton	'Room in Wood-street'	Scenes from John Watkins's John Frost
NS 16.01.1841; 23.01.1841	'Monday evening' [18.01.1841]	Keighley	Working Man's Hall	Trial of Robert Emmett
NS 27.02.1841	'Tuesday' [23.02.1841]	East Bierley	Unknown	Trial of Robert Emmet
Freeman's Journal 3.03.1841	'Yesterday week' [25.02.1841?]	Preston	'In their rooms'	Trial of Robert Emmett
Freeman's Journal 3.03.1841	Unknown but future	Preston	'In their rooms'	Trial of Robert Emmett
NS 29.05.1841	'Whit-Monday', 31.05.1841	London	Marylebone and Paddington Working Men's Hall	'Selection from Wat Tyler'
NS 24.07.1841	2.08.1841	London	Working Man's Hall, Marylebone	'Dramatic readings'
NS 31.07.1841; 7.08.1841; 21.08.1841	14.08.1841	Hyde	Working Man's Institution	Trial of Robert Emmett
NS 14.08.1841	'Monday last' [9.08.1841]	London	City Rooms, Old Bailey	Scenes from John Watkins's John Frost
NS 4.09.1841	11.09.1841	Hyde	Working Man's Institution	Trial of Robert Emmett
NS 4.09.1841	13.09.1841	London	Pantheon Theatre	Venice Preserved; Wreck Ashore
Bradford Observer 2.12.1841	'Monday previous' [29.11.1841]	Bradford	Social Institution	Scene from Hofer, Tell of the Tyrol

(continued)

Table 5.1 Chartist dramatic performances

Source and date (Northern Star indicated as NS)	Date performed	Place	Location	Work(s) performed
NS 24.12.1841	'Saturday evening last' [17.12.1841]	Failsworth	Pole-lane school room	Trial of Robert Emmett
NS 24.12.1841	'New Year's Day' [1842]	Hollinwood	Primitive Methodist schoolroom	Trial of Robert Emmett
NS 22.01.1842	'Tuesday evening last' [18.01.1842?]	Leeds	Chartist Association Room, Fish Market, Shambles	William Tell
NS 29.01.1842	'Monday evening' [31.01.1842]	Manchester	Hall of Science, Camp field	Trial of the Patriot Emmett
NS 26.03.1842	30.03.1842	London	Pavilion Theatre	The Yew Tree Ruin; 'A New Drama of intense interest', The Queen of Cyprus
NS 9.04.1842	'Monday' 11.04.1842	Stockport	Hall of Science	The Trial of Robert Emmett
NS 9.04.1842	'Easter Tuesday'	Coventry	George Inn, Little Park Street	'several pieces … from Wat Tyler, William Tell &c.'
NS 23.04.1842	'Saturday evening last' [16.04.1842]	Winlaton	Unknown	John Watkins's John Frost
NS 23.04.1842; 12.05.1842 Morning Advertiser 23.04.1842	12.05.1842	London	Albert Saloon	The Rake's Progress; State Secrets
NS 14.05.1842	23.04.1842	London	Victoria Theatre	William Tell, the Hero of Switzerland; Nature and Art!; The Last Witness; or, the Fate of St Marc
	'Tuesday evening' [17.05.1842]	Sutton-in-Ashfield	Unknown	William Tell
NS 4.06.1842	8.06.1842	London	Victoria Theatre	The Wreck of the Heart; Andreas Hofer, the Tell of the Tyrol; Wallace, the Hero of Scotland

Source	Performances	Location	Venue	Play
NS 19.11.1842	2 performances 'Saturday and Monday' [12.11.1842 and 14.11.1842?]	Clitheroe	King's Arms Inn	Wat Tyler
NS 17.12.1842	Unknown but previous 'Tuesday last' [13.12.1842?]	Nottingham	Unknown	Unknown
NS 17.12.1842; Leicestershire Mercury 17.12.1842		Leicester	Amphitheatre	Douglas; 'musical drama' The Floating Beacon
Leicestershire Mercury 17.12.1842; 24.12.1842	19.12.1842	Leicester	Amphitheatre	Unknown but likely as above, Douglas and The Floating Beacon
Stamford Mercury 3.02.1843; Leicester Chronicle 4.02.1843; Cooper, Life of Thomas Cooper 228–29	2 performances 9.01.1843; 16.01.1843	Leicester	Amphitheatre	Hamlet
NS 1.04.1843	2 performances 'Saturday evening'; 'Monday evening' [24.03.1843? 26.03.1843?]	Glasgow	Cooke's Circus	Emmet's Trial
Waterford Weekly Chronicle 22.04.1843; NS 13.05.1843	2 performances Unknown but previous	Glasgow	Cooke's Circus	Trial of Robert Emmet [possibly same performances as above but likely not]
Waterford Weekly Chronicle 22.04.1843	2 performances 8.04.1843; 10.04.1843	Glasgow	City Hall	Trial of Robert Emmet

(continued)

Table 5.1 Chartist dramatic performances

Source and date (*Northern Star* indicated as NS)	Date performed	Place	Location	Work(s) performed
NS 22.04.1843	Unknown	[See play title]	Unknown	*Trial of Robert Emmett*. Tour of Hamilton, Airdrie, Campsie, Kilmarnock, Ayr, Falkirk, Stirling, Edinburgh, Dundee, Aberdeen, Coalsnaughton, Allos, Tillicoultry, Arbroath, Kilmarnock, Kirkcudbright, Lanark, Barrhead, Strathaven, Perth, and Irvine (Scotland) and possibly other towns. Not known which performances occurred, but some did.
NS 13.05.1843	Unknown but previous	Greenock (Scotland)	Mechanic's Institution	*Trial of Robert Emmet*
NS 13.05.1843	**2 performances** Unknown but previous	Vale of Leven (Scotland)	Unknown	*Trial of Robert Emmet*
NS 13.05.1843	Unknown but previous	Paisley (Scotland)	Unknown	*Trial of Robert Emmet*
NS 13.05.1843	Unknown but previous	Johnstone (Scotland)	Unknown	*Trial of Robert Emmet*
NS 29.07.1843; Dorothy Thompsons, *Chartists*, p. 118	Unknown but future	Nottingham	Unknown	*Trial of Robert Emmett*
NS 21.10.1843	26.10.1842	Unknown	Unknown	'Theatrical entertainment' (*Star* publishes no details because report 'rated *too old*')

Date	Location	Venue	Performance
NS 11.11.1843	Unknown	Unknown	John Watkins's *John Frost*; *The Inch Cap Bell, a Nautical Burletta*
NS 25.11.1843 **2 performances** 'Friday and Saturday last' [3.11.1843; 4.11.1843]	Hamilton (Scotland)		
NS 25.11.1843	London	Standard Theatre	*Ella Rosenberg*; 'the fourth act of *Venice Preserved*'; 'the farce of *The Weathercock*'
NS 3.02.1844; *Nottingham Review* 16.02.1844 'Shrove Tuesday' [2.20.1844]	Nottingham	Democratic Chapel, Rice-place	*John Frost*
NS 4.05.1844	Nottingham	Unknown	*John Frost*
NS 6.07.1844	London	Hall of Science	'Songs and recitations, given by gentlemen from the various theatres'
NS 6.12.1845	London	Standard Theatre	'Theatrical benefit'
NS 7.02.1846	London	Grecian Saloon	'Popular opera' *The Daughter of the Regiment*; the 'farce' *A Spanking Legacy*
NS 21.03.1846, 18.04.1846; *Morning Advertiser* 29.04.1846	London	Victoria Theatre	*Laid up in Port, or Sharks along Shore*; *The Bride's Journey, or the Escapes of Adelaide of Dresden*; *The Factory Lads! or the Workmen's Saturday Night*
NS 30.05.1846; 11.07.1846	London	City Theatre	Unknown
NS 31.10.1846; 14.11.1846	London	City Theatre	*The Black Doctor, or the Siege of the Bastile, and Revolution of 1793*; *My Wife's Dentist*; *The Reprobate*
NS 21.11.1846; 28.11.1846; 5.12.1846	London	Marylebone Theatre	*John Bull, or, an Englishman's Fire-Side*; 'musical Drama' *The Little Devil*
NS 6.02.1847; 27.02.1847; 6.03.1847	London	Marylebone Theatre	Sheridan Knowles's *William Tell*; 'the sketch from the French Revolution of 1793' *Robert le Grange*; 'the nautical drama' *Black Eyed Susan*

(continued)

Table 5.1 Chartist dramatic performances

Source and date (Northern Star indicated as NS)	Date performed	Place	Location	Work(s) performed
NS 3.04.1847; 10.04.1847; 24.04.1847; 1.05.1847	28.04.1847	London	Pavilion Theatre	'The melodrama' *Gypsey King*; *A New Divertissement*; 'the domestic drama' *The Lawless Witness*
NS 1.05.1847	1.05.1847	Todmorden	Unknown	*Trial of Robert Emmett*
NS 18.09.1847	'Wednesday evening' [15.09.1847?]	Manchester	Queen's Theatre	Unknown
NS 5.02.1848	9.02.1848	Manchester	'Large Hall' in the People's Institute	*William Tell*; 'the farce of *Bathing*'
NS 11.03.1848	Unknown but future	Manchester	Queen's Theatre	*Hofer of the Tyrol*; *Wallace, the Hero of Scotland*
NS 14.10.1848; 21.10.1848	16.10.1848	London	Milton Street Theatre	Unknown
NS 21.10.1848	'Monday Week' [30.10.1848]	London	Milton Street Theatre	Unknown
NS 21.10.1848	13.10.1848	London	Strand Theatre	Unknown
NS 16.12.1848	'Thursday next' [21.12.1848]	London	Strand Theatre	*Henry IV*; *Damon and Pythias*
NS 3.02.1849	7.02.1849	London	Standard Theatre	*Punishment in Six Stages*; "The Model Pantomime'
NS 10.03.1849; 24.03.1849	21.03.1849	London	Victoria Theatre	*Ruth; or, the Lass that loves a Sailor*; *The Wild Irish Girl*; 'the burlesque' *Fayre Rosamonde*
NS 6.10.1849; Morning Advertiser 24.10.1849	24.10.1849	London	Standard Theatre	'Nautical domestic drama' by T. P. Taylor *The Anchors Weighed* ; 'a farce'; *The North Pole or the Frozen Regions*

NS 29.12.1849	11.12.1849	Dundee (Scotland)	Dundee Democratic School	*Trial of Robert Emmett*
NS 6.04.1850	22.03.1850	Kilbarchan	Mason Arm's Inn	*Othello*; 'Payne's comedy' *Charles the II*
NS 25.05.1850; 1.06.1850	29.05.1850	London	Standard Theatre	*Peter Wilkins or the Flying Indians*; *Matrimony*; *The Haunted Grange, or The Heart and the Key*
Red Republican 29.06.1850; NS 6.07.1850	4.07.1850	London	City Theatre	*The Grape Girl of Madrid*; *Luke the Labourer*; *An Irish Engagement*
NS 16.11.1850; 7.12.1850	'Monday last' [2.12.1850?]	Ashton	Unknown	*Trial of Robert Emmett*
NS 7.12.1850	Unknown but previous	Dukinfield	Unknown	*Trial of Robert Emmett*
NS 7.12.1850	Unknown but future	Oldham	Unknown	*Trial of Robert Emmett*
NS 18.01.1851; 1.02.1851	Unknown but previous	Longton	Working Man's Hall	*Castle Spectre*; *The Lottery Ticket*
NS 8.03.1851	10.03.1851	London	Literary Institute, Fitzroy Square	'Dramatic readings'
NS 15.03.1851	17.03.1851	London	Astley's Theatre	Unknown
NS 22.03.1851	Unknown but early March 1851	London	Astley's Theatre	Unknown
NS 24.05.1851	22.05.1851	London	Standard Theatre	*The Extorted Oath*; Webb's *The Secretary*
NS 24.05.1851	26.05.1851	London	Literary Institution, Bethnal-green	'Dramatic Entertainment'
Ben Brierley's *Home Memories* (1886), pp. 30–42	**Several performances** 'every Easter Monday for years'	Failsworth	Pole-lane school room	Southey's *Wat Tyler*; *William Tell*; *Othello*; *The Stranger*; *Virginius*; *The Lear of Private Life*; *Black-eyed Susan*; *Douglas*

Appendix 2

Newport sonnets

As a way of showing the diversity of Chartist literary responses to the Newport rising, a sequence of sonnets by the pseudonymous poet 'Iota' is included.

Iota, 'Sonnet Devoted to Chartism', *Northern Star* **(9 May 1840), p. 7.**

I.

ONCE more I visit thee, sweet rural walk,
   'Tis long since last I came this pleasant way,
   And many a sad event hath had its day
In yonder little town since then. The talk
   Of all the empire it hath been. The gay
Have laughed – the sober heaved a heartfelt sigh
When Newport hath been named. The tearful eye
Hath been its tribute o'er the grave to pay,
Where mothers, widows, sisters, brothers wept
O'er those who there in death untimely slept,
   The fallen brave! – fall'n in a glorious cause,
Howe'er mistaken in their way; – to gain
Their country's liberty they strove; though slain,
   Not fruitless was their fight, but worthy our applause.

– Newport, Monmouthshire, May, 1840.

'Sonnets Devoted to Chartism', *Northern Star* **(27 June 1840), p. 7.**

II.

Even yet thou shal't not be unknown to fame –
   Some future bard shall sing thy triumph, SHELL!
   And all thy virtues, all thy worth shall tell.
Thy countrymen shall glory in thy name,

Thy fall reflects upon thy foes a shame
   Which ages shall not wipe away. The yell
That tyranny raised o'er thy ruined frame
   Hath sunk no more o'er murdered worth to swell.
Thy patriot spirit hovering o'er the land
   That gave thee birth, and far too soon a grave,
   In spite of all the tyrant's power shall have
The joy, e'er long, to see the glorious stand
   Which Walia-Scotia-England's slaves can make
For Labour – Virtue – Honour – Freedom's sake!

III.

Along this favourite walk was wont to wend,
   One of the noblest patriots of the age;
Each step I take reminds me of that friend
   Of man – and victim of the tyrant's rage,
But late he wandered o'er this pleasant way,
   With heart-felt ardour for his country's weal,
And fond anticipations of the day
When England's glory – FREEDOM, should be real.
When worth and virtuous labour should obtain
   Their rights untrammelled by oppression's law;
When men no more should be the slaves of gain,
   Nor infants die to fill the Moloch maw
Of despot lordlings – tyrants of the loom,
Who yearly hurl their thousands to th' untimely tomb.

– Gold-tops, May, 1840.

    'Sonnets Devoted to Chartism', *Northern Star* (1 August 1840), p. 3.

IV.

WHAT fury maddened yonder mountain race,
   And unto desperation drove their chiefs?
   Was it their own severe heart-rending griefs,
Because th' oppressor ground the poor man's face,
And want was likely, from the earth, to chase
   Them and their offspring? Was wanton mischief's power
Sufficient all their soul's t' inspire
   With fearful resolution to destroy
The guilty and the innocent by fire,
   Or sword, or musket shot? Was it the joy

They hoped to realize by rapine's gains
    That urged them on with too industrious speed
    To dare the execution of a deed
Which, failing, must result in death or chains?

V.

Think not the PATRIOT formed so wild a plan;
    Or that his mind had grown so desperate;
    Whatever natural cause he had to hate
(And cause he had enough) his fellow man;
    He loved his wife too well to step one span
    Aside from virtue's path, to contemplate
Murder, cold-blooded and deliberate,
    Of victims innocent. But virtue can
Herself conceive, determine, execute,
    The ridding of the world of tyranny,
    Whatever form the monster may assume,
To minimise the sum of misery
    Endured by man. But who will dare impute
Foul murder to the tyrant slayer? No one will presume.

VI.

But e'en the brutal tyrant to destroy
    The patriot ne'er contemplated: not he.
He would have let him live – but not enjoy
    His power to exercise his tyranny.
Yet e'en in justice, truth, and virtue's cause
    Some one amongst the mass may do amiss,
And thus, by disregarding wisdom's laws,
    Bring to the virtuous woe instead of bliss.
'That fatal firing,' thus the patriot said,
    'That mad, rash firing, unexpected all
By me, has ruined that which might have led
    To bloodless freedom from despotic thrall.'
    But he, though innocent, was doomed to be
The victim of another's drunk insanity.

VII.

Shall tyranny have rest whilst Patriots roam
    In foreign lands far from their native climes?
Shall those who drove them from their cherished home,
    Have peace, prosperity, and happy times?

Shall no disaster o'er them spread its gloom;
    And pierce their hearts with well-deserved woe?
    Shall tyrants still *inflict*, but never *know*,
The pangs that hasten human beings to the tomb?
    Justice is retributive; soon or late.
    Reward will follow the oppressor's wrong.
The king, the peer, the proud man, and the strong
    Must bow to their inevitable fate.
    Th' eternal principles of truth and right;
    And equity shall overcome the tyrant's might.

– Newport, Monmouthshire.

'Sonnets Devoted to Chartism', *Northern Star* (15 August 1840), p. 7.

VIII.

ALAS! no more o'er these delightful fields
    To roam – no more those cheerful birds to hear –
    No more inhale this sweet, salubrious air –
No more the pleasures which the country yields,
To share, the patriot THREE are doomed. He builds,
    They say, too low, who builds upon this sphere
    His pinnacle of bliss. Thus lately here,
Beneath the lofty oak whose branches shield
Alike from sun or storm, the PATRIOT stood
    Contemplating the *future*, when the rights
        Of man would be secured to all the sons
    Of toil – when all their moral, mental fights,
        Free from the trenchant swords or thund'ring guns,
Should end in triumph innocent of blood.

IX.

Peace, plenty, and content in peasant's cot,
    And closely-huddled houses of the poor,
    As well as in the palace, through whose door
It is the prince, the peer, the priest's proud lot
To tread. Strife, wrath, and rage being all forgot,
    And lost in love and concord evermore.
    Laws administered impartially o'er
All the land; being themselves without spot,
Or shadow of injustice. Magistrates
    Extensively informed in all the laws,

    And men of soundest sense, free from the fear
Of man, which brings a 'snare'; whom not applause
    Nor scorn would move from Virtue's stern career:
Such and superior good the patriot contemplates.

– Newport, Monmouthshire.

Appendix 3

Passages omitted in Cleave's trial version as they appear in Cleave's source, *The Life, Trial and Conversations of Robert Emmet, Esq., Leader of the Irish Insurrection of 1803*.[1]

In contrast with Cleave's memoir, the very popular chapbook *The Life, Trial and Conversations of Robert Emmet* was not explicitly Chartist. It did, however, circulate widely among members of the movement and was likely a second source from which trial re-enactments drew. Except for the omitted passages, Cleave's version of the trial generally copies *Life, Trial, and Conversations* verbatim. Omitted passages comprise the testimony of six witnesses, the judge's final interruption of Emmet, and the Attorney General's opening address. The latter is the most important as newspaper accounts make clear the speech was a regular feature of performances. Footnotes in Cleave's version indicate where these passages occur in the trial.

Address of Standish O'Grady, the Attorney-General

The indictment was then opened, in substance, to the following effect, by
THE ATTORNEY-GENERAL.
My Lord, and Gentlemen of the Jury,
   It is my duty to state as concisely as I can, the nature of the charge which has been preferred against the prisoner at the bar, and also the nature of the evidence, which will be produced to substantiate the charge. It will require on your part the most deliberate consideration: because it is not only the highest crime of which at all times the subject can be guilty, but it receives, if possible, additional aggravation when we consider the state of Europe, and the lamentable consequences which revolution has already brought upon it.
   Perhaps at former periods some allowance might be made for the heated imaginations of enthusiasts; perhaps an extravagant love of liberty, might for a moment supersede a rational understanding, and might be induced, for want of sufficient experience or capacity, to look for that liberty in revolution. But it is not the road to liberty. It throws the mass of the people into agitation only to

---

[1] Manchester: John Doherty, 1836.

bring the worst and the most profligate to the surface. It originates in anarchy, proceeds in bloodshed, and ends in cruel and unrelenting despotism.

Therefore, Gentlemen, the crime of which the prisoner stands charged, demands the most serious and deep investigation, because it is in its nature a crime of the blackest dye, and which, under all existing circumstances, does not admit of a momentary explanation.

Gentlemen, the prisoner stands indicted under a very ancient statute – the 25th of Edward III. – and the indictment is grounded on three clauses. The first relates to compassing and imagining the death of the king – the second in adhering to his enemies – and the third in compassing to levy war against him. The two latter, namely, that of adhering to the king's enemies, and that of compassing to levy war, are so intelligible in themselves that they do not require any observation upon them. But the first admits of some technical considerations, and may require upon my part a short explanation.

In the language of the law, compassing the death of the king, does not mean or imply necessarily any immediate attack upon his person. But any conspiracy, which has for its object all alteration of the laws, constitution, and government of the country by force, uniformly leads to anarchy and general destruction, and finally tends to endanger the life of the king. And, therefore, where that design is substantiated, and manifested by overt acts, whenever the party entertaining the design, uses any means to carry his traitorous intentions into execution, the crime of compassing and imagining the death of the king is complete.

Accordingly, gentlemen, this indictment particularly states overt acts, by which the prisoner disclosed the traitorous imagination of his heart – and, if it shall be necessary, those particular overt acts, and the applicability of the evidence which will be produced to support them, will be stated at large to you by the court, and therefore, it will not be necessary for me now to trespass upon the public time, by a minute examination of them.

Gentlemen, having heard the charge against the prisoner, you will naturally feel that your duty will require an investigation into two distinct points: first, whether there has, or has not existed a traitorous conspiracy and rebellion for the purpose of altering the law, the constitution, and the government of the country by force? – And, secondly, whether the prisoner has in any, and in what degree, participated in that conspiracy and rebellion?

Gentlemen, I do not wish to undertake to speak in the prophetic. But when I consider the vigilance and firmness of his majesty's government, the spirit and discipline of his majesty's troops, and that armed valour and loyalty which, from one end of the country to the other has raised itself for the purpose of crushing domestic treason, and, if necessary, of meeting and repelling a foreign foe, I do not think it unreasonable to indulge a sanguinary hope, that a continuance of the same conduct upon the part of government, and of the same exertions upon the part of the people, will long preserve the nation free, happy and independent.

Gentlemen, upon former occasions, persons were brought to the bar of this court, implicated in the rebellion, in various, though inferior degrees. But if I am rightly instructed, we have now brought to the bar of justice, not a person who has been seduced by others, but a gentleman to whom the rebellion may be traced, as the origin, the life, and soul of it. If I mistake not, it will appear that some time before christmas last, the prisoner who had visited foreign countries, and who for several months before had made a continental tour, embracing France, returned to this country, full of those mischievous designs which have been so fully exposed. He came from that country, in which he might well have learned the necessary effects of revolution; and therefore, if he be guilty of treason, he embarked in it with his eyes open, and with a previous knowledge of all its inevitable consequences. But, notwithstanding, I am instructed that he persevered in fomenting a rebellion, which I will be bold to say, is unexampled in any country, ancient or modern. A rebellion which does not complain of any existing grievances, which does not flow from any immediate oppression, and which is not pretended to have been provoked by our mild and gracious king, or by the administration employed by him to execute his authority. No, gentlemen, it is a rebellion which avows itself to come, not to remove any evil which the people feel, but to recal the memory of grievances which, if they ever existed, must have long since passed away.

You will recollect, gentlemen, that in the large proclamation there was a studied endeavour to persuade a large portion of the people that they had no religious feuds to apprehend from the establishment of a new government. But the manifesto upon which I am now about animadverting has taken somewhat a different course, and has revived religious distinctions at the very moment in which it expresses a desire to extinguish them.

'Orangemen, add not to the catalogue of your follies and crimes, already have you been duped to the ruin of the country in the legislative union with its tyrant; attempt not an opposition; return from the paths of delusion; return to the arms of your countrymen who will receive and hail your repentance. Countrymen of all descriptions, let us act with union and concert, all sects, Catholic, Protestant, Presbyterian, are equal and indiscriminately embraced in the benevolence of our object.' I will not apply to this passage all the observations that press upon my mind, because I am sincerely desirous that one feeling and one spirit should animate us all. I cannot but lament that there should be so many sectaries in religion, but trust in God there will be found amongst us but one political faith. But this manifesto is equally unfortunate in every instance in which it prescribes moderation. Attend to the advice by which it instigates the citizens of Dublin: 'In a city each street becomes a defile and each house a battery; impede the march of your oppressors, charge them with the arms of the brave, the pike, and from the windows and roofs, hurl stones, bricks, bottles, and all other convenient implements on the heads of the satellites of your tyrant, the mercenary, the sanguinary, soldiery of England.'

Having thus roused them, it throws in a few words of composure, 'repress, prevent, and discourage excesses, pillage, and intoxication'; and to ensure that calmness of mind which is so necessary to qualify them for the adoption of this salutary advice, it desires that they will 'remember against whom they fight, their oppressors for 600 years; remember their massacres, their tortures, remember your murdered friends, your burned houses, your violated females'. Thus affecting to recommend moderation, every expedient is resorted to, which could tend to inflame sanguinary men to the commission of sanguinary deeds.

Gentlemen, you must by this time be somewhat anxious to know the progress of the general, who escaped the memorable action which was to be fought; and the first place in which I am enabled to introduce him to you, is at the house of one Doyle, who resides near the Wicklow mountains. There the general and his companions took refuge at the commencement of the following week; they arrived there at a late hour; the general was still dressed in his full uniform, with suitable lace and epaulettes, and a military cocked hat, with a conspicuous feather. Two other persons were also decorated in green and gold. From thence, they proceeded to the house of Mrs Bagnall, and returned to the city of Dublin. What became of the other persons is foreign to the present inquiry, but we trace the prisoner from those mountains to the same house in Harolds'-cross, in which he formerly resided, and assuming the old name of Hewit; he arrived there the Saturday after the rebellion.

Having remained a month in this concealment, information was had, and Major Sirr, to whose activity and intrepidity the loyal citizens of Dublin are under much obligation, did confer an additional, and a great one, by the zealous discharge of his duty on this occasion. He came by surprise on the house, having sent a countryman to give a single rap, and the door being opened, the Major rushed in, and caught Mrs Palmer and the prisoner sitting down to dinner; the former withdrew, and the Major immediately asked the prisoner his name, and as if he found a gratification in assuming a variety of titles, he said his name was Cunningham, that he had that day arrived in the house, having been upon a visit with some friends in the neighbourhood: the Major then left him in charge of another person, and went to enquire of Mrs Palmer concerning him; she said he was a very proper young man of the name of Hewit, and that he had been in her house about a month; the Major at this moment heard a noise, and he found that the prisoner was endeavouring to make his escape, but having been struck with a pistol by the person who had the custody of him, he was by that means detained; immediately further assistance was called in from a neighbouring guard-house, and an additional sentry was put upon him. The Major then again proceeded further to interrogate Mrs Palmer, when the prisoner made another effort, got into the garden through the parlour window, but was at length overtaken by the Major, who at the peril of his own life, fortunately secured him. When the Major apologised for the roughness with which he was obliged to treat him, the prisoner replied, *'all was fair in war.'*

Gentlemen, you have the life of a fellow subject in your hands, and by the benignity of our laws, he is presumed to be an innocent man until your verdict shall find him guilty.

If upon the evidence you shall be so satisfied that this man is guilty, you must discharge your duty to your king, your country, and to your God. If, on the other hand, nothing shall appear sufficient to affect him, we shall acknowledge that we have grievously offended him, and will heartily participate in the common joy that must result from the acquittal of an innocent man.

Testimony of tailor Terence Colgan

TERENCE COLGAN, the tailor named in the foregoing evidence, sworn. Deposed, that on the Sunday previous to the insurrection, he came to town from Lucan, where he lived, and having met with a friend, they went to Dillon's, the White Bull Inn, in Thomas-street, and drank, until the witness, overcome with liquor, fell asleep, when he was conveyed in this state of insensibility, into the depot, in Marshal-lane, and when he awoke the next morning, he was set to work making green jackets and white pantaloons. He saw the prisoner there by whose directions everything was done, and who, he understood, was the chief. He recollected seeing the last witness frequently in the depot while he was there. He also saw the prisoner often at the desk writing. The witness corroborated the general preparations of arms, ammunition, &c., for the insurrection.

Full testimony of Patrick Fraser/Farrell

PATRICK FARRELL, sworn. Deposed, that as he was passing through Marshal-lane, between the hours of nine and ten o'clock on the evening of Friday, the 22nd of July, he stopped before the malt stores, or depot, on hearing a noise therein, which surprised him, as he considered it a waste house. Immediately the door opened, and a man came forth who caught him, and asked him what he was doing there? The witness was then brought into the depot, and again asked what brought him there, or had he been ever there before? He said he had not. They asked him did he know Graham? He replied he did not. One of the persons then said the witness was a spy, and called out to 'drop him immediately', by which the witness understood they meant to shoot him. They brought him up stairs, and after some consultation, they agreed to wait for some person to come in, who would decide what should be done with him. That person having arrived, he asked the witness if he knew Graham? He replied that he did not.

A light was brought in at the same time, and the witness having looked about, was asked if he knew any one there? He replied he knew Quigley. He was asked where? He replied that he knew him five or six years ago in the College of Maynooth, as a bricklayer or mason. The witness understood that Quigley was the person who went by the name of Graham. Here the witness identified the prisoner as the person who came in and decided he should not be killed, but he should be taken care of, and not let out. The witness was detained there that night, and the whole of the next day, Saturday, the 23rd, and was made to assist at the different kinds of work.

He assisted in taking boards off a car; the boards, he said, were made into cases, and pikes put into them. These cases the witness described as being made of the outside slabs of a long beam, taken off about an inch or more thick – four or five inches at each end of the beam was cut off – the slabs were nailed together, and these pieces put in at the ends, so that it appeared like a rough plank or beam of timber. He saw several such cases filled with pikes sent out. The witness stated that on the evening of the 23rd, he saw three men dressed in green uniforms, richly laced; one of whom was the prisoner, who wore two gold epaulettes, but the other two only one each. The prisoner had also a cocked hat, sword, and pistols. When the witness was helping out one of the beams prepared for explosion, he contrived to effect his escape.

On his cross-examination, in which the interrogatories were suggested by the prisoner, the only thing remarkable in the evidence of the witness was, that he heard a printed paper read, part of which was, that nineteen counties were ready to rise at the same time, to second the attempt in Dublin. The witness also heard them say, that 'they had no idea as to French relief, but would make it good themselves'. In answer to a question from the Court, the witness said, that he gave information of the circumstance deposed in his evidence, the next morning, to Mr Ormsby in Thomas-street, to whom he was steward.

Several minor witnesses

COLONEL SPENCER THOMAS VASSAL being sworn, deposed that he was field officer of the day on the 23rd of July; that having gone to the depot in Marshal-lane, he found there several small proclamations, addressed to the citizens of Dublin, and which were quite wet. He identified one of them. The witness also identified the desk which the prisoner used in the depot. Having remained about a quarter of an hour in the depot, he committed to Major Greville the care of its contents.

Questioned by the Court: The witness said, that he visited the depot between three and four o'clock on Sunday morning, it having been much advanced in day light before he was suffered to go his rounds.

ALDERMAN FREDERICK DARLEY sworn. Proved having found in the depot a paper directed to 'Robert Ellis, Butterfield'. Also a paper entitled, a 'Treatise on the Art of War'. The latter had been handed, at the time, to Captain Evelyn.

CAPT. HENRY EVELYN sworn. Deposed having been at the rebel depot on the morning of Sunday, the 23rd of July, to see the things removed to the barracks; and that he found a paper there, which, being shewn to him, he identified. This paper was a manuscript draft of the greater part of the Proclamation of the Provisional Government, altered and interlined in a great many places.

ROBT. LINDSAY, a soldier, and Michael Clement Frayne, quarter-master-sergeant of the 38th regiment, proved the conveyance of the desk (then in court) to the barracks; and the latter identified a letter which he found therein. The letter was signed, 'Thomas Addis Emmet,' and directed to 'Mrs Emmet, Miltown, near Dublin,' and began with, 'My dearest Robert'. It bore a foreign post-mark.

Norbury's final interruption of Emmet

(Here Lord Norbury told Mr Emmet that his sentiments and language disgraced his family and education, but more particularly, his father, Dr Emmet, who was a man, if alive, that would not countenance such opinions.)

Appendix 4

Advertising placard for a performance of *The Trial of Robert Emmett, Esq.*

A newspaper hostile to Chartism quoted in full an advertising placard for a Manchester performance of *The Trial of Robert Emmett* (note the variant spelling of Emmet's name), providing valuable evidence about how and to whom the Chartists promoted their productions and some suggestion of what productions looked like.

From 'The Irish in England', *Freeman's Journal* (21 December 1840), p. 2.

ARISE! YE SONS OF ERIN! YOUR BRAVE PATRIOTS ARE GONE.

The members of the Ashton branch of the National Charter Association have great pleasure in announcing to their friends, and the public in general, that they intend to perform, in court uniform, the trial of Robert Emmett. Esq., in the Hall of Science, Campfield, Manchester, on Saturday, 19th December, 1840.

Attend, then, O ye sons of liberty, and detesters of tyranny. Show by your number on this occasion that you love and respect the name and principle of that unflinching advocate of his country's rights and liberties, who fell a sacrifice to the wrath of tyranny and injustice, for endeavouring to drive from his native country, that tyranny and oppression which the poor unhappy and degraded people of Ireland have so long and so patiently suffered to prevail. Several persons will appear as witnesses against him, and a young man, appearing in the character of Robert Emmett, will deliver, in full, the splendid and eloquent address, as delivered by him before Judge Norbury, at his ever-memorable, and never-to-be-forgotten trial in 1803.

EU authorised representative for GPSR:
Easy Access System Europe, Mustamäe tee 50,
10621 Tallinn, Estonia
gpsr.requests@easproject.com

www.ingramcontent.com/pod-product-compliance
Lightning Source LLC
Chambersburg PA
CBHW070237240426
43673CB00044B/1820